With expert readings and forecasts, you can chart a course to romance, adventure, good health, or career opportunities while gaining valuable insight into yourself and others. Offering a daily outlook for 18 full months, this fascinating guide shows you:

- The important dates in your life
- What to expect from an astrological reading
- How the stars can help you stay healthy and fit And more!

Let this sound advice guide you through a year of heavenly possibilities—for today and for every day of 2006!

SYDNEY OMARR'S® DAY-BY-DAY ASTROLOGICAL GUIDE FOR

ARIES—March 21–April 19
TAURUS—April 20–May 20
GEMINI—May 21–June 20
CANCER—June 21–July 22
LEO—July 23–August 22
VIRGO—August 23–September 22
LIBRA—September 23–October 22
SCORPIO—October 23–November 21
SAGITTARIUS—November 22–December 21
CAPRICORN—December 22–January 19
AQUARIUS—January 20–February 18
PISCES—February 19–March 20

IN 2006

Sydney Omarr's®

DAY-BY-DAY ASTROLOGICAL GUIDE FOR

CAPRICORN

DECEMBER 22–JANUARY 19

2006

By Trish MacGregor
with Carol Tonsing

A SIGNET BOOK

SIGNET
Published by New American Library, a division of
Penguin Group (USA) Inc., 375 Hudson Street,
New York, New York 10014, USA
Penguin Group (Canada), 10 Alcorn Avenue, Toronto,
Ontario M4V 3B2, Canada (a division of Pearson Penguin Canada Inc.)
Penguin Books Ltd., 80 Strand, London WC2R 0RL, England
Penguin Ireland, 25 St. Stephen's Green, Dublin 2,
Ireland (a division of Penguin Books Ltd.)
Penguin Group (Australia), 250 Camberwell Road, Camberwell, Victoria 3124,
Australia (a division of Pearson Australia Group Pty. Ltd.)
Penguin Books India Pvt. Ltd., 11 Community Centre, Panchsheel Park,
New Delhi - 110 017, India
Penguin Group (NZ), cnr Airborne and Rosedale Roads, Albany,
Auckland 1310, New Zealand (a division of Pearson New Zealand Ltd.)
Penguin Books (South Africa) (Pty.) Ltd., 24 Sturdee Avenue,
Rosebank, Johannesburg 2196, South Africa

Penguin Books Ltd., Registered Offices:
80 Strand, London WC2R 0RL, England

First published by Signet, an imprint of New American Library,
a division of Penguin Group (USA) Inc.

First Printing, June 2005
10 9 8 7 6 5 4 3 2 1

Copyright © The Estate of Sydney Omarr, 2005
All rights reserved

Sydney Omarr's is a registered trademark of Writers House, LLC.

Sydney Omarr® is syndicated worldwide by
Los Angeles Times Syndicate.

REGISTERED TRADEMARK—MARCA REGISTRADA

Printed in the United States of America

Without limiting the rights under copyright reserved above, no part of this publication may be reproduced, stored in or introduced into a retrieval system, or transmitted, in any form, or by any means (electronic, mechanical, photocopying, recording, or otherwise), without the prior written permission of both the copyright owner and the above publisher of this book.

PUBLISHER'S NOTE
While the author has made every effort to provide accurate telephone numbers and Internet addresses at the time of publication, neither the publisher nor the author assumes any responsibility for errors, or for changes that occur after publication. Further, publisher does not have any control over and does not assume any responsibility for author or third-party Web sites or their contents.

If you purchased this book without a cover you should be aware that this book is stolen property. It was reported as "unsold and destroyed" to the publisher and neither the author nor the publisher has received any payment for this "stripped book."

The scanning, uploading and distribution of this book via the Internet or via any other means without the permission of the publisher is illegal and punishable by law. Please purchase only authorized electronic editions, and do not participate in or encourage electronic piracy of copyrighted materials. Your support of the author's rights is appreciated.

CONTENTS

Introduction: Ancient Roots, Modern Flowering 1

1. The Big Trends of 2006 5
2. Optimum Time Management by the Stars: Take Advantage of Your Best Days This Year! 12
3. The Moon: Your Emotional Barometer 25
4. Those Mysterious Eclipses: How They Can Shake Up Your Life! 32
5. Solving the Mystery of Astrology: Your Big Questions Answered Here! 42
6. Your Planetary Power Sources 55
7. The Astrology Code: The History and Mystery of Those Symbols on Your Chart 113
8. Your Rising Sign Makes Your Horoscope Unique 126
9. Join Astrology Fans Around the World 136
10. Empower Yourself with a Personal Reading 147
11. Are You Having a Baby This Year? An Astrological Portrait of Children Born This Year 153
12. The Love Detective: Your Star Guide for Finding the Most Compatible Partner 164
13. Hot Careers for 2006: Where Are the Future Billionaires? 172
14. Your Capricorn Sign Power: Your Capricorn Potential, Possibilities, and Passion! 178

15. Capricorn at Home and Away: Home Decor, Music, Color, Vacation Getaways	185
16. Your Capricorn Fashion Stylist	189
17. Stay Healthy and Slim the Capricorn Way	192
18. Your Capricorn Career Coach	195
19. Capricorn Celebrity Sightings: Look Who's Born on Your Birthday!	198
20. The Capricorn Connections: Your Love, Lust, or Break-up Potential with Every Other Sign	203
21. Astrological Overview for Capricorn in 2006	212
22. Eighteen Months of Day-by-Day Predictions—July 2005 to December 2006	215

INTRODUCTION

Ancient Roots, Modern Flowering

Since the beginning of time, man has been fascinated by the relationship of heaven and earth, nowhere more than in ancient Mesopotamia, the place that is now modern Iraq. Cities buried deep in the sand with fabled names like Ur of the Chaldees and Babylon contain the 3000-year-old roots of astrology. Crumbling ruins of ziggurats, towers where astrologer priests studied the stars, evoke a time when rulers routinely consulted their predictions and warnings etched on clay tablets. In Ur of the Chaldees, the "city of astrologers," priests first learned to calculate the cycles of eclipses. Even the founding of the city of Baghdad is said to have been astrologically timed.

The horoscope of modern Iraq (founded on August 23, 1921, after World War I) reveals the current turbulence in that country. We see activity in the planet Uranus, a force of sudden upheaval and rebellion leading to freedom and individuation. Known to astrologers as "the awakener," Uranus has returned to Pisces, associated with petroleum, the same sign placement as modern Iraq's chart. It has been crossing back and forth over the degree of the foundation chart's Uranus during the past year, making its final pass in January 2006. After it finishes this important transit of the Iraqi horoscope, we can hope that Iraq will go from chaos to clarity, find its own individual voice, a fully awakened one that is resonant with modern times, and then realize the peace it deserves.

In the West, astrology has become very much a part

of today's consciousness, giving us practical tools to improve our lives. You might use astrology every day to schedule routine matters, such as planning a vacation or buying a car. Or you can analyze personal relationships, learning to resolve conflicts and improve communication. On a deeper level, astrology can be a tool for personal growth or for insight into your special place in the cosmos. We've learned that through the study of the planets we can study ourselves and bring into balance the inner and outer universe. No wonder this ancient art has become more popular, relevant, and dynamic today than it was many thousands of years ago.

To celebrate 2006, we've included some helpful astrological tips for every sign, including how to get along with every other sign. Just knowing another person's sun sign can give you many clues to how to improve your relationship. Astrology gives you a way to troubleshoot potential problems and, if they crop up, find a way to turn them around.

The moon is considered by many astrological systems to be as important as the sun. This year, we consider the mystery of lunar eclipses as well as how the moon influences our actions every day. You'll want to look up the daily moon sign under the daily forecasts in this book to follow along in your own activities.

We'll deal in many ways with the question of timing—the difficult times (which also present positive challenges), times with potential for delays and misunderstandings, the best times to take risks, and when to kick back and relax.

For those who would like to know more about astrology, there is basic information to start you on your astrological journey. Then you can put your whole astrological portrait together by looking up the other planets in your horoscope.

Anyone with access to the Internet has a world of astrological connections available. We'll show you the best astrology Web sites, where you can find sophisticated astrology software and virtually a free education. And if you're interested in connecting with other astrologers, we provide an extensive resource list of contacts and organizations, as well as computer program recommendations for fun or serious study.

Bring astrology into your life every day with our astonishingly accurate day-by-day forecasts. Let this book become your astrological partner and companion, ready to enhance every aspect of your life. Here's wishing you love, happiness, health, and success in 2006!

CHAPTER 1

The Big Trends of 2006

Astrologers judge the trends of a year by following the slow-moving planets, from Jupiter through Pluto. A change in sign indicates a new cycle, with new emphasis. The farthest planets (Uranus, Neptune, and Pluto), which stay in a sign for at least seven years, cause a very significant change in the atmosphere when they change signs. Shifts in Jupiter, which changes every year, and Saturn, every two years, are more obvious in current events and daily lives. Jupiter generally brings a fortunate, expansive emphasis to its new sign, while Saturn's two-year cycle is a reality check, bringing tests of maturity, discipline, and responsibility.

This year, there are no major outer planet changes, so we should witness trends developing that began last year.

Saturn Continues in Leo: The Maturing of the Baby Boomers

Saturn, the planet of limitation, testing, and restriction, has been transiting Leo since mid-July 2005, forcing us to grow up and get serious in the Leo areas of our lives. Many of the fun things in life fall under the banner of Leo: entertainment, show business, children, play, recreation, love affairs, hobbies, performing, talent, the creative arts, and recognition by others. Since Saturn tends to put a damper on Leo's fun, expect some restrictions on the entertainment business, shows with more serious themes and actors. Leo is associated with children, and with Saturn come the burdens and responsibilities of bringing them up.

The subject of aging in general belongs to Saturn, and the Leo archetype in this area is the aging film star determined to hold on to youth. Love affairs and flirtations, part of Leo's sunny side, may this year involve older people. Maturing baby boomers will demand more awareness from the media. Therefore we will see more older people on television and in films, more entertainment tailored to an aging population, a harbinger of the even stronger Saturnian trends coming up in 2008. Since Leo is also associated with speculation and gambling, in fact all games, expect more stringent regulation and controversy around big-time casinos and sports.

Saturn in Leo demands hard work in creative ventures, responsibility when interacting with others. Leo types can't get away with casual love affairs, being highhanded, arrogant, or divalike in any way. Leo divas will have to earn their applause. This could tone down the blatant celebrity-worshipping culture that has arisen over the past few years. No longer will it be enough to be famous for being famous. The emphasis will be on true values rather than the trappings of success. Flashy lifestyles, bling bling jewelry, and showing off will be out.

Jupiter in Scorpio and Sagittarius

When Jupiter enters a sign where it stays for a year, the fields associated with that sign are the ones that currently arouse excitement and enthusiasm, usually providing excellent opportunities for expansion, fame, and fortune.

Since November 2005, Jupiter has been in Scorpio, which creates an intense atmosphere, especially as it interacts with Saturn in Leo and the Sun and Neptune in Aquarius in February 2006. Scorpio is concerned with all things sexual, waste disposal, underground areas, police and detective work, the meat trade, and leather in fashion. Expect one of the most sex-oriented years ever in mass market culture. Think X with Scorpio: X-treme and X-rated. (Scorpio does nothing halfway.)

Scorpio is also concerned with police work, espionage, and undercover operation, so look for an increase in security devices and operations. Computer spyware, which has become invasive at this writing, and the antispyware business should be booming.

Since Scorpio is associated with science and research, Jupiter could bring positive breakthroughs in medicine and surgery, perhaps a cure for sexually transmitted diseases.

One place we notice the Jupiter influence is in fashion, and compared to the previous year's more feminine style-consciousness (Jupiter in Libra), this year should bring back the sleek minimalism of designers like Calvin Klein or the extreme looks of Comme des Garcons. Black and dark red or purple should return as strong colors. The overall look will be sensual with fur, leather, and reptile fabrics, a darker, more extreme style with transgender androgynous looks, tomboy style, and male-female role switching. Films are sure to feature more explicit love scenes than ever as well as more gory views of surgery.

Surgery, especially that which works a transformation, is associated with Scorpio. This offers new opportunities, especially in sexually related surgery, such as sex-change operations or forms of reproductive surgery. Drastic plastic surgery that encourages us to transform our bodies could become even more widespread under this planetary influence.

It will be interesting to see what develops in the Scorpio area of finance and credit, also in the field of taxes. Jupiter usually means more rather than less, so it's possible that there will be more borrowing and creative financing, new types of credit cards.

Those born under Scorpio should have many opportunities during the year. However, the key is to keep your feet on the ground. The flip side of Jupiter is that there are no limits. You can expand off the planet under a Jupiter transit, which is why the planet is often called the Gateway to Heaven. If something is going to burst (such as an artery) or overextend or go over the top in some way, it could happen under a supposedly lucky Jupiter transit, so be aware.

Those born under Taurus may find their best opportunities working with partners this year, as Jupiter will be transiting their seventh house of relationships.

After an intense Jupiter in Scorpio and the damper of Saturn in Leo, we'll need a lot of fun and laughter. Jupiter finishes the year on a much more upbeat note, moving into fun-loving Sagittarius, the sign it rules in late November. This is the strongest place for Jupiter, so we should have a banner time for Sagittarius-related things: comedy, fun, travel, laughter! Expect one of the most jovial holiday seasons ever. Not a moment too soon!

Continuing Trends

Uranus and Neptune continue to do a kind of astrological dance called a mutual reception. This is a supportive relationship where Uranus is in Pisces, the sign ruled by Neptune, while Neptune is in Aquarius, the sign ruled by Uranus. When this dance is over in 2011, it is likely that we will be living under very different political and social circumstances.

Uranus in Pisces

Uranus, known as the Great Awakener, tends to cause both upheaval and innovation in the sign it transits. During previous episodes of Uranus in Pisces, great religions and spiritual movements have come into being, most recently Mormonism and Christian Fundamentalism. In its most positive mode, Pisces promotes imagination and creativity, the art of illusion in theater and film, the inspiration of great artists. A water sign, Pisces is naturally associated with all things liquid—oceans, oil, alcohol—and with those creatures that live in the water—fish, the fishing industry, fish habitats, and fish farming. Currently there is a great debate going on about overfishing, contamination of fish, and fish farming. The underdog, the enslaved, and the disenfranchised should also benefit from Uranus in Pisces.

Pisces is associated with the prenatal phase of life, which is related to regenerative medicine. The controversy over embryonic stem cell research should continue to be debated. Petroleum issues, both in the oil-producing countries and offshore oil drilling, will come to a head. Uranus in Pisces suggests that development of new hydroelectric sources may provide the power we need to continue our current power-thirsty lifestyle.

As in previous eras, there should continue to be a flourishing of the arts. We are seeing many new artistic forms developing now, such as computer-created actors and special effects. The sky's the limit on this influence.

Those who have problems with Uranus are those who resist change, so the key is to embrace the future.

Neptune in Aquarius

Neptune is a planet of imagination and creativity, but also of deception and illusion. Neptune is associated with hospitals, which have been the subject of much controversy. On the positive side, hospitals are acquiring cutting-edge technology. The atmosphere of many hospitals is already changing from the intimidating and sterile environment of the past to that of a health-promoting spa. Alternative therapies, such as massage, diet counseling, and aromatherapy, are becoming commonplace, which expresses this Neptune trend. New procedures in plastic surgery, also a Neptune glamour field, and anti-aging therapies are restoring the illusion of youth.

However, issues involving the expense and quality of health care and the evolving relationship between doctors, drug companies, and HMOs reflect a darker side of this trend.

Pluto in Sagittarius

The slow-moving planet Pluto is our guide to life-changing, long-term trends. In Sagittarius until 2008, Pluto has been emphasizing everything associated with this sign to prepare us philosophically and spiritually for things to come. Perhaps the most pervasive sign of Pluto in Sagittarius over the past few years has been globalization in all its forms. We are re-forming boundaries, creating new forms of travel, and interacting with exotic cultures and religions as never before.

In true Sagittarius fashion, Pluto will shift our emphasis away from acquiring wealth to a quest for the meaning of it all, as upward strivers discover that money and power are not enough and religious extremists assert themselves. Sagittarius is the sign of linking everything together; therefore, the trend will be to find ways to interconnect on a spiritual, philosophical, and intellectual level.

The spiritual emphasis of Pluto in Sagittarius has already filtered down to our home lives. Home altars and private sanctuaries are becoming a part of our personal environment.

Pluto in Sagittarius has expanded the experience of religion into other areas of our lives. For example, vast church complexes are now being built. They combine religious activities with sports centers, health clubs, malls, and theme parks. Look for an expansion in religious education and religious book publishing as well.

Sagittarius is known for love of animals, especially horses. Horse racing has become popular again, and America has never been more pet happy. Look for extremes related to animal welfare, such as vegetarianism, which will become even more popular and widespread as a lifestyle. As habitats are destroyed, the care, feeding, and control of wild animals will become a larger issue, especially when deer, bears, and coyotes invade our backyard.

The Sagittarius love of the outdoors combined with Pluto's power has already promoted extreme sports, especially those that require strong legs, like rock climbing, trekking, or snowboarding. Rugged, sporty all-terrain vehicles continue to be popular. Expect the trend toward more adventurous travel as well as fitness or sports-oriented vacations to accelerate. Exotic hiking trips to unexplored territories, mountain-climbing expeditions, spa vacations, and sports-associated resorts are part of this trend.

Publishing, which is associated with Sagittarius, has been transformed by global conglomerates and the Internet. It is fascinating that the online bookstore Amazon.com took the Sagittarius-influenced name of the fierce female tribe of archer warriors. There should continue to be more inspirational books, aimed at those who are interested in spirituality outside of traditional religions.

CHAPTER 2

Optimum Time Management by the Stars: Take Advantage of Your Best Days This Year!

Have you ever wanted to coordinate your schedule with the cosmos, like many celebrities who have personal astrologers do? Astrology is one of the oldest and best ways to manage your time by going with the flow of the universe. You can do it yourself by studying the movement of the planets and then using this information to pick the perfect time for coming events in your life.

Set your schedule on a successful course by coordinating your activities with the most beneficial times and knowing when the stars say it's time to kick back and review where you're going. For instance, when mischievous Mercury creates havoc with communications and you can't seem to make progress with projects, you'll use the time to best advantage by backing up your vital computer files, clearing out your files and closets and reading between the lines of contracts. That's the time to be extra patient with coworkers and double-check all messages. Mark your social calendar when Venus passes through your sign—that's when you're the flavor of the month. You've got extra sex appeal, time to get a knock-out new outfit or hairstyle. Then ask someone you'd like to know better to dinner. Venus timing can also help you charm clients with a stunning sales pitch or make an offer they won't refuse.

In this chapter, you will learn how to find your best times as well as which times to avoid. You will also learn how to read the moods of the moon and make them work for you. Use the information and tables in this chapter and the planet tables in this book, and also use the moon sign listings in your daily forecasts.

Here are the happenings to note on your agenda:

- Dates of your sun sign (high-energy period)
- The month previous to your sun sign (low-energy period)
- Dates of planets in your sign this year
- Full and new moons (Pay special attention when these fall in your sun sign!)
- Eclipses
- Moon in your sun sign every month, as well as moon in the opposite sign (listed in daily forecast)
- Mercury retrogrades
- Other retrograde periods

Switch on the Power During the Month of Your Sign

You should feel a new surge of vitality as the powerful sun enters your sign. This is the time when predominant energies are most favorable to you. So go for it! Start new projects, make your big moves (especially when the new moon is in your sign, doubling your charisma). You'll get the recognition you deserve now, when everyone is attuned to your sun sign. Look in the tables in this book to see if other planets will also be passing through your sun sign at this time. Venus (love, beauty), Mars (energy, drive), and Mercury (communication, mental sharpness) reinforce the sun and give an extra boost to your life in the areas they affect. Venus will rev up your social and love life, making you seem especially attractive. Mars amplifies your energy and drive. Mercury fuels your brainpower and helps you communicate. Jupiter signals an especially lucky period of expansion.

There are two downtimes related to the sun. During the month before your birthday period, when you are winding up your annual cycle, you could be feeling especially vulnerable and depleted. So at that time get extra rest, watch your diet, and take it easy. Don't overstress yourself. Use this time to gear up for a big "push" when the sun enters your sign.

Another downtime is when the sun is in a sign opposite your sun sign (six months from your birthday). That's when the prevailing energies are very different from yours. You may feel at odds with the world. You'll have to work harder for recognition because people are not on your wavelength. However, this could be a good time to work on a team, in cooperation with others, or behind the scenes.

Make the Moon Your Daily Planner

The moon is a powerful tool to divine the mood of the moment. You can work with the moon in two ways. Plan by the *sign* the moon is in; plan by the *phase* of the moon. The sign will tell you the kind of activities that suit the moon's mood. The phase will tell you the best time to start or finish a certain activity.

Working with the phases of the moon is as easy as looking up at the night sky. During the new moon, when both the sun and moon are in the same sign, begin new ventures—especially activities that are favored by that sign. Then you'll utilize the powerful energies pulling you in the same direction. You'll be focused outward, toward action, and in a doing mode. Postpone breaking off, terminating, deliberating, or reflecting—activities that require introspection and passive work. These are better suited to a later moon phase.

Get your project under way during the first quarter. Then go public at the full moon, a time of high intensity, when feelings come out into the open. This is your time to shine—to express yourself. Be aware, however, that because pressures are being released, other people will also be letting off steam. Since confrontations are possible, take advantage of this time either to air grievances or to avoid arguments. Traditionally, astrologers often advise against surgery at this time, which could produce heavier bleeding.

About three days after the full moon comes the disseminating phase, a time when the energy of the cycle begins to wind down. From the last quarter of the moon to the next new moon, it's a time to cut off unproductive relationships, do serious thinking, and focus on inward-directed activities.

You'll feel some new and full moons more strongly than others, especially those new moons that fall in your sun sign and full moons in your opposite sign. Because that full moon happens at your low-energy time of year, it is likely to be an especially stressful time in a relationship, when any hidden problems or unexpressed emotions could surface.

Full and New Moons in 2006

All dates are calculated for eastern standard time and eastern daylight time.

Full Moon—January 14 in Cancer
New Moon—January 29 in Aquarius

Full Moon—February 12 in Leo
New Moon—February 27 in Pisces

Full Moon—March 14 in Virgo (lunar eclipse)
New Moon—March 29 in Aries (total solar eclipse)

Full Moon—April 13 in Libra
New Moon—April 27 in Taurus

Full Moon—May 13 in Scorpio

New Moon—May 27 in Gemini

Full Moon—June 11 in Sagittarius
New Moon—June 25 in Cancer

Full Moon—July 10 in Capricorn
New Moon—July 25 in Leo

Full Moon—August 9 in Aquarius
New Moon—August 23 in Virgo

Full Moon—September 7 in Pisces (lunar eclipse)
New Moon—September 22 in Virgo (solar eclipse)

Full Moon—October 6 in Aries
New Moon—October 22 in Libra

Full Moon—November 5 in Taurus
New Moon—November 20 in Scorpio

Full Moon—December 4 in Gemini
New Moon—December 20 in Sagittarius

How to Time by the Moon Sign

To forecast the daily emotional "weather," to determine your monthly high and low days, or to synchronize your activities with the cycles of the moon, take note of the moon sign under your daily forecast at the end of the book. Here are some of the activities favored and the moods you are likely to encounter under each moon sign.

Moon in Aries: Get Moving!

The new moon in Aries is an ideal time to start new projects. Everyone is pushy, raring to go, rather impatient, and short-tempered. Leave details and follow-up for later. Competitive sports or martial arts are great ways to let off steam. Quiet types could use some assertiveness, but it's a great day for dynamos. Be careful not to step on too many toes.

Moon in Taurus: Lay the Foundations for Success

Do solid, methodical tasks like follow-through or backup work. Make investments, buy real estate, do appraisals, do some hard bargaining. Attend to your property. Get out in the country or spend some time in your garden. Enjoy creature comforts, music, a good dinner, sensual lovemaking. Forget starting a diet—this is a day when you'll feel self-indulgent.

Moon in Gemini: Communicate

Talk means action today. Telephone, write letters, fax! Make new contacts, stay in touch with steady customers. You can juggle lots of tasks today. It's a great time for mental activity of any kind. Don't try to pin people down—they, too, are feeling restless. Keep it light. Flirtations and socializing are good. Watch gossip—and don't give away secrets.

Moon in Cancer: Pay Attention to Loved Ones

This is a moody, sensitive, emotional time. People respond to personal attention, to mothering. Stay at home, have a family dinner, call your mother. Nostalgia, memories, and psychic powers are heightened. You'll want to hang on to people and things (don't clean out your closets now). You could have shrewd insights into what others really need and want. Pay attention to dreams, intuition, and gut reactions.

Moon in Leo: Be Confident

Everybody is in a much more confident, warm, generous mood. It's a good day to ask for a raise, show what you can do, dress like a star. People will respond to flattery, enjoy a bit of drama and theater. You may be extravagant, treat yourself royally, and show off a bit—but don't break the bank! Be careful you don't promise more than you can deliver.

Moon in Virgo: Be Practical

Do practical down-to-earth chores. Review your budget, make repairs, be an efficiency expert. Not a day to ask for a raise. Tend to personal care and maintenance. Have a health checkup, go on a diet, buy vitamins or health food. Make your home spotless. Take care of details and piled-up chores. Reorganize your work and life so they run more smoothly and efficiently. Save money. Be prepared for others to be in a critical, faultfinding mood.

Moon in Libra: Be Diplomatic

Attend to legal matters. Negotiate contracts. Arbitrate. Do things with your favorite partner. Socialize. Be romantic. Buy a special gift, a beautiful object. Decorate yourself or your surroundings. Buy new clothes. Throw a party. Have an elegant, romantic evening. Smooth over any ruffled feathers. Avoid confrontations. Stick to civilized discussions.

Moon in Scorpio: Solve Problems

This is a day to do things with passion. You'll have excellent concentration and focus. Try not to get too intense emotionally. Avoid sharp exchanges with loved ones. Others may tend to go to extremes, get jealous, overreact. Great for troubleshooting, problem solving, research, scientific work—and making love. Pay attention to those psychic vibes.

Moon in Sagittarius: Sell and Motivate

A great time for travel, philosophical discussions, setting long-range career goals. Work out, do sports, buy athletic equipment. Others will be feeling upbeat, exuberant, and adventurous. Risk taking is favored. You may feel like taking a gamble, betting on the horses. visiting a local casino, buying a lottery ticket. Teaching, writing, and spiritual activities also get the green light. Relax outdoors. Take care of animals.

Moon in Capricorn: Get Organized

You can accomplish a lot now, so get on the ball! Attend to business. Issues concerning your basic responsibilities, duties, family, and elderly parents could crop up. You'll be expected to deliver on promises. Weed out the deadwood from your life. Get a dental checkup. Not a good day for gambling or taking risks.

Moon in Aquarius: Join the Group

A great day for doing things with groups—clubs, meetings, outings, politics, parties. Campaign for your candidate. Work for a worthy cause. Deal with larger issues that affect humanity—the environment and metaphysical questions. Buy a computer or electronic gadget. Watch TV. Wear something outrageous. Try something you've never done before. Present an original idea. Don't stick to a rigid schedule—go with the flow. Take a class in meditation, mind control, yoga.

Moon in Pisces: Be Creative

This can be a very creative day, so let your imagination work overtime. Film, theater, music, ballet could inspire you. Spend some time alone, resting and reflecting, reading or writing poetry. Daydreams can also be profitable. Help those less fortunate. Lend a listening ear to someone who may be feeling blue. Don't overindulge in self-pity or escapism, however. People are especially vulnerable to substance abuse now. Turn your thoughts to romance and someone special.

Retrogrades: When the Planets Seem to Backstep

All the planets, except for the sun and moon, have times when they appear to move backward—or retrograde—as it seems from our point of view on earth. At these times, planets do not work as they normally do. So it's best to "take a break" from that planet's energies in our life and to do some work on an inner level.

Mercury Retrograde: The Key Is in "Re"

Mercury goes retrograde most often, and its effects can be especially irritating. When it reaches a short distance ahead of the sun several times a year, it seems to move backward from our point of view. Astrologers often compare retrograde motion to the optical illusion that occurs when we ride on a train that passes another train traveling at a different speed—the second train appears to be moving in reverse.

What this means to you is that the Mercury-ruled areas of your life—analytical thought processes, communications, scheduling—are subject to all kinds of confusion. Be prepared. Communications equipment can break down. Schedules may be changed on short notice. People are late for appointments or don't show up at all. Traffic is terrible. Major purchases malfunction, don't work out, or get delivered in the wrong color. Letters don't arrive or are delivered to the wrong address. Employees will make errors that have to be corrected later. Contracts don't work out or must be renegotiated.

Since most of us can't put our lives on "hold" during Mercury retrogrades, we should learn to tame the trickster and make it work for us. The key is in the prefix *re-*. This is the time to go back over things in your life, *re*flect on what you've done during the previous months. Now you can get deeper insights, spot errors you've missed. So take time to *re*view and *re*evaluate what has happened. *R*est and *re*ward yourself—it's a good time to take a vacation, especially if you *re*visit a favorite place. *Re*organize your work and finish up projects that are backed up. Clean out your desk and closets. Throw away what you can't *re*cycle. If you must sign contracts or agreements, do so with a contingency clause that lets you *re*evaluate the terms later.

Postpone major purchases or commitments for the time being. Don't get married (unless you're *re*marrying the same person). Try not to *re*ly on other people keeping appointments, contracts, or agreements to the letter; have several alternatives. Double-check and *re*ad between the lines. Don't buy anything connected with communications or transportation (if you must, be sure to cover yourself).

Mercury retrograding through your sun sign will intensify its effect on your life.

If Mercury was retrograde when you were born, you may be one of the lucky people who don't suffer the frustrations of this period. If so, your mind probably works in a very intuitive, insightful way.

The sign in which Mercury is retrograding can give you an idea of what's in store—as well as the sun signs that will be especially challenged.

Mercury Retrogrades in 2006

Mercury has three retrograde periods this year.
  March 2 to March 25 in Pisces

July 4 to July 28 from Leo back to Cancer
October 28 to November 17 in Scorpio

Venus Retrograde: Relationships Are Affected

Retrograding Venus can cause your relationships to take a backward step, or it can make you extravagant and impractical. Shopping till you drop and buying what you cannot afford are problems at this time. It's *not* a good time to redecorate—you'll hate the color of the walls later. Postpone getting a new hairstyle. Try not to fall in love either. But if you wish to make amends in an already troubled relationship, make peaceful overtures at this time.

Venus Retrogrades in 2006

Venus turns retrograde in Aquarius on December 24, 2005, until February 3, 2006 (back in Capricorn).

Use the Go Power of Mars

Mars shows how and when to get where you want to go. Timing your moves with Mars on your side can give you a big push. On the other hand, pushing Mars the wrong way can guarantee that you'll run into frustrations in every corner. Your best times to forge ahead are during the weeks when Mars is traveling through your sun sign or your Mars sign (look these up in the tables in this book). Also consider times when Mars is in a compatible sign (fire with air signs, or earth with water signs). You'll be sure to have planetary power on your side.

Mars Retrogrades in 2006

There is no Mars retrograde period in 2006.

When Other Planets Retrograde

The slower-moving planets stay retrograde for months at a time (Jupiter, Saturn, Neptune, Uranus, and Pluto).

When Saturn is retrograde, it's an uphill battle with self-discipline. You may not be in the mood for work. You may feel more like hanging out at the beach than getting things done.

Neptune retrograde promotes a dreamy escapism from reality, when you may feel you're in a fog (Pisces will feel this, especially).

Uranus retrograde may mean setbacks in areas where there have been sudden changes, when you may be forced to regroup or reevaluate the situation.

Pluto retrograde is a time to work on establishing proportion and balance in areas where there have been recent dramatic transformations.

When the planets move forward again, there's a shift in the atmosphere. Activities connected with each planet start moving ahead, plans that were stalled get rolling. Make a special note of those days on your calendar and proceed accordingly.

Other Retrogrades in 2006

The five slower-moving planets all go retrograde in 2006. Jupiter retrogrades from March 4 to July 6 in Scorpio. Saturn retrogrades in Leo from November 22, 2005, to April 5, 2006. It turns retrograde again on December 5, 2006, also in Leo, for the duration of the year.

Uranus retrogrades from June 19 to November 20 in Pisces.

Neptune retrogrades from May 22 to October 29 in Aquarius.

Pluto retrogrades from March 29 to September 4 in Sagittarius.

CHAPTER 3

The Moon: Your Emotional Barometer

Your sun sign reveals your personality—but for information about your feelings and inner emotional life, astrologers look at your moon sign. In some astrology-conscious lands, the moon placement is given as much importance in a horoscope as the sun. The moon sign is the best barometer of your moods and needs. How you react to life's problems, what you care about, what you need to feel comfortable, secure, and romantic are a few secrets revealed by the moon.

Astrologers often refer to the sun and moon as the lights, an apt term, since they shed the most light upon our personality in a horoscope reading. This also is a more technically appropriate description, since the sun and moon are not really planets, but a star and a satellite. Since ancient times, the moon has symbolized nurturing, caring, protecting. Imagine what would happen if the moon were somehow caused to change its orbit, perhaps by a bombarding asteroid. What would happen to the tides, to ocean and plant life, which respond to the moon, or to our own bodies, which are mostly water? The state of shellfish, animals, and planets is affected by the moon. Without the moon in its current orbit, life on earth would be impossible.

Through the centuries, the moon has been represented by a mother goddess figure, symbolizing the ultimate in feminine caring. This follows through in your horoscope, where the moon represents your receptive, reflective, female, nurturing self. It also reflects who you were nurtured by—the mother or mother figure in your chart. In a man's chart, the moon position describes his receptive, emotional, yin side, as well as the woman in his life who will have the deepest effect, usually his mother. (Venus reveals the kind of woman who will attract him physically.)

The sign the moon was passing through at birth reveals much about your inner life, your needs and secrets, as well as those of the people you'd like to know better. You can learn what appeals to people subconsciously by knowing their moon sign, which reflects their instinctive emotional nature.

It's well worth having an accurate chart cast to determine your moon sign, which several Internet sites listed in this book will do for you. (See chapter 9.) Since accurate moon tables are too extensive for this book, check through the following listing to find the moon sign that feels most familiar.

The moon is more at home in some signs than others. It rules maternal Cancer and is exalted in Taurus—both comforting, home-loving signs where the natural emotional energies of the moon are easily and productively expressed. But when the moon is in the opposite signs—Capricorn and Scorpio—it leaves the comfortable nest and deals with emotional issues of power and achievement in the outside world. Those of you with the moon in these signs are likely to find your emotional role more challenging in life.

Moon in Aries

This placement makes you both independent and ardent. An idealist, you tend to fall in and out of love easily. You love a challenge but could cool once your quarry is captured. Your emotional reactions are fast and fiery, quickly expressed and quickly forgotten. You may not think before expressing your feelings. It's not easy to hide how you feel. Channeling all your emotional energy could be one of your big challenges.

Moon in Taurus

A sentimental soul, you are very fond of the good life, and you gravitate toward solid, secure relationships. You like displays of affection and creature comforts—all the tangible trappings of a cozy, safe, calm atmosphere. You are sensual and steady emotionally, but very stubborn, possessive, and determined. You can't be pushed, and you tend to dislike changes. You should make an effort to broaden your horizons and to take a risk sometimes. You may become very attached to your home turf. You may also be a collector of objects that are meaningful to you.

Moon in Gemini

You crave mental stimulation and variety in life, which you usually get through either an ever-varied social life, the excitement of flirtation and/or multiple professional involvements. You may marry more than once and have a rather chaotic emotional life due to your difficulty with commitment and settling down, as well as your need to be constantly on the go. (Be sure to find a partner who is as outgoing as you are.) You will have to learn at some point to focus your energies because you tend to be somewhat fragmented—to do two things at once, to have two homes or even two lovers. If you can find a creative way to express your many-faceted nature, you'll be ahead of the game.

Moon in Cancer

This is the most powerful lunar position, which is sure to make a deep imprint on your character. Your needs are very much associated with your reaction to the needs of others. You are very sensitive, caring, and self-protective, though some of you may mask this with a hard shell, like the moon-sensitive crab. This placement also gives an excellent memory, keen intuition, and an uncanny ability to perceive the needs of others. All of the lunar phases will affect you, especially full moons and eclipses, so you would do well to mark them on your calendar. Because you're happiest at home, you may work at home or turn your office into a second home, where you can nurture and comfort people. (You may tend to mother the world.) With natural psychic, intuitive ability, you might be drawn to occult work in some way. Or you may get professionally involved with providing food and shelter to others.

Moon in Leo

This warm, passionate moon takes everything to heart. You are attracted to all that is noble, generous, and aristocratic in life (and may be a bit of a snob). You have an innate ability to take command emotionally, but you do need strong support, loyalty, and loud applause from those you love. You are possessive of your loved ones and your turf and will roar if anyone threatens to take over your territory.

Moon in Virgo

You are rather cool until you decide if others measure up. But once someone or something meets your ideal standards, you hold up your end of the arrangement perfectly. You may, in fact, drive yourself too hard to attain some notion of perfection. Try to be a bit easier on yourself and others. Don't always act the censor! You love to be the teacher and are drawn to situations where you can change others for the better, but sometimes you must learn to accept others for what they are—enjoy what you have!

Moon in Libra

Like other air-sign moons, you think before you feel. Therefore, you may not immediately recognize the emotional needs of others. However, you are relationship oriented and may find it difficult to be alone or to do things alone. After you have learned emotional balance by leaning on yourself first, you can have excellent partnerships. It is best for you to avoid extremes, which set your scales swinging and can make your love life precarious. You thrive in a rather conservative, traditional, romantic relationship, where you receive attention and flattery—but not possessiveness—from your partner. You'll be your most charming in an elegant, harmonious atmosphere.

Moon in Scorpio

This is a moon that enjoys and responds to intense, passionate feelings. You may go to extremes and have a very dramatic emotional life, full of ardor, suspicion, jealousy, and obsession. It would be much healthier to channel your need for power and control into meaningful work. This is a good position for anyone in the fields of medicine, police work, research, the occult, psychoanalysis, or intuitive work, because life-and-death situations don't faze you. However, you do take personal disappointments very hard.

Moon in Sagittarius

You take life's ups and downs with good humor and the proverbial grain of salt. You'll love 'em and leave 'em—take off on a great adventure at a moment's notice. Born free could be your slogan. Attracted by the exotic, you have wanderlust mentally and physically. You may be too much in search of new mental and spiritual stimulation to ever settle down.

Moon in Capricorn

Are you ever accused of being too cool and calculating? You have an earthy side, but you take prestige and position very seriously. Your strong drive to succeed extends to your romantic life, where you will be devoted to improving your lifestyle, rising to the top. A structured situation where you can advance methodically makes you feel wonderfully secure. You may be attracted to someone older or very much younger or from a different social world. It may be difficult to look at the lighter side of emotional relationships. Though this moon is placed in the sign of its detriment, the good news is that you tend to be very dutiful and responsible to those you care for.

Moon in Aquarius

You are a people collector with many friends of all backgrounds. You are happiest surrounded by people and may feel uneasy when left alone. Though you usually stay friends with lovers, intense emotions and demanding one-on-one relationships turn you off. You don't like anything to be too rigid or scheduled. Though tolerant and understanding, you can be emotionally unpredictable and may opt for an unconventional love life. With plenty of space, you will be able to sustain relationships with liberal, freedom-loving types.

Moon in Pisces

You are very responsive and empathetic to others, especially if they have problems or are the underdog. (Be on guard against attracting too many people with sob stories.) You'll be happiest if you can express your creative imagination in the arts or in the spiritual or healing professions. Because you may tend to escape in fantasies or overreact to the moods of others, you need an emotional anchor to help you keep a firm foothold in reality. Steer clear of too much escapism (especially in alcohol) or reclusiveness. Places near water soothe your moods. Working in a field that gives you emotional variety will also help you be productive.

Your Happiness Meter

When the daily moon is in your moon sign (or the same element as your moon), your emotions are especially sensitive, your ESP is activated, and you should be in an upbeat mood.

You'll be happiest in the element of your moon sign. Water sign moons (Cancer, Scorpio, Pisces) should head for the nearest body of water—that could be a shower, indoor waterfall, or hot tub—when blue moods hit. A ride on a local ferry could be the perfect mood lifter. Audio tapes with the sound of water—waterfalls or raindrops—could lift your spirits.

Earth sign moons (Taurus, Virgo, Capricorn) resonate to the beauties of nature—hikes in the country, working in the garden, rock climbing. Or the sensual pleasures of listening to music, enjoying a delicious meal. Engaging your mind with shopping or bargaining at a flea market could distract you from problems.

Air sign moons (Gemini, Libra, Aquarius) need to give themselves more space and get rid of any closed-in feeling. Contact with new people and fresh ideas banishes the blues. Parties and other social events, lectures, a mentally stimulating book will restore your equilibrium. Finding a worthy cause and promoting it puts you on a positive track.

Fire sign moons (Aries, Sagittarius, Leo) need a productive place to put their emotional energy. You need to be proactive, to do something positive. Traveling, exercising, and starting a new project rekindle your fiery enthusiasm. A sports event, a contest, training for a race or political campaign, volunteering to help make a difference, putting on a play, or starring in one should recharge your energy.

CHAPTER 4

Those Mysterious Eclipses: How They Can Shake Up Your Life!

Have you ever considered the amazing fact that one of the smallest bodies in our solar system, our moon, appears almost the same size as the sun, the largest body in our solar system? This is most evident during a total solar eclipse, when the moon so neatly covers the sun that scientists can study the solar flares that light up the rim of the eclipse. Imagine what would happen if the moon were somehow caused to change its orbit, perhaps by bombarding asteroids. What would happen to the tides, to ocean and plant life, which respond to the moon, or to our own bodies, which are mostly water? Life on earth would be impossible!

In case we've been taking the moon for granted, the eclipse seasons, which occur about every six months, remind us how important the moon is for our survival. Perhaps that is why eclipses have always had an ominous reputation. The eclipse is a popular theme in Mexican art, with many colorful ceramic or beaded representations available in the markets. Folklore all over the world blames eclipses for catastrophes, such as birth defects, crop failures, and hurricanes. Villagers on the peninsula of Baja California paint their fruit trees red and wear red ribbons and underwear to deflect evil rays. During a total eclipse, everyone retreats safely indoors to follow it on television. In other native societies, people play drums and make loud noises to frighten off heavenly monsters believed to destroy the light of the sun and moon. Only the romantic Tahitians seem to have positive feelings about an eclipse. In this sensual tropical paradise, legend declares that the lights go out when the sun and moon make love and create the stars.

Ancient Chaldean astrologer priests were the first to time eclipses accurately. They discovered that 6,585 days after an eclipse, another eclipse would happen. By counting ahead after all the eclipses in a given year, they could predict eclipses eighteen years into the future. This technique was practiced by navigators through the centuries, including Christopher Columbus, who used his knowledge of an upcoming lunar eclipse to extort food from the frightened inhabitants of Jamaica in 1504. In pre-Columbian Mexico, Mayan astronomer priests also discovered that eclipses occur at regular intervals and recorded them with a hieroglyph of a serpent swallowing the sun.

What Causes an Eclipse?

A solar eclipse is the passage of the new moon directly across the face of the sun. It is a very exciting and awesome event, which causes the sky to darken suddenly. Though the effect lasts only a few minutes, it is enough to strike panic in the uninformed viewer.

A lunar eclipse happens when the full moon passes through the shadow of the earth on the opposite side from the sun; as a result, the earth blocks the sun's light from reaching the moon. The moon must be in level alignment with the sun and earth for a lunar eclipse to occur.

This year, there will be four eclipses: a lunar eclipse on March 14 in Virgo, a total solar eclipse on March 29 in Aries, a lunar eclipse on September 7 in Pisces, and a solar eclipse on September 22 in Virgo.

Conditions are ripe for an eclipse twice a year, when a full or new moon is most likely to cross the path of the sun at two points known as the nodes.

What to Know About Nodes

To understand the nodes, visualize two rings, one inside the other. As you move the rings, you'll notice that the two circles intersect at opposite points. Now imagine one ring as the moon's orbit and the other as the sun's (as seen from earth). The crossing points are called the moon's nodes.

For an eclipse to happen, two conditions must be met. First, the path of the orbiting moon must be close enough to a node. Second, this must happen at a time when there is either a new or full moon. (Not every new or full moon happens close enough to the nodes to create an eclipse.) The axis of the nodes is continually moving backward through the zodiac at the rate of about one and a half degrees per month; therefore, eclipses eventually occur in every sign of the zodiac.

How Often Do Eclipses Occur?

Whenever the sun draws close to one of the nodes, any new or full moon happening near that time will align to create an eclipse. This eclipse season happens twice a year, approximately six months apart. There are at least four eclipses each year, and there can be as many as seven.

Eclipses Have Family Ties

One of the most interesting things about eclipses is that they belong to a string of related eclipses that pop up regularly. As mentioned before, the ancient Chaldeans, who were the first great skywatchers, discovered that eclipses recur in patterns, repeating themselves after approximately eighteen years plus nine to eleven days, in a cycle lasting a total of approximately 1300 years. Much later, in the eleventh century A.D., these patterns became known as the Saros Series. (In ancient Greek, *saros* means repetition.)

How Does a Solar Eclipse Interpretation Differ from a Lunar One?

The lineup of energy in a solar eclipse is quite different from that in a lunar eclipse. Lunar eclipses happen at the full moon, a time in the normal monthly lunar cycle when it's natural for emotions (ruled by the moon) to come to a head and be released. At a lunar eclipse, however, when the earth passes between the sun and moon, the tense pull of energy created by the powerful opposition is temporarily short circuited. During this time, we might become more objective and find relief from destructive emotional patterns, such as addictions, which would normally be intensified. The momentary turnoff of the full moon's emotional energies might give us a different perspective that helps us turn our lives around. On the other hand, this break in the normal cycle could cause a bewildering disorientation that intensifies insecurities and sends us off balance.

The solar eclipse occurs when the moon and sun are directly aligned, with the moon temporarily blocking the sun's energy. Now it is the moon's forces that dominate, interfering with the normal communication between the earth and the sun. When subconscious lunar forces take over, we are more likely to be ruled by our emotions and to make decisions based on subconscious feelings, rather than reason. Our self-esteem may also be weakened, as the sun (our ego force) darkens. However, this can be an opportunity to work on a deep inner spiritual level. Psychic experiences are also possibilities as the doorway to the unconscious opens wide.

Because eclipses bring about such a concentration of energy, these can be intense, unbalanced times, when the rhythms of everything in nature—birds, animals, fish, even oysters—are thrown off. But if we look behind a crisis that occurs at this time, we often find that there is some deep positive force bubbling beneath the surface that needed some kind of upheaval to manifest.

What Is the Purpose of an Eclipse in Your Life?

Eclipses can bring on milestone events in your life, if they aspect a key point in your horoscope. In general, they shake up the status quo, bringing hidden areas out into the open. During this time, problems you've been avoiding or have brushed aside can surface to demand your attention. A good coping strategy is to accept whatever comes up as a challenge. It could make a big difference in your life. And don't forget the power of your sense of humor. If you can laugh at something, you'll never be afraid of it.

Second-guessing the eclipses is easy if you have a copy of your horoscope calculated by a computer. This enables you to pinpoint the area of your life which will be affected. However, you can make an educated guess, by setting up a rough diagram on your own. If you'd like to find out which area of your life this year's eclipses are most likely to affect, follow these easy steps. First, you must know the time of day you were born and look up your rising sign listed on the tables in this book. Set up an estimated horoscope by drawing a circle; then divide it into four parts by making a cross directly through the center. Continue to divide each of the parts into thirds, as if you were dividing a cake, until you have twelve slices. Write your rising sign on the middle left-hand slice, which would be the nine o'clock point, if you were looking at your watch. Then continue counterclockwise until you have listed all twelve signs of the zodiac.

You should now have a basic diagram of your horoscope chart (minus the planets, of course). Starting with your rising sign slice, number each portion consecutively, working counterclockwise. Since this year's eclipses will fall in Aries, Pisces, and Virgo, find the number of these slices or houses on the chart and read the following descriptions for the kinds of issues that are likely to be emphasized.

If an eclipse falls in your FIRST HOUSE

Events cause you to examine the ways you are acting independently, push you to become more visible, to assert yourself. This is a time when you feel compelled to make your own decisions, do your own thing. There is an emphasis on how you are coming across to others. You may want to change your physical appearance, body image, or style of dress in some way. Under affliction, there might be illness or physical harm.

If an eclipse falls in your SECOND HOUSE

This is the place where you consider all matters of security. You consolidate your resources, earn money, acquire property, decide what you value, what you want to own. On a deeper level, this house reveals your sense of self-worth, the inner values that draw wealth in various forms.

If an eclipse falls in your THIRD HOUSE

Here you communicate, reach out to others, express your ideas, explore different courses of action. You may feel especially restless, have confrontations with neighbors or siblings. In your search for more knowledge, you may decide to improve your skills, get more education, or sign up for a course that interests you. Local transportation, especially your car, might be affected by an eclipse here.

If an eclipse falls in your FOURTH HOUSE

Here is where you put down roots, establish your home base. You'll consider what home really means to you. Issues involving parents, the physical setup or location of your home, your immediate family demand your attention. You may be especially concerned with parenting or relationships with your own mother. You may consider moving your home to a new location or leaving home.

If an eclipse falls in your FIFTH HOUSE

Here is where you express yourself, either through your personal talents or through creating children. You are interested in making your special talents visible. This is also the house of love affairs and the romantic aspect of life, where you flirt, have fun, enjoy the excitement of love. Hobbies and crafts, the ways you explore the playful child within, fall in this area.

If an eclipse falls in your SIXTH HOUSE

This is your care and maintenance department, where you take care of your health, organize your life, set up a daily routine. It is also the place where you perfect your skills, add polish to your life. The chores you do every day, the skills you learn, the techniques you use fall here. If something doesn't work in your life, an eclipse is sure to bring this to light. If you've been neglecting your health, diet, and fitness, you'll probably pay the consequences during an eclipse. Or you may be faced with work that requires much routine organization and steady effort, rather than creative ability. Or you may be required to perform services for others.

If an eclipse falls in your SEVENTH HOUSE

This is the area of committed relationships, of those which involve legal agreements, of working in a close relationship with another. Here you'll be dealing with how you relate, what you'll be willing to give up for the sake of a marriage or partnership. Eclipses here can put extra pressure on a relationship and, if it's not working, precipitate a breakup. Lawsuits and open enemies also reside here.

If an eclipse falls in your EIGHTH HOUSE

This area is concerned with power and control. Consider what you are willing to give up in order that something might happen. Power struggles, intense relationships, desire to penetrate a deeper mystery belong here. Debts, loans, financial matters that involve another party, and wheeling and dealing also come into focus. So does sex, where you surrender your individual power to create a new life together. Matters involving birth and death are also involved here.

If an eclipse falls in your NINTH HOUSE

Here is where you look at the big picture, how everything relates to form a pattern. You'll seek information that helps you find meaning in life: higher education, religion, travel, global issues. Eclipses here can push you to get out of your rut, explore something you've never done before, expand your horizons.

If an eclipse falls in your TENTH HOUSE

This is the high profile point in your chart. Here is where you consider how society looks at you, what your position is in the outside world. You'll be concerned about whether you receive proper credit for your work and if you're recognized by higher-ups. Promotions, raises and other forms of recognition can be given or denied. Your standing in your career or community can be challenged, or you'll get publicly acknowledged for achieving a goal. An eclipse here can make you famous . . . or burst your balloon if you've been too ambitious or neglecting other areas of your life.

If an eclipse falls in your ELEVENTH HOUSE

Your relationship with groups of people comes under scrutiny during an eclipse. Who are you identified with, who do you socialize with, how well are you accepted by other members of your team. Activities of clubs, political parties, networking, social interactions become important. You'll be concerned about what other people think.

If an eclipse falls in your TWELFTH HOUSE

This is the time when the focus turns to your inner life. An especially favorable eclipse here might bring you great insight and inspiration. Or events may happen which cause you to retreat from public life. Here is where we go to be alone, do spiritual or reparatory work in retreats, hospitals, religious institutions, psychotherapy. Here is where you deliver selfless service, through charitable acts. Good aspects from an eclipse could promote an ability to go with the flow, to rise above the competition and find an inner, almost mystical strength that enables you to connect with the deepest needs of others.

What Is the Best Thing to Do During an Eclipse?

When the natural rhythms of the sun and moon are disturbed, it's best to postpone important activities. Be sure to mark eclipse days on your calendar, especially if the eclipse falls in your birth sign. This year, those born under Aries, Pisces, and Virgo should take special note of the feelings that arise. With lunar eclipses, some possibilities could be a break from attachments, or the healing of an illness or substance abuse which had been triggered by the subconscious. The temporary event could be a healing time, when you gain perspective. During solar eclipses, when you might be in a highly subjective state, pay attention to the hidden subconscious patterns that surface, the emotional truth that is revealed at this time.

The effect of the eclipse can reverberate for some time, often months after the event. But it is especially important to stay cool and make no major moves during the period known as the shadow of the eclipse, which begins about a week before and lasts until at least three days after the eclipse. After three days, the daily rhythms should return to normal and you can proceed with business as usual.

Back in 1648, an astrologer named William Lilly wrote a treatise on eclipses that listed the effect of an eclipse in each of the astrological signs. Though his predictions stressed the negative side of the eclipse, some have been quite accurate. Solar eclipses in Pisces, for instance, were said to portend the destruction and waste in sea towns, an earthquake, and churchmen "questioned and called to account for knavery." In 1989, there was a solar eclipse in Pisces (reinforced by a conjunction of Saturn and Neptune, ruler of Pisces). In the following few months, there was a devastating earthquake in San Francisco, much concern about water pollution and oil spills, and the sensational trial of TV evangelist Jim Bakker, whose financial and sexual scandals surfaced and sent him to prison.

However, it is a more positive way to view eclipses as very special times, when we can receive great insight through a changed perspective. By blacking out the emotional pressure of the full moon, a lunar eclipse could be a time of reason, rather than confusion, a time when we can take a break from our problems. A solar eclipse, when the new moon blocks out the sun (or ego), could be a time when the moon's most positive qualities are expressed, bringing us a feeling of oneness, nurturing, and compassion.

CHAPTER 5

Solving the Mystery of Astrology: Your Big Questions Answered Here!

Is astrology a mystery to you? Once you get beyond sun signs, the symbols and terminology of this subject can often be confusing to the beginner. Here are some of the basic questions asked about how astrology works. The answers should help solve some of astrology's mysteries for you. Like so many readers, you'll find that it's easy to get hooked on astrology. The more you know, the more deeply you'll want to investigate this fascinating subject.

What is the difference between an astrological sign and a constellation?

This is one of the most frequently asked questions. Everyone knows that the constellations of the zodiac are specific configurations of stars. But not everyone knows that the sign the constellation represents may be in a different place!

A sign is actually a 30 degree division of a circular belt of sky called the zodiac. These divisions never change. They are the basic real estate of astrology. (The word *zodiac* comes from the Greek word meaning "circle of animals".) Originally, each division was marked by a constellation, some of which were named after animals or sea creatures: a lion, a bull, a goat, a ram, a fish, etc.

But as the earth's axis changed over thousands of years, so did the celestial signposts. However, the namesake division of the circle, which is what astrologers call a sign, always remains in the same place.

Then what is a sun sign?

A sun sign is the sign (or 30-degree segment of the zodiac) that the sun was passing through at the time of your birth. Your sun sign is really the foundation of your horoscope, the base of your astrological character. It takes on color and nuances with nine other planets (including the moon, which is most often referred to as a planet) and the signs in which they fall.

What does it mean that Pisces is a water sign or Aquarius is an air sign?

The definitions of the signs evolved systematically from four components that interrelate. These four different criteria are a sign's element: its quality, its polarity or sex, and its order in the progression of the zodiac. All these factors work together to tell us what the sign is like.

The system is magically mathematical. The number 12—as in the twelve signs of the zodiac—is divisible by 4, by 3, and by 2. There are four elements, three qualities, and two polarities, which follow each other in sequence around the zodiac.

The four elements (earth, air, fire, and water) are the building blocks of astrology. The use of an element to describe a sign probably dates from man's first attempts to categorize what he saw. Ancient sages believed that all things were composed of combinations of these basic elements—earth, air, fire, and water. This included the human character, which was fiery/choleric, earthy/melancholy, airy/sanguine, or watery/phlegmatic. The elements also correspond to our emotional (water), physical (earth), mental (air) and spiritual (fire) natures. The energies of each of the elements were then observed to be related to the time of year when the sun was passing through a certain segment of the zodiac.

Those born with the sun in fire signs—Aries, Leo, Sagittarius—embody the characteristic of that element. Optimism, warmth, hot tempers, enthusiasm, and spirit are typical of these signs. Taurus, Virgo, and Capricorn are earthy—more grounded, physical, materialistic, organized and deliberate than fire sign people. Air-sign people—Gemini, Libra, and Aquarius—are mentally oriented communicators. Water signs—Cancer, Scorpio, and Pisces—are emotional, sensitive, and creative.

Think of what each element does to the others. Water puts out fire or evaporates under heat. Air fans the flames or blows them out. Earth smothers fire, drifts and erodes with too much wind, becomes mud or fertile soil with water. Those are often perfect analogies for the relationships between people of different sun sign elements. This astrochemistry was one of the first ways man described his relationships. Fortunately, no one is entirely air or fire. We all have a bit, or a lot, of each element in our horoscopes. It is this unique mix that defines each astrological personality.

Within each element, there are three qualities that describe types of behavior associated with the sign. Those of cardinal signs are activists, go-getters. These four signs—Aries, Cancer, Libra, and Capricorn—begin each season. Fixed signs, which happen in the middle of the season, are associated with builders, stabilizers. You'll find that sun signs Taurus, Leo, Scorpio, and Aquarius are usually gifted with concentration, stamina, and focus. Mutable signs—Gemini, Virgo, Sagittarius, and Pisces—fall at the end of each season and thus are considered catalysts for change. People born under mutable signs are flexible, adaptable.

The polarity of a sign is either its positive or negative charge. It can be masculine, active, positive, and yang like air or fire signs. Or feminine, reactive, negative, and yin like the water and earth signs.

Finally, we consider the sign's place in the order of

the zodiac. This is vital to the balance of all the forces and the transmission of energy moving through the signs. You may have noticed that your sign is quite different from your neighboring sign on either side. Yet each seems to grow out of its predecessor like links in a chain and transmits a synthesis of energy gathered along the chain to the following sign, beginning with the fire-powered, active, positive charge of Aries.

What if a person has no planets in an element?

Usually that person will be especially challenged in the areas of that low-function element. For instance, someone who has no planets in earth signs may have to work very hard to manifest the material side of life. Or the person may overcompensate in that area and want to be around earthy things—have a beautiful garden, for instance.

It's appropriate here to remember that, in astrology, there are no pat answers. How a chart works out depends on the individual—a missing element could be an area of great self-expression and self-development, as well as a difficult area. The missing element could also be emphasized in the placement of the houses. Someone with no planets in the water element might have a water rising sign or one in another powerful angular position.

Does my sign have a special planet?

Each sign has a ruling planet that is most compatible with its energies. Mars adds its fiery assertive characteristics to Aries. The sensual beauty and comfort-loving side of Venus rules Taurus, whereas the idealistic side of Venus rules Libra. Quick-moving Mercury rules two mutable signs, Gemini and Virgo. Its mental agility belongs to Gemini while its analytical, critical side is best expressed in Virgo. The changeable emotional moon is associated with Cancer, while the outgoing Leo personality is ruled by the sun. Scorpio originally shared Mars, but when Pluto was discovered in this century, its powerful magnetic energies were deemed more suitable to the intense vibrations of the fixed water sign Scorpio. Disciplined Capricorn is ruled by Saturn, and expansive Sagittarius by Jupiter. Unpredictable Aquarius is ruled by Uranus and creative, imaginative Pisces by Neptune. In a horoscope, if a planet is placed in the sign it rules, it is sure to be especially powerful.

How does an astrologer cast a horoscope?

An astrologer first gathers information about the subject that will enable the horoscope to have a specific time and place. A horoscope can be cast about anything that has a specific time and place. This could be the birth of someone, a meeting, an event, etc. It is very important that the time be as accurate as possible, because this influences the setup of the horoscope chart.

After obtaining an accurate time and place, the astrologer calculates the exact placement of the moon and planets at that moment. Most astrologers today can do this very quickly using sophisticated computer software that will accurately place the planets around a horoscope chart. The astrologer then will interpret the chart according to the client's needs, perhaps calculating several other charts for related events. (See the chapter in this book on astrological readings for more details.)

What does a house mean in astrology?

A horoscope chart is a map of the heavens at a given moment in time. It looks somewhat like a wheel divided with twelve spokes. In between each of the "spokes" is a section called a *house*.

Each house deals with a different area of life and is influenced by a special sign and a planet. In addition, the house is governed by the sign passing over the spoke (or cusp of the house) at that particular moment. For example, the first house is naturally associated with Aries and Mars. However, if Capricorn was the sign passing over the house cusp at the time the chart was cast, that house would have a Capricorn influence as well.

The houses start at the left center spoke (the number 9 position if you were reading a clock) and are read *counterclockwise* around the chart.

Astrologers look at the houses to tell in what area of a subject's life an event is happening or about to happen in the subject's career, finances, health, or other area designated by the house.

The First House: Home of Aries and Mars

The sign passing over the first house at the time of your birth is known as your *ascendant,* or *rising sign.* The first house is the house of "firsts"—the first impression you make, how you initiate matters, the image you choose to project. This is where you advertise yourself, where you project your personality. Planets that fall here will intensify the way you come across to others. Often the first house will project an entirely different type of personality than the sun sign. For instance, a Capricorn with Leo in the first house will come across as much more flamboyant than the average Capricorn.

The Second House: Home of Taurus and Venus

This house is where you experience the material world—what you value. Here are your attitudes about money, possessions, finances, whatever belongs to you, and what you own, as well as your earning and spending capacity. On a deeper level, this house reveals your sense of self-worth, the inner values that draw wealth in various forms.

The Third House: Home of Gemini and Mercury

This house describes how you communicate with others, how you reach out to others nearby, and how you interact with the immediate environment. It shows how your thinking process works and the way you express your thoughts. Are you articulate or tongue-tied? Can you think on your feet? This house also shows your first relationships, your experiences with brothers and sisters, and how you deal with people close to you such as your neighbors or pals. It's where you take short trips, write letters, or use the telephone. It shows how your mind works in terms of left-brain logical and analytical functions.

The Fourth House: Home of Cancer and the Moon

The fourth house shows the foundation of life, the psychological underpinnings. At the bottom of the chart, this house shows how you are nurtured and made to feel secure—your roots! It shows your early home environment and the circumstances at the end of your life (your final "home") as well as the place you call home now. Astrologers look here for information about the parental nurturers in your life.

The Fifth House: Home of Leo and the Sun

The fifth house is where the creative potential develops. Here you express yourself and procreate in the sense that children are outgrowths of your creative ability. But this house most represents your inner childlike self who delights in play. If your inner security has been established by the time you reach this house, you are now free to have fun, romance, and love affairs and to give of yourself. This is also the place astrologers look for playful love affairs, flirtations, and brief romantic encounters (rather than long-term commitments).

The Sixth House: Home of Virgo and Mercury

The sixth house has been called the "care and maintenance" department. This house shows how you take care of your body and organize yourself to perform efficiently in the world. Here is where you get things done, where you look after others, and fulfill service duties such as taking care of pets. Here is what you do to survive on a day-to-day basis. The sixth house demands order in your life; otherwise there would be chaos. This house is your "job" (as opposed to your career, which is the domain of the tenth house), your diet, and your health and fitness regimens.

The Seventh House: Home of Libra and Venus

This house shows your attitude toward partners and those with whom you enter into commitments, contracts, or agreements. Here is the way you relate to others, as well as your close, intimate, one-on-one relationships (including open enemies—those you "face off" with). Open hostilities, lawsuits, divorces, and marriages happen here. If the first house represents the "I," the seventh or opposite house is the "not-I"—the complementary partner you attract by the way you come across. If you are having trouble with partnerships, consider what you are attracting by the energies of your first and seventh house.

The Eighth House: Home of Scorpio and Pluto (also Mars)

The eighth house refers to how you merge with something or someone, and how you handle power and control. This is one of the most mysterious and powerful houses, where your energy transforms itself from "I" to "we." As you give up power and control by uniting with something or someone, two kinds of energies merge and become something greater, leading to a regeneration of the self on a higher level. Here are your attitudes toward sex, shared resources, taxes (what you share with the government). Because this house involves what belongs to others, you face issues of control and power struggles, or undergo a deep psychological transformation as you bond with another. Here you transcend yourself with dreams, drugs, and occult or psychic experiences that reflect the collective unconscious.

The Ninth House: Home of Sagittarius and Jupiter

The ninth house shows your search for wisdom and higher knowledge—your belief system. As the third house represents the "lower mind," its opposite on the wheel, the ninth house, is the "higher mind"—the abstract, intuitive, spiritual mind that asks "big" questions like "Why are we here?" After the third house has explored what was close at hand, the ninth stretches out to broaden you mentally with higher education and travel. Here you stretch spiritually with religious activity. Since you are concerned with how everything is related, you tend to push boundaries, take risks. Here is where you express your ideas in a book or thesis, where you pontificate, philosophize, or preach.

The Tenth House: Home of Capricorn and Saturn

The tenth house is associated with your public life and high-profile activities. Located directly overhead at the "high noon" position on the horoscope wheel, this is the most "visible" house in the chart, the one where the world sees you. It deals with your career (but not your routine "job") and your reputation. Here is where you go public, take on responsibilities (as opposed to the fourth house, where you stay home). This will affect the career you choose and your "public relations." This house is also associated with your father figure or the main authority figure in your life.

The Eleventh House: Home of Aquarius and Uranus

The eleventh house is where you extend yourself to a group, a goal, or a belief system. This house is where you define what you really want, the kinds of friends you have, your political affiliations, and the kind of groups you identify with as an equal. Here is where you become concerned with "what other people think" or where you rebel against social conventions. Here is where you could become a socially conscious humanitarian or a partygoing social butterfly. It's where you look to others to stimulate you and discover your kinship to the rest of humanity. The sign on this house can help you understand what you gain and lose from friendships.

The Twelfth House: Home of Pisces and Neptune

The twelfth house is where the boundaries between yourself and others become blurred, and you become selfless. Old-fashioned astrologers used to put a rather negative spin on this house, calling it the "house of self-undoing." When we "undo ourselves," we surrender control, boundaries, limits, and rules. But instead of being self-undoing, the twelfth house can be a place of great creativity and talent. It is the place where you can tap into the collective unconscious, where your imagination is limitless.

Are some houses more important than others?

Houses are stronger or weaker depending on how many planets are inhabiting them. If there are many planets in a given house, it follows that the activities of that house will be especially important in your life. If the planet that rules the house is also located there, this also adds power to the house.

If someone has the same birthday as mine, why aren't our lives similar? What about twins?

Even a few moments' difference in time can change a horoscope chart. However, the difference in development of the charts involves how the individual uses the energies. Though astrology may indicate certain strengths and weaknesses, every person can choose positive or negative ways to express them. We often see strikingly similar charts, belonging to people who bear little resemblance to each other, who have used their energies in radically different ways. Twins may often choose to express different facets of very similar charts, simply from the desire not to be alike.

Besides my sun sign, how many other signs do I have?

In compiling your astrological database, we consider eight planets, besides the moon and sun. The three closest planets to the earth—Mercury, Mars, Venus—and the moon affect your personal character. The next farthest out, Jupiter and Saturn, affect influences from others, turning points, and significant cycles in your life. As we get farther out, the slower-moving planets Uranus, Neptune, and Pluto deal with mass trends that influence your whole generation.

In the Western system of astrology, we confine our charts to the planets and stars within the zodiac. We would not consider the influence of the Big Dipper or Orion or black holes or supernovas.

What about the new planets being discovered, the asteroids, and Chiron?

With ten planets to juggle, what more do astrologers need? The answer could come from our quest for depth, richness, and relationship to the issues of today, which emerges in the archetypes and symbolism of the most recent discoveries. Women's consciousness, deep psychological issues, healing and ecology, as well as our approach to the afterlife, all have a place in astrological readings and can be clarified by components discovered in our own time.

The asteroids, a ring of thousands of oddly shaped objects between Mars and Jupiter, have recently been noticed by astrologers who have begun to chart the effects of the larger ones—Pallas, Vesta, Ceres, and Juno—in the horoscopes of clients and have found a correlation with the reemergence of feminine consciousness.

Chiron is a small body orbiting between Saturn and Uranus, which some scientists think is a comet captured from outer space. Astrologers have discovered that it has very deep psychological meaning in our chart.

It was discovered in 1977 and named after mythological centaur, half man and half horse, who was known for his wisdom and learning and who became a teacher to both the gods and man. The mythological Chiron was severely disabled by an arrow wound, which gives a special meaning to the planetoid. It is believed to relate to the area in life where we are wounded, emotionally or physically, and must learn from those experiences to teach and heal others. To benefit from Chiron's wisdom, we must rise above our wounds to choose a higher, noble path. It is then that Chiron has the power to unlock higher consciousness.

New planets far out in space, plus asteroids and other objects, are constantly being discovered and interpreted by astrologers. Who knows, even satellites and space stations may affect our charts. Whatever is out there or whatever we put out there has a place in the energies that affect us all.

Will astrology conflict with my religious beliefs?

Many religious people disapprove of astrologers, first because they confuse modern-day astrologers with charlatans or fortune-tellers of the past, or because they feel someone interested in astrology will turn away from religion. However, the study of astrology actually brings one closer to a religious understanding of the dynamic interchange between the universal cycles, the material world, and man's place in it.

There is no religious dogma attached to astrology—although it can be found in the spiritual history of all races. It is an objective study with no definite rules for behavior, moral codes or concept of a particular god. Most astrologers stress strongly that you are in charge of your horoscope. It is a diagnostic tool for enlightenment, a helpful method of analysis, but by no means an arbitrary dictator and should not conflict with any form of spiritual self-development.

I would like to use my computer to learn more about astrology by doing some charts for friends. What kind of software would you recommend for a nonprofessional student of astrology?

If you have a PC or Mac, the world of astrology really opens up for you. Since you will be using the astrology program only occasionally for fun, then you won't need expensive or complicated software. You might even download a free chart calculation program from the Internet. Contact one of the software companies listed in chapter 9 for suggestions and perhaps free demo software. You should also learn the astrology symbols (or glyphs), which are explained in chapter 7 since they are universally used in astrology software.

CHAPTER 6

Your Planetary Power Sources

Besides the sun and moon, there are eight planets in your horoscope that make up the composite energy picture that is uniquely you. Each is a special power source representing a basic force in life. The location of a planet in your horoscope can determine how strongly that planet will affect you. A planet that's close to your rising sign will be emphasized in your chart. If two or more planets are grouped together in one sign, they usually operate together, playing off each other, rather than expressing their energy singularly. A lone planet that stands far away from the others is usually outstanding and often calls the shots in a horoscope.

The sign of each planet also has a powerful influence. In some signs, the planetary energies are very much at home and can easily express themselves. In others, the planet has to work harder and is slightly out of sorts. The sign that most corresponds to the energies of a planet is said to be ruled by that planet and obviously is the best place for it to be. The next best place is in a sign where it is exalted, or especially harmonious. On the other hand, there are places in the horoscope where a planet has to work harder to play its role, such as the sign opposite a planet's rulership, which embodies the opposite area of life, and the sign opposite its exaltation. However, a planet that must work harder can actually be more complete, because it must stretch itself to meet the challenges of living in a more difficult sign. Like world leaders who've had to struggle for greatness, this planet may actually develop great strength and character.

Here's a list of the best places for each planet to be. Note that, as new planets were discovered, they replaced the traditional rulers of signs which best complemented their energies.

ARIES—Mars
TAURUS—Venus, in its most sensual form
GEMINI—Mercury, in its communicative role
CANCER—the moon
LEO—the sun
VIRGO—also Mercury, this time in its more critical capacity
LIBRA—also Venus, in its more aesthetic, judgmental form
SCORPIO—Pluto, replacing Mars, the sign's original ruler
SAGITTARIUS—Jupiter
CAPRICORN—Saturn
AQUARIUS—Uranus, replacing Saturn, its original ruler
PISCES—Neptune, replacing Jupiter, its original ruler

A person who has many planets in exalted signs is lucky indeed, for here is where the planet can accomplish the most and be its most influential and creative.

SUN—exalted in Aries, where its energy creates action
MOON—exalted in Taurus, where instincts and reactions operate on a highly creative level
MERCURY—exalted in Aquarius, where it can reach analytical heights
VENUS—exalted in Pisces, a sign whose sensitivity encourages love and creativity
MARS—exalted in Capricorn, a sign that puts energy to work productively
JUPITER—exalted in Cancer, where it encourages nurturing and growth
SATURN—at home in Libra, where it steadies the scales of justice and promotes balanced, responsible judgment

URANUS—powerful in Scorpio, where it promotes transformation

NEPTUNE—especially favored in Cancer, where it gains the security to transcend to a higher state

PLUTO—exalted in Pisces, where it dissolves the old cycle to make way for transition to the new

The Personal Planets: Mercury, Venus, and Mars

These planets work in your immediate personal life.

Mercury affects how you communicate and how your mental processes work. Are you a quick study who grasps information rapidly? Or do you learn more slowly and thoroughly? How is your concentration? Can you express yourself easily? Are you a good writer? All these questions can be answered by your Mercury placement.

Venus shows what you react to. What turns you on? What appeals to you aesthetically? Are you charming to others? Are you attractive to look at? Your taste, your refinement, your sense of balance and proportion are all Venus-ruled.

Mars is your outgoing energy, your drive and ambition. Do you reach out for new adventures? Are you assertive? Are you motivated? Self-confident? Hot-tempered? How you channel your energy and drive is revealed by your Mars placement.

Mercury Shows How Your Mind Works

Mercury shows how you think and speak, how logical you are. Since it stays close to the sun, read the description for Mercury in your sun sign, then the sign preceding and following it. Then decide which reflects the way you think.

Mercury in Aries

Your mind is very active and assertive. You never hesitate to say what you think, never shy away from a battle. In fact, you may relish a verbal confrontation. Tact is not your strong point, so you may have to learn not to trip over your tongue.

Mercury in Taurus

Though you may be a slow learner, you have good concentration and mental stamina. You want to make your ideas really happen. You'll attack a problem methodically and consider every angle thoroughly, never jumping to conclusions. You'll stick with a subject until you master it.

Mercury in Gemini

You are a wonderful communicator with great facility for expressing yourself both verbally and in writing. You love gathering all kinds of information. You probably finish other people's sentences, and express yourself with eloquent hand gestures. You can talk to anybody anytime . . . and probably have phone and e-mail bills to prove it. You read anything from sci-fi to Shakespeare, and might need an extra room just for your book collection. Though you learn fast, you may lack focus and discipline. Watch a tendency to jump from subject to subject.

Mercury in Cancer

You rely on intuition more than logic. Your mental processes are usually colored by your emotions, so you may seem shy or hesitant to voice your opinions. However, this placement gives you the advantage of great imagination and empathy in the way you communicate with others.

Mercury in Leo

You are enthusiastic and very dramatic in the way you express yourself. You like to hold the attention of groups, and could be a great public speaker. Your mind thinks big, so you prefer to deal with the overall picture rather than with the details.

Mercury in Virgo

This is one of the best places for Mercury. It should give you critical ability, attention to details, and thorough analysis. Your mind focuses on the practical side of things. This type of thinking is very well suited to being a teacher or editor.

Mercury in Libra

You're either a born diplomat who smooths over ruffled feathers or a talented debater. Many lawyers have this placement. However, since you're forever weighing the pros and cons of a situation, you may vacillate when making decisions.

Mercury in Scorpio

This is an investigative mind that stops at nothing to get the answers. You may have a sarcastic, stinging wit or a gift for the cutting remark. There's always a grain of truth to your verbal sallies, thanks to your penetrating insight.

Mercury in Sagittarius

You are a supersalesman with a tendency to expound. Though you are very broad-minded, you can be dogmatic when it comes to telling others what's good for them. You won't hesitate to tell the truth as you see it, so watch a tendency toward tactlessness. On the plus side, you have a great sense of humor. This position of Mercury is often considered by astrologers to be at a disadvantage because Sagittarius opposes Gemini, the sign Mercury rules, and squares off with Virgo, another Mercury-ruled sign. What often happens is that Mercury in Sagittarius oversteps its bounds and loses sight of the facts in a situation. Do a reality check before making promises you may not be able to deliver.

Mercury in Capricorn

This placement endows good mental discipline. You have a love of learning and a very orderly approach to your subjects. You will patiently plod through the facts and figures until you have mastered the tasks. You grasp structured situations easily, but may be short on creativity.

Mercury in Aquarius

An independent, original thinker, you'll have more cutting-edge ideas than the average person. You will be quick to check out any unusual opportunities. Your opinions are so well-researched and grounded that once your mind is made up, it is difficult to change.

Mercury in Pisces

You have the psychic and intuitive mind of a natural poet. Learn to make use of your creative imagination. You may think in terms of helping others, but check a tendency to be vague and forgetful of details.

Your Power to Relate: Venus

Venus tells how you relate to others and to your environment. It shows where you receive pleasure, what you love to do. Find your Venus placement from the charts at the end of this chapter by looking for the year of your birth in the left-hand column. Then follow the line of that year across the page until you reach the time period of your birthday. The sign heading that column will be your Venus. If you were born on a day when Venus was changing signs, check the signs preceding or following that day to determine if that sign feels more like your Venus nature.

Venus in Aries

You can't stand to be bored, confined, or ordered around. But a good challenge, maybe even a rousing row, turns you on. Confess—don't you pick a fight now and then just to get someone stirred up? You're attracted by the chase, not the catch, which could cause some problems in your love life if the object of your affection becomes too attainable. You like to wear red, and you can spot a trend before anyone else.

Venus in Taurus

All your senses work in high gear. You love to be surrounded by glorious tastes, smells, textures, sounds, and visuals. Austerity is not for you! Neither is being rushed. You like time to enjoy your pleasures. Soothing surroundings with plenty of creature comforts are your cup of tea. You like to feel secure in your nest, with no sudden jolts or surprises. You like familiar objects—in fact, you may hate to let anything or anyone go.

Venus in Gemini

You are a lively, sparkling personality who thrives in a situation that affords a constant variety and a frequent change of scenery. A varied social life is important to you, with plenty of stimulation and a chance to engage in some light flirtation. Commitment may be difficult, because playing the field is so much fun.

Venus in Cancer

An atmosphere where you feel protected, coddled, and mothered is best for you. You love to be surrounded by children in a cozy, homelike situation. You are attracted to those who are tender and nurturing, who make you feel secure and well provided for. You may be quite secretive about your emotional life, or attracted to clandestine relationships.

Venus in Leo

First-class attention in large doses turns you on, and so does the glitter of real gold and the flash of mirrors. You like to feel like a star at all times, surrounded by your admiring audience. The side effect is that you may be attracted to flatterers and tinsel, while the real gold requires some digging.

Venus in Virgo

Everything neatly in its place? On the surface, you are attracted to an atmosphere where everything is in perfect order, but underneath are some basic, earthy urges. You are attracted to those who appeal to your need to teach, to be of service, or to play out a Pygmalion fantasy. You are at your best when you are busy doing something useful.

Venus in Libra

Elegance and harmony are your key words. You can't abide an atmosphere of contention. Your taste tends toward the classic, with light harmonies of color—nothing clashing, trendy, or outrageous. You love doing things with a partner, and should be careful to pick one who is decisive but patient enough to let you weigh the pros and cons. And steer clear of argumentative types!

Venus in Scorpio

Hidden mysteries intrigue you. In fact, anything that is too open and aboveboard is a bit of a bore. You surely have a stack of whodunits by the bed, along with an erotic magazine or two. You like to solve puzzles, and may also be fascinated with the occult, crime, or scientific research. Intense, all-or-nothing situations add spice to your life, and you love to ferret out the secrets of others. But you could get burned by your flair for living dangerously. The color black, spicy food, dark wood furniture, and heady perfume all get you in the right mood.

Venus in Sagittarius

If you are not actually a world traveler, your surroundings are sure to reflect your love of faraway places. You like a casual outdoor atmosphere and a dog or two to pet. There should be plenty of room for athletic equipment and suitcases. You're attracted to kindred souls who love to travel and who share your freedom-loving philosophy of life. Athletics and spiritual or New Age pursuits could be other interests.

Venus in Capricorn

No fly-by-night relationships for you! You want substance in life, and you are attracted to whatever will help you get where you are going. Status objects turn you on. And so do those who have a serious, responsible, businesslike approach as well as those who remind you of a beloved parent. It is characteristic of this placement to be attracted to someone of a different generation. Antiques, traditional clothing, and dignified behavior are becoming to you.

Venus in Aquarius

This Venus wants to make friends, to be "cool." You like to be in a group, particularly one pushing a worthy cause. You feel quite at home surrounded by people, and could even court fame. Yet all the while you remain detached from any intense commitment. Original ideas and unpredictable people fascinate you. You don't like everything to be planned out in advance, preferring spontaneity and delightful surprises.

Venus in Pisces

This Venus loves to give of yourself, and you find plenty of takers. Stray animals and people appeal to your heart and your pocketbook, but be careful to look at their motives realistically once in a while. You are extremely vulnerable to sob stories of all kinds. Fantasy, the arts (especially film, dance, and theater), and psychic or spiritual activities also speak to you.

Mars Is Your Go Power

Mars is the mover and shaker in your life. It shows how you pursue your goals, whether you have energy to burn or proceed in a slow, steady pace. It will also show how you get angry. Do you explode or do a slow burn or hold everything inside, then get revenge later?

To find your Mars, turn to the charts on pages 100–8. Then find your birth year in the left-hand column and trace the line across horizontally until you come to the column headed by the month of your birth. There you will find an abbreviation of your Mars sign. If the description of your Mars sign doesn't ring true, read the description of the sign preceding and following it. You may have been born on a day when Mars was changing signs, in which case your Mars might be in the adjacent sign.

Mars in Aries

In the sign it rules, Mars shows its brilliant fiery nature. You have an explosive temper and can be quite impatient. On the other hand, you have tremendous courage, energy, and drive. You'll let nothing stand in your way as you race to be first! Obstacles are met head-on and broken through by force. However, those that require patience and persistence can have you exploding in rage. You're a great starter, but not necessarily around for the finish.

Mars in Taurus

Slow, steady, concentrated energy gives you staying power to last until the finish line. You have great stamina, and you never give up. Your tactic is to wear away obstacles with your persistence. Often you come out a winner because you've had the patience to hang in there. When angered, you do a slow burn.

Mars in Gemini

You can't sit still for long. This Mars craves variety. You often have two or more things going on at once—it's all an amusing game to you. Your life can get very complicated, but that only adds spice and stimulation. What drives you into a nervous, hyper state? Boredom, sameness, routine, and confinement. You can do wonderful things with your hands, and you have a way with words.

Mars in Cancer

You rarely attack head-on. Instead, you'll keep things to yourself, make plans in secret, and always cover your actions. This might be interpreted by some as manipulative, but you are only being self-protective. You get furious when anyone knows too much about you. But you do like to know all about others. Your mothering and feeding instincts can be put to good use if you work in the food, hotel, or child-care businesses. You may have to overcome your fragile sense of security, which prompts you not to take risks and to get physically upset when criticized. Don't take things so personally!

Mars in Leo

You have a very dominant personality that takes center stage. Modesty is not one of your traits, nor is taking a backseat. You prefer giving the orders, and have been known to make a dramatic scene if they are not obeyed. Properly used, this Mars confers leadership ability, endurance, and courage.

Mars in Virgo

You are the faultfinder of the zodiac. You notice every detail. Mistakes of any kind make you very nervous. You may worry, even if everything is going smoothly. You may not express your anger directly, but you sure can nag. You have definite likes and dislikes, and you are sure you can do the job better than anyone else. You are certainly more industrious and detail-oriented than other signs. Your Mars energy is often most positively expressed in some kind of teaching role.

Mars in Libra

This Mars will have a passion for beauty, justice, and art. Generally, you will avoid confrontations at all costs. You prefer to spend your energy finding diplomatic solutions or weighing pros and cons. Your other techniques are passive aggression or exercising your well-known charm to get people to do what you want.

Mars in Scorpio

This is a powerful placement, so intense that it demands careful channeling into worthwhile activities. Otherwise, you could become obsessed with your sexuality or might use your need for power and control to manipulate others. You are strong-willed, shrewd, and very private about your affairs, and you'll usually have a secret agenda behind your actions. Your great stamina, focus, and discipline would be excellent assets for careers in the military or medical fields, especially research or surgery. When angry, you don't get mad—you get even!

Mars in Sagittarius

This expansive Mars often propels people into sales, travel, athletics, or philosophy. Your energies function well when you are on the move. You have a hot temper, and are inclined to say what you think before you consider the consequences. You shoot for high goals—and talk endlessly about them—but you may be weak on groundwork. This Mars needs a solid foundation. Watch a tendency to take unnecessary risks.

Mars in Capricorn

This is an ambitious Mars with an excellent sense of timing. You have an eye for those who can be of use to you, and you may dismiss people ruthlessly when you're angry. But you drive yourself hard and deliver full value. This is a good placement for an executive. You'll aim for status and a high material position in life, and you'll keep climbing despite the odds. A great Mars to have!

Mars in Aquarius

This is the most rebellious Mars. You seem to have a drive to assert yourself against the status quo. You may enjoy provoking people, shocking them out of traditional views. Or this placement could express itself in an offbeat sex life. Somehow you often find yourself in unconventional situations. You enjoy being a leader of an active group, which pursues forward-looking studies, politics, or goals.

Mars in Pisces

This Mars is a good actor who knows just how to appeal to the sympathies of others. You create and project wonderful fantasies, or you use your sensitive antennae to crusade for those less fortunate. You get what you want through creating a veil of illusion and glamour. This is a good Mars for someone in the creative and imaginative fields—a dancer, performer, photographer, actor. Many famous film stars have this placement. Watch a tendency to manipulate by making others feel sorry for you.

Jupiter Is Your Power of Expansion

This big, bright, swirling mass of gases is associated with abundance, prosperity, and the kind of windfall you get without too much hard work. You're optimistic under Jupiter's influence, when anything seems possible. You'll travel, expand your mind with higher education, and publish to share your knowledge widely. On the other hand, Jupiter's influence is neither discriminating nor disciplined. It represents the principle of growth without judgment, and therefore could result in extravagance, weight gain, laziness, and carelessness, if not kept in check.

Be sure to look up your Jupiter in the tables in this book. When the current position of Jupiter is favorable, you may get that lucky break. This is a great time to try new things, take risks, travel, or get more education. Opportunities seem to open up easily, so take advantage of them.

Once a year, Jupiter changes signs. That means you

are due for an expansive time every twelve years, when Jupiter travels through your sun sign. You'll also have up periods every four years, when Jupiter is in the same element as your sun sign.

Jupiter in Aries

You are the soul of enthusiasm and optimism. Your luckiest times are when you are getting started on an exciting project or selling an idea that you really believe in. You may have to watch a tendency to be arrogant with those who do not share your enthusiasm. You follow your impulses, often ignoring budget or other commonsense limitations. To produce real, solid benefits, you'll need patience and follow-through wherever this Jupiter falls in your horoscope.

Jupiter in Taurus

You'll spend on beautiful material things, especially those that come from nature—items made of rare woods, natural fabrics, or precious gems, for instance. You can't have too much comfort or too many sensual pleasures. Watch a tendency to overindulge in good food, or to overpamper yourself with nothing but the best. Spartan living is not for you! You may be especially lucky in matters of real estate.

Jupiter in Gemini

You are the great talker of the zodiac, and you may be a great writer, too. But restlessness could be your weak point. You jump around, talk too much, and could be a jack-of-all-trades. Keeping a secret is especially difficult, so you'll also have to watch a tendency to spill the beans. Since you love to be at the center of a beehive of activity, you'll have a vibrant social life. Your best opportunities will come through your talent for language—speaking, writing, communicating, and selling.

Jupiter in Cancer

You are luckiest in situations where you can find emotional closeness or deal with basic security needs such as food, nurturing, or shelter. You may be a great collector. Or you may simply love to accumulate things—you are the one who stashes things away for a rainy day. You probably have a very good memory and love children. In fact, you may have many children to care for. The food, hotel, child-care, and shipping businesses hold good opportunities for you.

Jupiter in Leo

You are a natural showman who loves to live in a larger-than-life way. Yours is a personality full of color that always finds its way into the limelight. You can't have too much attention or applause. Showbiz is a natural place for you, and so is any area where you can play to a crowd. Exercising your flair for drama, your natural playfulness, and your romantic nature brings you good fortune. But watch a tendency to be overly extravagant or to monopolize center stage.

Jupiter in Virgo

You actually love those minute details others find boring. To you, they make all the difference between the perfect and the ordinary. You are the fine craftsman who spots every flaw. You expand your awareness by finding the most efficient methods and by being of service to others. Many of you will be drawn to medical or teaching fields. You'll also have luck in publishing, crafts, nutrition, and service professions. Watch out for a tendency to overwork.

Jupiter in Libra

This is an other-directed Jupiter that develops best with a partner. The stimulation of others helps you grow. You are also most comfortable in harmonious, beautiful situations, and you work well with artistic people. You have a great sense of fair play and an ability to evaluate the pros and cons of a situation. You usually prefer to play the role of diplomat rather than adversary.

Jupiter in Scorpio

You love the feeling of power and control, of taking things to their limit. You can't resist a mystery. Your shrewd, penetrating mind sees right through to the heart of most situations and people. You have luck in work that provides for solutions to matters of life and death. You may be drawn to undercover work, behind-the-scenes intrigue, psychotherapy, the occult, and sex-related ventures. Your challenge will be to develop a sense of moderation and tolerance for other beliefs. This Jupiter can be fanatical. You may have luck in handling other people's money—insurance, taxes, and inheritance can bring you a windfall.

Jupiter in Sagittarius

Independent, outgoing, and idealistic, you'll shoot for the stars. This Jupiter compels you to travel far and wide, both physically and mentally, via higher education. You may have luck while traveling in an exotic place. You also have luck with outdoor ventures, exercise, and animals, particularly horses. Since you tend to be very open about your opinions, watch a tendency to be tactless and to exaggerate. Instead, use your wonderful sense of humor to make your point.

Jupiter in Capricorn

Jupiter is much more restrained in Capricorn, the sign of rules and authority. Here, Jupiter can make you overwork and heighten any ambition or sense of duty you may have. You'll expand in areas that advance your position, putting you farther up the social or corporate ladder. You are lucky working within the establishment in a very structured situation where you can show off your ability to organize and reap rewards for your hard work.

Jupiter in Aquarius

This is another freedom-loving Jupiter, with great tolerance and originality. You are at your best when you are working for a humanitarian cause and in the company of many supporters. This is a good Jupiter for a political career. You'll relate to all kinds of people on all social levels. You have an abundance of original ideas, but you are best off away from routine and any situation that imposes rigid rules. You need mental stimulation!

Jupiter in Pisces

You are a giver whose feelings and pocketbook are easily touched by others, so choose your companions with care. You could be the original sucker for a hard-luck story. Better find a worthy hospital or a charity that will appreciate your selfless support. You have a great creative imagination. You may attract good fortune in fields related to oil, perfume, pharmaceuticals, petroleum, dance, footwear, and alcohol. But beware of overindulgence in alcohol—focus on a creative outlet instead.

Saturn Is Your Power of Discipline

Jupiter speeds you up with *lucky breaks,* then along comes Saturn to slow you down with the *disciplinary brakes.* Saturn has unfairly been called a malefic planet, one of the bad guys of the zodiac. On the contrary, Saturn is one of our best friends, the kind who tells you what you need to hear even if it's not good news. Under a Saturn transit, we grow up, take responsibility for our lives, and emerge from whatever test this planet has in store as far wiser, more capable, and mature human beings. It is when we are under pressure that we grow stronger.

When Saturn hits a critical point in your horoscope, you can count on an experience that will make you slow up, pull back, and reexamine your life. It is a call to eliminate what is not working and to shape up. By the end of its twenty-eight-year trip around the zodiac, Saturn will have tested you in all areas of your life. The major tests happen in seven-year cycles, when Saturn passes over the *angles* of your chart—your rising sign, midheaven, descendant, and nadir. This is when the real life-changing experiences happen. But you are also in for a testing period whenever Saturn passes a *planet* in your chart or stresses that planet from a distance. Therefore, it is useful to check your planetary positions with the timetable of Saturn to prepare in advance, or at least to brace yourself.

When Saturn returns to its location at the time of your birth, at approximately age twenty-eight, you'll have your first Saturn return. At this time, a person usually takes stock or settles down to find his or her mission in life and assumes full adult duties and responsibilities.

Another way Saturn helps us is to reveal the karmic lessons from previous lives and to give us the chance to overcome them. So look at Saturn's challenges as much-needed opportunities for self-improvement. Under a Jupiter influence, you'll have more fun. But Saturn gives you solid, long-lasting results.

Look up your natal Saturn in the tables in this book for clues on where you need work.

Saturn in Aries

Saturn here puts the brakes on Aries' natural drive and enthusiasm. There is often an angry side to this placement. You don't let anyone push you around, and you know what's best for yourself. Following orders is not your strong point, and neither is diplomacy. You tend to be quick to go on the offensive in relationships, attacking first, before anyone attacks you. Because no one quite lives up to your standards, you often wind up doing everything yourself. You'll have to learn to cooperate and tone down self-centeredness. Both Pat Buchanan and Saddam Hussein have this Saturn.

Saturn in Taurus

A big issue is getting control of the cash flow. There will be lean periods that can be frightening, but you have the patience and endurance to stick them out and the methodical drive to prosper in the end. Learn to take a philosophical attitude, like Ben Franklin who also had this placement and who said, "A penny saved is a penny earned."

Saturn in Gemini

You are a serious student of life, but you may have difficulty communicating or sharing your knowledge. You may be shy, speak slowly, or have fears about communicating, like Eleanor Roosevelt. You dwell in the realms of science, theory, or abstract analysis—even when you are dealing with the emotions, like Sigmund Freud who also had this placement.

Saturn in Cancer

Your tests come with establishing a secure emotional base. In doing so, you may have to deal with some very basic fears centering on your early home environment. Most of your Saturn tests will have emotional roots in those early childhood experiences. You may have difficulty remaining objective in terms of what you try to achieve. So it will be especially important for you to deal with negative feelings such as guilt, paranoia, jealousy, resentment, and suspicion. Galileo and Michelangelo also navigated these murky waters.

Saturn in Leo

This is an authoritarian Saturn—a strict, demanding parent who may deny the pleasure principle in your zeal to see that rules are followed. Though you may feel guilty about taking the spotlight, you are very ambitious and loyal. You have to watch a tendency toward rigidity, also toward overwork and holding back affection. Joseph Kennedy and Billy Graham share this placement.

Saturn in Virgo

This is a cautious, exacting Saturn. You are intensely hard on yourself. Most of all, you give yourself the roughest time with your constant worries about every little detail, often making yourself sick. You may have difficulties setting priorities and getting the job done. Your tests will come in learning tolerance and understanding of others. Charles de Gaulle, Mae West, and Nathaniel Hawthorne had this meticulous Saturn.

Saturn in Libra

Saturn is exalted here, which makes this planet an ally. You may choose very serious, older partners in life, perhaps stemming from a fear of dependency. You need to learn to stand solidly on your own before you commit to another. You are extremely cautious as you deliberate every involvement—with good reason. It is best that you find an occupation that makes good use of your sense of duty and honor. Steer clear of fly-by-night situations. Both Khruschev and Mao Tse-tung had this placement.

Saturn in Scorpio

You have great staying power. This Saturn tests you in situations involving the control of others. You may feel drawn to some kind of intrigue or undercover work, like J. Edgar Hoover. Or there may be an air of mystery surrounding your life and death, like Marilyn Monroe and Robert Kennedy who both had this placement. There are lessons to be learned from your sexual involvements. Often sex is used for manipulation or is somehow out of the ordinary. The Roman emperor Caligula and the transsexual Christine Jorgensen are extreme cases.

Saturn in Sagittarius

Your challenges and lessons will come from tests of your spiritual and philosophical values, as happened to Martin Luther King and Gandhi. You are high-minded and sincere with this reflective, moral placement. Uncompromising in your ethical standards, you could become a benevolent despot.

Saturn in Capricorn

With the help of Saturn at maximum strength, your judgment will improve with age. And like Spencer Tracy's screen image, you'll be the gray-haired hero with a strong sense of responsibility. You advance in life slowly but steadily, always with a strong hand at the helm and an eye for the advantageous situation. Like Pat Robertson, you're likely to stand for conservative values. Negatively, you may be a loner, prone to periods of melancholy.

Saturn in Aquarius

Your tests come from relationships with groups. Do you care too much about what others think? Do you feel like an outsider, like Greta Garbo? You may fear being different from others and therefore slight your own unique, forward-looking gifts. Or like Lord Byron and Howard Hughes, you may take the opposite tack and rebel in the extreme. You can apply discipline to accomplish great humanitarian goals, as Albert Schweitzer did.

Saturn in Pisces

Your fear of the unknown and the irrational may lead you to the safety and protection of an institution. You may go on the run like Jesse James, who had this placement, to avoid looking too deeply inside. Or you might go in the opposite, more positive direction and develop a disciplined psychoanalytic approach, which puts you more in control of your feelings. Some of you will take refuge in work with hospitals, charities, or religious institutions. Queen Victoria, who had this placement, symbolized an era when institutions of all kinds were sustained. Discipline applied to artistic work, especially poetry and dance, or to spiritual work, such as yoga or meditation, might be helpful.

How Uranus, Neptune, and Pluto Influence a Whole Generation

These three planets remain in signs such a long time that a whole generation bears the imprint of the sign. Mass movements, great sweeping changes, fads that characterize a generation, even the issues of the conflicts and wars of the time are influenced by these "outer three" planets. When one of these distant planets changes signs, there is a definite shift in the atmosphere, the feeling of the end of an era.

Since these planets are so far away from the sun—too distant to be seen by the naked eye—they pick up signals from the universe at large. These planetary receivers literally link the sun with distant energies, and then perform a similar function in your horoscope by linking your central character with intuitive, spiritual, transformative forces from the cosmos. Each planet has a special domain, and will reflect this in the area of your chart where it falls.

Uranus Is Your Power to Break Through

There is nothing ordinary about this quirky green planet that seems to be traveling on its side, surrounded by a swarm of moons. Is it any wonder that astrologers assigned it to Aquarius, the most eccentric and gregarious sign? Uranus seems to wend its way around the sun, marching to its own tune.

Significantly, Uranus follows Saturn, the planet of limitations and structures. Often we get caught up in the structures we have created to give ourselves a sense of security. However, if we lose contact with our spiritual roots, then Uranus is likely to jolt us out of our comfortable rut and wake us up.

Uranus energy is electrical, happening in sudden flashes. It is not influenced by karma or past events, nor does it regard tradition, sex, or sentiment. The Uranus key words are surprise and awakening. Suddenly, there's that flash of inspiration, that bright idea, that totally new approach to revolutionize whatever scheme you were undertaking. A Uranus event takes you by surprise; it happens from out of the blue, for better or for worse. The Uranus place in your life is where you awaken and become your own person, leaving the structures of Saturn behind. And it is probably the most unconventional place in your chart.

Look up the sign of Uranus at the time of your birth and see where you follow your own tune.

Uranus in Aries

Birth Dates:
   March 31, 1927–November 4, 1927

January 13, 1928–June 6, 1934
October 10, 1934–March 28, 1935

Your generation is original, creative, pioneering. It developed the computer, the airplane, and the cyclotron. You let nothing hold you back from exploring the unknown, and you have a powerful mixture of fire and electricity behind you. Women of your generation were among the first to be liberated. You were the unforgettable style setters. You have a surprise in store for everyone. Like Yoko Ono, Grace Kelly, and Jacqueline Onassis, your life may be jolted by sudden and violent changes.

Uranus in Taurus

Birth Dates:
June 6, 1934–October 10, 1934
March 28, 1935–August 7, 1941
October 5, 1941–May 15, 1942

The great territorial shake-ups of World War II began during your generation. You are independent, probably self-employed or would like to be. You have original ideas about making money, and you brace yourself for sudden changes of fortune. This Uranus can cause shake-ups, particularly in finances, but it can also make you a born entrepreneur.

Uranus in Gemini

Birth Dates:
August 7, 1941–October 5, 1941
May 15, 1942–August 30, 1948
November 12, 1948–June 10, 1949

You were the first children to be influenced by television. Now, in your adult years, your generation stocks up on answering machines, cell phones, computers, and fax machines—any new way you can communicate. You have an inquiring mind, but your interests may be rather short-lived. This Uranus can be easily fragmented if there is no structure and focus.

Uranus in Cancer

Birth Dates:
August 30, 1948–November 12, 1948
June 10, 1949–August 24, 1955
January 28, 1956–June 10, 1956

This generation came at a time when divorce was becoming commonplace, so your home image is unconventional. You may have an unusual relationship with your parents; you may have come from a broken home or an unconventional one. You'll have unorthodox ideas about parenting, intimacy, food, and shelter. You may also be interested in dreams, psychic phenomena, and memory work.

Uranus in Leo

Birth Dates:
August 24, 1955–January 28, 1956
June 10, 1956–November 1, 1961
January 10, 1962–August 10, 1962

This generation understood how to use electronic media. Many of your group are now leaders in the high-tech industries, and you also understand how to use the new media to promote yourself. Like Isadora Duncan, you may have a very eccentric kind of charisma and a life that is sparked by unusual love affairs. Your children, too, may have traits that are out of the ordinary. Where this planet falls in your chart, you'll have a love of freedom, be a bit of an egomaniac, and show the full force of your personality in a unique way, like tennis great Martina Navratilova.

Uranus in Virgo

Birth Dates:
 November 1, 1961–January 10, 1962
 August 10, 1962–September 28, 1968
 May 20, 1969–June 24, 1969

You'll have highly individual work methods. Many of you will be finding newer, more practical ways to use computers. Like Einstein, who had this placement, you'll break the rules brilliantly. Your generation came at a time of student rebellions, the civil rights movement, and the general acceptance of health foods. Chances are, you're concerned about pollution and cleaning up the environment. You may also be involved with nontraditional healing methods.

Uranus in Libra

Birth Dates:
 September 28, 1968–May 20, 1969
 June 24, 1969–November 21, 1974
 May 1, 1975–September 8, 1975

Your generation will be always changing partners. Born during the era of women's liberation, you may have come from a broken home and have no clear image of what a marriage entails. There will be many sudden splits and experiments before you settle down. Your generation will be much involved in legal and political reforms and in changing artistic and fashion looks.

Uranus in Scorpio

Birth Dates:
 November 21, 1974–May 1, 1975
 September 8, 1975–February 17, 1981
 March 20, 1981–November 16, 1981

Interest in transformation, meditation, and life after death signaled the beginning of New Age consciousness. Your generation recognizes no boundaries, no limits, and no external controls. You'll have new attitudes toward death and dying, psychic phenomena, and the occult. Like Mae West and Casanova, you'll shock 'em sexually, too.

Uranus in Sagittarius

Birth Dates:
February 17, 1981–March 20, 1981
November 16, 1981–February 15, 1988
May 27, 1988–December 2, 1988

Could this generation be the first to travel in outer space? An earlier generation with this placement included Charles Lindbergh and a time when the first zeppelins and the Wright Brothers were conquering the skies. Uranus here forecasts great discoveries, mind expansion, and long-distance travel. Like Galileo and Martin Luther, those born in these years will generate new theories about the cosmos and mankind's relation to it.

Uranus in Capricorn

Birth Dates:
December 20, 1904–January 30, 1912
September 4, 1912–November 12, 1912
February 15, 1988–May 27, 1988
December 2, 1988–April 1, 1995
June 9, 1995–January 12, 1996

This generation, now growing up, will challenge traditions with the help of electronic gadgets. In these years, we got organized with the help of technology put to practical use. The Internet was born following the great economic boom of the 1990s. Great leaders who were movers and shakers of history, like Julius Caesar and Henry VIII, were born under this placement.

Uranus in Aquarius

Birth Dates:
January 30, 1912–September 4, 1912
November 12, 1912–April 1, 1919
August 16, 1919–January 22, 1920
April 1, 1995–June 9, 1995
January 12, 1996–March 10, 2003
September 15, 2003–December 30, 2003

The last generation with this placement produced great innovative minds such as Leonard Bernstein and Orson Welles. The next will become another radical breakthrough generation, much concerned with global issues that involve all humanity. Already this is a time of high-tech experimentation on every level, when home computers are becoming as ubiquitous as television. It is also a time of globalization, of surprise attacks (9/11), and of "wake-up" calls, as underdeveloped countries demand attention.

Uranus in Pisces

Birth Dates:
April 1, 1919–August 16, 1919
January 22, 1920–March 31, 1927
November 4, 1927–January 12, 1928
March 10, 2003–September 15, 2003
December 20, 2003–May 28, 2010

Uranus is ushering in a new generation that will surely spark innovations and creativity in the arts as well as in the sciences. In the past century, Uranus in Pisces focused attention on the rise of such electronic entertainment as radio and the cinema as well as the secretiveness of Prohibition. This produced a generation of idealists exemplified by Judy Garland's theme, "Somewhere Over the Rainbow." Uranus in Pisces hints at stealth activities, at hospital and prison reform, at high-tech drugs and medical experiments, at shake-ups and reforms in the Pisces-ruled petroleum industry.

Neptune Is Your Power to Imagine

Neptune is often called the planet of dissolution. It is the "dissolver" of reality. It is often maligned as the planet of illusions, drugs, and alcohol where you escape the real world. Under Neptune's influence, you see what you want to see. But Neptune also encourages you to create, to let your imagination run free. Neptune embodies the energy of glamour, subtlety, mystery and mysticism. It governs anything that takes you beyond the mundane world, including out-of-body experiences.

Neptune acts to transcend your ordinary perceptions to take you to another level of reality where you experience either confusion or ecstasy. Neptune's force can pull you off course, but only if you allow this to happen. Those who use Neptune wisely can translate their daydreams into poetry, theater, design, or inspired moves in the business world, avoiding the tricky "con artist" side of this planet.

Find your Neptune listed below.

Neptune in Cancer

Birth Dates:
  July 19, 1901–December 25, 1901
  May 21, 1902–September 23, 1914
  December 14, 1914–July 19, 1915
  March 19, 1916–May 2, 1916

Dreams of the homeland, idealistic patriotism, and glamorization of the nurturing assets of women characterized this time. You who were born here have unusual psychic ability and deep insights into basic needs of others.

Neptune in Leo

Birth Dates:
  September 23, 1914–December 14, 1914
  July 19, 1915–March 19, 1916
  May 2, 1916–September 21, 1928
  February 19, 1929–July 24, 1929

Neptune in Leo brought us the glamour and high living of the 1920s and the big spenders of that time. The Neptune temptations of gambling, seduction, theater, and lavish entertaining distracted from the realities of the age. Those born in that generation also made great advances in the arts.

Neptune in Virgo

Birth Dates:
  September 21, 1928–February 19, 1929
  July 24, 1929–October 3, 1942
  April 17, 1943–August 2, 1943

Neptune in Virgo encompassed the 1930s, the Great Depression, and the beginning of World War II, when a new order was born. There was a time of facing "what doesn't work." Many were unemployed and found solace at the movies, watching the great Virgo star Greta Garbo or the escapist dance films of Busby Berkeley. New public services were born. Those with Neptune in Virgo later spread the gospel of health and fitness. This generation's devotion to spending hours at the office inspired the term *workaholic*.

Neptune in Libra

Birth Dates:
  October 3, 1942–April 17, 1943
  August 2, 1943–December 24, 1955
  March 12, 1956–October 19, 1956
  June 15, 1957–August 6, 1957

This was the time of World War II and the postwar period, when the world regained balance and returned to relative stability. Neptune in Libra was the romantic generation who would later be concerned with relating. As this generation matured, there was a new trend toward marriage and commitment. Racial and sexual equality became important issues, as they redesigned traditional roles to suit modern times.

Neptune in Scorpio

Birth Dates:
  December 24, 1955–March 12, 1956
  October 19, 1956–June 15, 1957
  August 6, 1957–January 4, 1970
  May 3, 1970–November 6, 1970

Neptune in Scorpio brought in a generation that would become interested in transformative power. Born in an era that glamorized sex, drugs, rock and roll, and Eastern religion, they matured in a more sobering time of AIDS, cocaine abuse, and New Age spirituality. As they evolve, they will become active in healing the planet from the results of the abuse of power.

Neptune in Sagittarius

Birth Dates:
  January 4, 1970–May 3, 1970
  November 6, 1970–January 19, 1984
  June 23, 1984–November 21, 1984

Neptune in Sagittarius was the time when space and astronaut travel became a reality. The Neptune influence glamorized new approaches to mysticism, religion, and mind expansion. This generation will take a new approach to spiritual life, with emphasis on visions, mysticism, and clairvoyance.

Neptune in Capricorn

Birth Dates:
January 19, 1984–June 23, 1984
November 21, 1984–January 29, 1998

Neptune in Capricorn brought a time when delusions about material power were glamorized in the mid-1980s and 1990s. There was a boom in the stock market, and the Internet era spawned young tycoons who later lost it all. It was also a time when the psychic and occult worlds spawned a new category of business enterprise, and sold services on television.

Neptune in Aquarius

Birth Dates:
January 29, 1998–April 4, 2011

This should continue to be a time of breakthroughs. Here the creative influence of Neptune reaches a universal audience. This is a time of dissolving barriers, of globalization—when we truly become one world. During this transit of high-tech Aquarius, new kinds of entertainment media reach across cultural differences. However, the transit of Neptune has also raised boundary issues between cultures, especially in Middle Eastern countries with Neptune-ruled oil fields. As Neptune raises issues of social and political structures not being as solid as they seem, this could continue to produce rebellion and chaos in the environment. However, by using imagination (Neptune) in partnership with a global view (Aquarius) we could reach creative solutions.

Those born with this placement should be true citizens of the world with a remarkable creative ability to transcend social and cultural barriers.

Pluto Is Your Power to Transform

Pluto is a mysterious little planet with a strange elliptical orbit that occasionally runs inside the orbit of its neighbor Neptune. Because of its eccentric path, the length of time Pluto stays in any given sign can vary from thirteen to thirty-two years. It covered only seven signs in the last century. Though it is a tiny planet, its influence is great. When Pluto zaps a strategic point in your horoscope, your life changes dramatically.

This little planet is the power behind the scenes. It affects you at deep levels of consciousness, causing events to come to the surface that will transform you and your generation. Nothing escapes, or is sacred, with this probing planet. Its purpose is to wipe out the past so something new can happen. The Pluto place in your horoscope is where you have invisible power (Mars governs the visible power)—where you can transform, heal, and affect the unconscious needs of the masses. Pluto tells lots about how your generation projects power, what makes it seem "cool" to others. And when Pluto changes signs, there's a whole new concept of what's "cool."

Pluto in Gemini

Birth Dates:
   Late 1800s–May 26, 1914

This was a time of mass suggestion and breakthroughs in communications, a time when many brilliant writers such as Ernest Hemingway and F. Scott Fitzgerald were born. Henry Miller, D. H. Lawrence, and James Joyce scandalized society by using explicit sexual images and language in their literature. "Muckraking" journalists exposed corruption. Pluto-ruled Scorpio President Theodore Roosevelt said, "Speak softly, but carry a big stick." This generation had an intense need to communicate and made major breakthroughs in knowledge. A compulsive restlessness and a thirst for a variety of experiences characterized many of this generation.

Pluto in Cancer

Birth Dates:
May 26, 1914–June 14, 1939

Dictators and mass media arose to wield emotional power over the masses. Women's rights was a popular issue. Deep sentimental feelings, acquisitiveness, and possessiveness characterized these times and people. Most of the great stars of the Hollywood era that embodied the American image were born during this period: Grace Kelly, Esther Williams, Frank Sinatra, Lana Turner, to name a few.

Pluto in Leo

Birth Dates:
June 14, 1939–August 19, 1957

The performing arts played on the emotions of the masses. Mick Jagger, John Lennon, and rock and roll were born at this time. So were "baby boomers" like Bill and Hillary Clinton. Those born here tend to be self-centered, powerful, and boisterous. This generation does its own thing, for better or for worse.

Pluto in Virgo

Birth Dates:
August 19, 1957–October 5, 1971
April 17, 1972–July 30, 1972

This is the "yuppie" generation that sparked a mass movement toward fitness, health, and career. It is a much more sober, serious, driven generation than the fun-loving Pluto in Leo. During this time, machines were invented to process detail work efficiently. Inventions took a practical turn with answering machines, fax machines, car phones, and home office equipment—all making the workplace far more efficient.

Pluto in Libra

Birth Dates:
  October 5, 1971–April 17, 1972
  July 30, 1972–November 5, 1983
  May 18, 1984–August 27, 1984

A mellower generation, people born at this time are concerned with partnerships, working together, and finding diplomatic solutions to problems. Marriage is important to this generation, and they will define it by combining traditional values with equal partnership. This was a time of women's liberation, gay rights, ERA, and legal battles over abortion, all of which transformed our ideas about relationships.

Pluto in Scorpio

Birth Dates:
  November 5, 1983–May 18, 1984
  August 27, 1984–January 17, 1995

Pluto was in the sign it rules for a comparatively short period of time. However, this was a time of record achievements, destructive sexually transmitted diseases, nuclear power controversies, and explosive political issues. Pluto destroys in order to create new understanding—the phoenix rising from the ashes—which should be some consolation for those of you who felt Pluto's force before 1995. Sexual shockers were par for the course during these intense years when black clothing, transvestites, body piercing, tattoos, and sexually explicit advertising pushed the boundaries of good taste.

Pluto in Sagittarius

Birth Dates:
January 17, 1995–April 20, 1995
November 10, 1995–January 26, 2008

During our current Pluto transit, we are being pushed to expand our horizons, to find deeper spiritual meaning in life. Pluto's opposition with Saturn in 2001 brought an enormous conflict between traditional societies and the forces of change. It signals a time when religious convictions will exert more power in our political life as well.

Since Sagittarius is the sign that rules travel, there's a good possibility that Pluto, the planet of extremes, will make space travel a reality for some of us. Already, we are seeing wealthy adventurers paying for the privilege of travel on space shuttles. Discovery of life-forms on other planets could transform our ideas about where we came from.

New dimensions in electronic publishing, concern with animal rights and the environment, and an increasing emphasis on extreme forms of religion are other signs of these times. Look for charismatic religious leaders to arise now. We'll also be developing far-reaching philosophies designed to elevate our lives with a new sense of purpose.

VENUS SIGNS 1901–2006

	Aries	Taurus	Gemini	Cancer	Leo	Virgo
1901	3/29–4/22	4/22–5/17	5/17–6/10	6/10–7/5	7/5–7/29	7/29–8/23
1902	5/7–6/3	6/3–6/30	6/30–7/25	7/25–8/19	8/19–9/13	9/13–10/7
1903	2/28–3/24	3/24–4/18	4/18–5/13	5/13–6/9	6/9–7/7	7/7–8/17 9/6–11/8
1904	3/13–5/7	5/7–6/1	6/1–6/25	6/25–7/19	7/19–8/13	8/13–9/6
1905	2/3–3/6 4/9–5/28	3/6–4/9 5/28–7/8	7/8–8/6	8/6–9/1	9/1–9/27	9/27–10/21
1906	3/1–4/7	4/7–5/2	5/2–5/26	5/26–6/20	6/20–7/16	7/16–8/11
1907	4/27–5/22	5/22–6/16	6/16–7/11	7/11–8/4	8/4–8/29	8/29–9/22
1908	2/14–3/10	3/10–4/5	4/5–5/5	5/5–9/8	9/8–10/8	10/8–11/3
1909	3/29–4/22	4/22–5/16	5/16–6/10	6/10–7/4	7/4–7/29	7/29–8/23
1910	5/7–6/3	6/4–6/29	6/30–7/24	7/25–8/18	8/19–9/12	9/13–10/6
1911	2/28–3/23	3/24–4/17	4/18–5/12	5/13–6/8	6/9–7/7	7/8–11/18
1912	4/13–5/6	5/7–5/31	6/1–6/24	6/24–7/18	7/19–8/12	8/13–9/5
1913	2/3–3/6 5/2–5/30	3/7–5/1 5/31–7/7	7/8–8/5	8/6–8/31	9/1–9/26	9/27–10/20
1914	3/14–4/6	4/7–5/1	5/2–5/25	5/26–6/19	6/20–7/15	7/16–8/10
1915	4/27–5/21	5/22–6/15	6/16–7/10	7/11–8/3	8/4–8/28	8/29–9/21
1916	2/14–3/9	3/10–4/5	4/6–5/5	5/6–9/8	9/9–10/7	10/8–11/2
1917	3/29–4/21	4/22–5/15	5/16–6/9	6/10–7/3	7/4–7/28	7/29–8/21
1918	5/7–6/2	6/3–6/28	6/29–7/24	7/25–8/18	8/19–9/11	9/12–10/5
1919	2/27–3/22	3/23–4/16	4/17–5/12	5/13–6/7	6/8–7/7	7/8–11/8
1920	4/12–5/6	5/7–5/30	5/31–6/23	6/24–7/18	7/19–8/11	8/12–9/4
1921	2/3–3/6 4/26–6/1	3/7–4/25 6/2–7/7	7/8–8/5	8/6–8/31	9/1–9/25	9/26–10/20
1922	3/13–4/6	4/7–4/30	5/1–5/25	5/26–6/19	6/20–7/14	7/15–8/9
1923	4/27–5/21	5/22–6/14	6/15–7/9	7/10–8/3	8/4–8/27	8/28–9/20
1924	2/13–3/8	3/9–4/4	4/5–5/5	5/6–9/8	9/9–10/7	10/8–11/12
1925	3/28–4/20	4/21–5/15	5/16–6/8	6/9–7/3	7/4–7/27	7/28–8/21

Libra	Scorpio	Sagittarius	Capricorn	Aquarius	Pisces
8/23–9/17	9/17–10/12	10/12–1/16	1/16–2/9	2/9–3/5	3/5–3/29
			11/7–12/5	12/5–1/11	
10/7–10/31	10/31–11/24	11/24–12/18	12/18–1/11	2/6–4/4	1/11–2/6
					4/4–5/7
8/17–9/6	12/9–1/5			1/11–2/4	2/4–2/28
11/8–12/9					
9/6–9/30	9/30–10/25	1/5–1/30	1/30–2/24	2/24–3/19	3/19–4/13
		10/25–11/18	11/18–12/13	12/13–1/7	
10/21–11/14	11/14–12/8	12/8–1/1/06			1/7–2/3
8/11–9/7	9/7–10/9	10/9–12/15	1/1–1/25	1/25–2/18	2/18–3/14
	12/15–12/25	12/25–2/6			
9/22–10/16	10/16–11/9	11/9–12/3	2/6–3/6	3/6–4/2	4/2–4/27
			12/3–12/27	12/27–1/20	
11/3–11/28	11/28–12/22	12/22–1/15			1/20–2/4
8/23–9/17	9/17–10/12	10/12–11/17	1/15–2/9	2/9–3/5	3/5–3/29
			11/17–12/5	12/5–1/15	
10/7–10/30	10/31–11/23	11/24–12/17	12/18–12/31	1/1–1/15	1/16–1/28
				1/29–4/4	4/5–5/6
11/19–12/8	12/9–12/31		1/1–1/10	1/11–2/2	2/3–2/27
9/6–9/30	1/1–1/4	1/5–1/29	1/30–2/23	2/24–3/18	3/19–4/12
	10/1–10/24	10/25–11/17	11/18–12/12	12/13–12/31	
10/21–11/13	11/14–12/7	12/8–12/31		1/1–1/6	1/7–2/2
8/11–9/6	9/7–10/9	10/10–12/5	1/1–1/24	1/25–2/17	2/18–3/13
	12/6–12/30	12/31			
9/22–10/15	10/16–11/8	1/1–2/6	2/7–3/6	3/7–4/1	4/2–4/26
		11/9–12/2	12/3–12/26	12/27–12/31	
11/3–11/27	11/28–12/21	12/22–12/31		1/1–1/19	1/20–2/13
8/22–9/16	9/17–10/11	1/1–1/14	1/15–2/7	2/8–3/4	3/5–3/28
		10/12–11/6	11/7–12/5	12/6–12/31	
10/6–10/29	10/30–11/22	11/23–12/16	12/17–12/31	1/1–4/5	4/6–5/6
11/9–12/8	12/9–12/31		1/1–1/9	1/10–2/2	2/3–2/26
9/5–9/30	1/1–1/3	1/4–1/28	1/29–2/22	2/23–3/18	3/19–4/11
	9/31–10/23	10/24–11/17	11/18–12/11	12/12–12/31	
10/21–11/13	11/14–12/7	12/8–12/31		1/1–1/6	1/7–2/2
8/10–9/6	9/7–10/10	10/11–11/28	1/1–1/24	1/25–2/16	2/17–3/12
	11/29–12/31				
9/21–10/14	1/1	1/2–2/6	2/7–3/5	3/6–3/31	4/1–4/26
	10/15–11/7	11/8–12/1	12/2–12/25	12/26–12/31	
11/13–11/26	11/27–12/21	12/22–12/31		1/1–1/19	1/20–2/12
8/22–9/15	9/16–10/11	1/1–1/14	1/15–2/7	2/8–3/3	3/4–3/27
		10/12–11/6	11/7–12/5	12/6–12/31	

VENUS SIGNS 1901–2006

	Aries	Taurus	Gemini	Cancer	Leo	Virgo
1926	5/7–6/2	6/3–6/28	6/29–7/23	7/24–8/17	8/18–9/11	9/12–10/5
1927	2/27–3/22	3/23–4/16	4/17–5/11	5/12–6/7	6/8–7/7	7/8–11/9
1928	4/12–5/5	5/6–5/29	5/30–6/23	6/24–7/17	7/18–8/11	8/12–9/4
1929	2/3–3/7	3/8–4/19	7/8–8/4	8/5–8/30	8/31–9/25	9/26–10/19
	4/20–6/2	6/3–7/7				
1930	3/13–4/5	4/6–4/30	5/1–5/24	5/25–6/18	6/19–7/14	7/15–8/9
1931	4/26–5/20	5/21–6/13	6/14–7/8	7/9–8/2	8/3–8/26	8/27–9/19
1932	2/12–3/8	3/9–4/3	4/4–5/5	5/6–7/12	9/9–10/6	10/7–11/1
			7/13–7/27	7/28–9/8		
1933	3/27–4/19	4/20–5/28	5/29–6/8	6/9–7/2	7/3–7/26	7/27–8/20
1934	5/6–6/1	6/2–6/27	6/28–7/22	7/23–8/16	8/17–9/10	9/11–10/4
1935	2/26–3/21	3/22–4/15	4/16–5/10	5/11–6/6	6/7–7/6	7/7–11/8
1936	4/11–5/4	5/5–5/28	5/29–6/22	6/23–7/16	7/17–8/10	8/11–9/4
1937	2/2–3/8	3/9–4/13	7/7–8/3	8/4–8/29	8/30–9/24	9/25–10/18
	4/14–6/3	6/4–7/6				
1938	3/12–4/4	4/5–4/28	4/29–5/23	5/24–6/18	6/19–7/13	7/14–8/8
1939	4/25–5/19	5/20–6/13	6/14–7/8	7/9–8/1	8/2–8/25	8/26–9/19
1940	2/12–3/7	3/8–4/3	4/4–5/5	5/6–7/4	9/9–10/5	10/6–10/31
			7/5–7/31	8/1–9/8		
1941	3/27–4/19	4/20–5/13	5/14–6/6	6/7–7/1	7/2–7/26	7/27–8/20
1942	5/6–6/1	6/2–6/26	6/27–7/22	7/23–8/16	8/17–9/9	9/10–10/3
1943	2/25–3/20	3/21–4/14	4/15–5/10	5/11–6/6	6/7–7/6	7/7–11/8
1944	4/10–5/3	5/4–5/28	5/29–6/21	6/22–7/16	7/17–8/9	8/10–9/2
1945	2/2–3/10	3/11–4/6	7/7–8/3	8/4–8/29	8/30–9/23	9/24–10/18
	4/7–6/3	6/4–7/6				
1946	3/11–4/4	4/5–4/28	4/29–5/23	5/24–6/17	6/18–7/12	7/13–8/8
1947	4/25–5/19	5/20–6/12	6/13–7/7	7/8–8/1	8/2–8/25	8/26–9/18
1948	2/11–3/7	3/8–4/3	4/4–5/6	5/7–6/28	9/8–10/5	10/6–10/31
			6/29–8/2	8/3–9/7		
1949	3/26–4/19	4/20–5/13	5/14–6/6	6/7–6/30	7/1–7/25	7/26–8/19
1950	5/5–5/31	6/1–6/26	6/27–7/21	7/22–8/15	8/16–9/9	9/10–10/3
1951	2/25–3/21	3/22–4/15	4/16–5/10	5/11–6/6	6/7–7/7	7/8–11/9

Libra	Scorpio	Sagittarius	Capricorn	Aquarius	Pisces
10/6–10/29	10/30–11/22	11/23–12/16	12/17–12/31	1/1–4/5	4/6–5/6
11/10–12/8	12/9–12/31	1/1–1/7	1/8	1/9–2/1	2/2–2/26
9/5–9/28	1/1–1/3	1/4–1/28	1/29–2/22	2/23–3/17	3/18–4/11
	9/29–10/23	10/24–11/16	11/17–12/11	12/12–12/31	
10/20–11/12	11/13–12/6	12/7–12/30	12/31	1/1–1/5	1/6–2/2
8/10–9/6	9/7–10/11	10/12–11/21	1/1–1/23	1/24–2/16	2/17–3/12
	11/22–12/31				
9/20–10/13	1/1–1/3	1/4–2/6	2/7–3/4	3/5–3/31	4/1–4/25
	10/14–11/6	11/7–11/30	12/1–12/24	12/25–12/31	
11/2–11/25	11/26–12/20	12/21–12/31		1/1–1/18	1/19–2/11
8/21–9/14	9/15–10/10	1/1–1/13	1/14–2/6	2/7–3/2	3/3–3/26
		10/11–11/5	11/6–12/4	12/5–12/31	
10/5–10/28	10/29–11/21	11/22–12/15	12/16–12/31	1/1–4/5	4/6–5/5
11/9–12/7	12/8–12/31		1/1–1/7	1/8–1/31	2/1–2/25
9/5–9/27	1/1–1/2	1/3–1/27	1/28–2/21	2/22–3/16	3/17–4/10
	9/28–10/22	10/23–11/15	11/16–12/10	12/11–12/31	
10/19–11/11	11/12–12/5	12/6–12/29	12/30–12/31	1/1–1/5	1/6–2/1
8/9–9/6	9/7–10/13	10/14–11/14	1/1–1/22	1/23–2/15	2/16–3/11
	11/15–12/31				
9/20–10/13	1/1–1/3	1/4–2/5	2/6–3/4	3/5–3/30	3/31–4/24
	10/14–11/6	11/7–11/30	12/1–12/24	12/25–12/31	
11/1–11/25	11/26–12/19	12/20–12/31		1/1–1/18	1/19–2/11
8/21–9/14	9/15–10/9	1/1–1/12	1/13–2/5	2/6–3/1	3/2–3/26
		10/10–11/5	11/6–12/4	12/5–12/31	
10/4–10/27	10/28–11/20	11/21–12/14	12/15–12/31	1/1–4/5	4/6–5/5
11/9–12/7	12/8–12/31		1/1–1/7	1/8–1/31	2/1–2/24
9/3–9/27	1/1–1/2	1/3–1/27	1/28–2/20	2/21–3/16	3/17–4/9
	9/28–10/21	10/22–11/15	11/16–12/10	12/11–12/31	
10/19–11/11	11/12–12/5	12/6–12/29	12/30–12/31	1/1–1/4	1/5–2/1
8/9–9/6	9/7–10/15	10/16–11/7	1/1–1/21	1/22–2/14	2/15–3/10
	11/8–12/31				
9/19–10/12	1/1–1/4	1/5–2/5	2/6–3/4	3/5–3/29	3/30–4/24
	10/13–11/5	11/6–11/29	11/30–12/23	12/24–12/31	
11/1–11/25	11/26–12/19	12/20–12/31		1/1–1/17	1/18–2/10
8/20–9/14	9/15–10/9	1/1–1/12	1/13–2/5	2/6–3/1	3/2–3/25
		10/10–11/5	11/6–12/5	12/6–12/31	
10/4–10/27	10/28–11/20	11/21–12/13	12/14–12/31	1/1–4/5	4/6–5/4
11/10–12/7	12/8–12/31		1/1–1/7	1/8–1/31	2/1–2/24

VENUS SIGNS 1901–2006

	Aries	Taurus	Gemini	Cancer	Leo	Virgo
1952	4/10–5/4	5/5–5/28	5/29–6/21	6/22–7/16	7/17–8/9	8/10–9/3
1953	2/2–3/3 4/1–6/5	3/4–3/31 6/6–7/7	7/8–8/3	8/4–8/29	8/30–9/24	9/25–10/18
1954	3/12–4/4	4/5–4/28	4/29–5/23	5/24–6/17	6/18–7/13	7/14–8/8
1955	4/25–5/19	5/20–6/13	6/14–7/7	7/8–8/1	8/2–8/25	8/26–9/18
1956	2/12–3/7	3/8–4/4	4/5–5/7 6/24–8/4	5/8–6/23 8/5–9/8	9/9–10/5	10/6–10/31
1957	3/26–4/19	4/20–5/13	5/14–6/6	6/7–7/1	7/2–7/26	7/27–8/19
1958	5/6–5/31	6/1–6/26	6/27–7/22	7/23–8/15	8/16–9/9	9/10–10/3
1959	2/25–3/20	3/21–4/14	4/15–5/10	5/11–6/6	6/7–7/8 9/21–9/24	7/9–9/20 9/25–11/9
1960	4/10–5/3	5/4–5/28	5/29–6/21	6/22–7/15	7/16–8/9	8/10–9/2
1961	2/3–6/5	6/6–7/7	7/8–8/3	8/4–8/29	8/30–9/23	9/24–10/17
1962	3/11–4/3	4/4–4/28	4/29–5/22	5/23–6/17	6/18–7/12	7/13–8/8
1963	4/24–5/18	5/19–6/12	6/13–7/7	7/8–7/31	8/1–8/25	8/26–9/18
1964	2/11–3/7	3/8–4/4	4/5–5/9 6/18–8/5	5/10–6/17 8/6–9/8	9/9–10/5	10/6–10/31
1965	3/26–4/18	4/19–5/12	5/13–6/6	6/7–6/30	7/1–7/25	7/26–8/19
1966	5/6–6/31	6/1–6/26	6/27–7/21	7/22–8/15	8/16–9/8	9/9–10/2
1967	2/24–3/20	3/21–4/14	4/15–5/10	5/11–6/6	6/7–7/8 9/10–10/1	7/9–9/9 10/2–11/9
1968	4/9–5/3	5/4–5/27	5/28–6/20	6/21–7/15	7/16–8/8	8/9–9/2
1969	2/3–6/6	6/7–7/6	7/7–8/3	8/4–8/28	8/29–9/22	9/23–10/17
1970	3/11–4/3	4/4–4/27	4/28–5/22	5/23–6/16	6/17–7/12	7/13–8/8
1971	4/24–5/18	5/19–6/12	6/13–7/6	7/7–7/31	8/1–8/24	8/25–9/17
1972	2/11–3/7	3/8–4/3	4/4–5/10 6/12–8/6	5/11–6/11 8/7–9/8	9/9–10/5	10/6–10/30
1973	3/25–4/18	4/18–5/12	5/13–6/5	6/6–6/29	7/1–7/25	7/26–8/19
1974	5/5–5/31	6/1–6/25	6/26–7/21	7/22–8/14	8/15–9/8	9/9–10/2
1975	2/24–3/20	3/21–4/13	4/14–5/9	5/10–6/6	6/7–7/9 9/3–10/4	7/10–9/2 10/5–11/9

Libra	Scorpio	Sagittarius	Capricorn	Aquarius	Pisces
9/4–9/27	1/1–1/2	1/3–1/27	1/28–2/20	2/21–3/16	3/17–4/9
	9/28–10/21	10/22–11/15	11/16–12/10	12/11–12/31	
10/19–11/11	11/12–12/5	12/6–12/29	12/30–12/31	1/1–1/5	1/6–2/1
8/9–9/6	9/7–10/22	10/23–10/27	1/1–1/22	1/23–2/15	2/16–3/11
	10/28–12/31				
9/19–10/13	1/1–1/6	1/7–2/5	2/6–3/4	3/5–3/30	3/31–4/24
	10/14–11/5	11/6–11/30	12/1–12/24	12/25–12/31	
11/1–11/25	11/26–12/19	12/20–12/31		1/1–1/17	1/18–2/11
8/20–9/14	9/15–10/9	1/1–1/12	1/13–2/5	2/6–3/1	3/2–3/25
		10/10–11/5	11/6–12/6	12/7–12/31	
10/4–10/27	10/28–11/20	11/21–12/14	12/15–12/31	1/1–4/6	4/7–5/5
11/10–12/7	12/8–12/31		1/1–1/7	1/8–1/31	2/1–2/24
9/3–9/26	1/1–1/2	1/3–1/27	1/28–2/20	2/21–3/15	3/16–4/9
	9/27–10/21	10/22–11/15	11/16–12/10	12/11–12/31	
10/18–11/11	11/12–12/4	12/5–12/28	12/29–12/31	1/1–1/5	1/6–2/2
8/9–9/6	9/7–12/31		1/1–1/21	1/22–2/14	2/15–3/10
9/19–10/12	1/1–1/6	1/7–2/5	2/6–3/4	3/5–3/29	3/30–4/23
	10/13–11/5	11/6–11/29	11/30–12/23	12/24–12/31	
11/1–11/24	11/25–12/19	12/20–12/31		1/1–1/16	1/17–2/10
8/20–9/13	9/14–10/9	1/1–1/12	1/13–2/5	2/6–3/1	3/2–3/25
		10/10–11/5	11/6–12/7	12/8–12/31	
10/3–10/26	10/27–11/19	11/20–12/13	2/7–2/25	1/1–2/6	4/7–5/5
			12/14–12/31	2/26–4/6	
11/10–12/7	12/8–12/31		1/1–1/6	1/7–1/30	1/31–2/23
9/3–9/26	1/1	1/2–1/26	1/27–2/20	2/21–3/15	3/16–4/8
	9/27–10/21	10/22–11/14	11/15–12/9	12/10–12/31	
10/18–11/10	11/11–12/4	12/5–12/28	12/29–12/31	1/1–1/4	1/5–2/2
8/9–9/7	9/8–12/31		1/1–1/21	1/22–2/14	2/15–3/10
9/18–10/11	1/1–1/7	1/8–2/5	2/6–3/4	3/5–3/29	3/30–4/23
	10/12–11/5	11/6–11/29	11/30–12/23	12/24–12/31	
	11/25–12/18	12/19–12/31		1/1–1/16	1/17–2/10
10/31–11/24					
8/20–9/13	9/14–10/8	1/1–1/12	1/13–2/4	2/5–2/28	3/1–3/24
		10/9–11/5	11/6–12/7	12/8–12/31	
			1/30–2/28	1/1–1/29	
10/3–10/26	10/27–11/19	11/20–12/13	12/14–12/31	3/1–4/6	4/7–5/4
11/10–12/7	12/8–12/31		1/1–1/6	1/7–1/30	1/31–2/23

VENUS SIGNS 1901–2006

	Aries	Taurus	Gemini	Cancer	Leo	Virgo
1976	4/8–5/2	5/2–5/27	5/27–6/20	6/20–7/14	7/14–8/8	8/8–9/1
1977	2/2–6/6	6/6–7/6	7/6–8/2	8/2–8/28	8/28–9/22	9/22–10/17
1978	3/9–4/2	4/2–4/27	4/27–5/22	5/22–6/16	6/16–7/12	7/12–8/6
1979	4/23–5/18	5/18–6/11	6/11–7/6	7/6–7/30	7/30–8/24	8/24–9/17
1980	2/9–3/6	3/6–4/3	4/3–5/12	5/12–6/5	9/7–10/4	10/4–10/30
			6/5–8/6	8/6–9/7		
1981	3/24–4/17	4/17–5/11	5/11–6/5	6/5–6/29	6/29–7/24	7/24–8/18
1982	5/4–5/30	5/30–6/25	6/25–7/20	7/20–8/14	8/14–9/7	9/7–10/2
1983	2/22–3/19	3/19–4/13	4/13–5/9	5/9–6/6	6/6–7/10	7/10–8/27
					8/27–10/5	10/5–11/9
1984	4/7–5/2	5/2–5/26	5/26–6/20	6/20–7/14	7/14–8/7	8/7–9/1
1985	2/2–6/6	6/7–7/6	7/6–8/2	8/2–8/28	8/28–9/22	9/22–10/16
1986	3/9–4/2	4/2–4/26	4/26–5/21	5/21–6/15	6/15–7/11	7/11–8/7
1987	4/22–5/17	5/17–6/11	6/11–7/5	7/5–7/30	7/30–8/23	8/23–9/16
1988	2/9–3/6	3/6–4/3	4/3–5/17	5/17–5/27	9/7–10/4	10/4–10/29
			5/27–8/6	8/28–9/22	9/22–10/16	
1989	3/23–4/16	4/16–5/11	5/11–6/4	6/4–6/29	6/29–7/24	7/24–8/18
1990	5/4–5/30	5/30–6/25	6/25–7/20	7/20–8/13	8/13–9/7	9/7–10/1
1991	2/22–3/18	3/18–4/13	4/13–5/9	5/9–6/6	6/6–7/11	7/11–8/21
					8/21–10/6	10/6–11/9
1992	4/7–5/1	5/1–5/26	5/26–6/19	6/19–7/13	7/13–8/7	8/7–8/31
1993	2/2–6/6	6/6–7/6	7/6–8/1	8/1–8/27	8/27–9/21	9/21–10/16
1994	3/8–4/1	4/1–4/26	4/26–5/21	5/21–6/15	6/15–7/11	7/11–8/7
1995	4/22–5/16	5/16–6/10	6/10–7/5	7/5–7/29	7/29–8/23	8/23–9/16
1996	2/9–3/6	3/6–4/3	4/3–8/7	8/7–9/7	9/7–10/4	10/4–10/29
1997	3/23–4/16	4/16–5/10	5/10–6/4	6/4–6/28	6/28–7/23	7/23–8/17
1998	5/3–5/29	5/29–6/24	6/24–7/19	7/19–8/13	8/13–9/6	9/6–9/30
1999	2/21–3/18	3/18–4/12	4/12–5/8	5/8–6/5	6/5–7/12	7/12–8/15
					8/15–10/7	10/7–11/9
2000	4/6–5/1	5/1–5/25	5/25–6/13	6/13–7/13	7/13–8/6	8/6–8/31
2001	2/2–6/6	6/6–7/5	7/5–8/1	8/1–8/26	8/26–9/20	9/20–10/15
2002	3/7–4/1	4/1–4/25	4/25–5/20	5/20–6/14	6/14–7/10	7/10–8/7
2003	4/21–5/16	5/16–6/9	6/9–7/4	7/4–7/29	7/29–8/22	8/22–9/15
2004	2/8–3/5	3/5–4/3	4/3–8/7	8/7–9/6	9/6–10/3	10/3–10/28
2005	3/22–4/15	4/15–5/10	5/10–6/3	6/3–6/28	6/28–7/23	7/23–8/17
2006	5/3–5/29	5/29–6/24	6/24–7/19	7/19–8/12	8/12–9/6	9/6–9/30

Libra	Scorpio	Sagittarius	Capricorn	Aquarius	Pisces
9/1–9/26	9/26–10/20	1/1–1/26	1/26–2/19	2/19–3/15	3/15–4/8
10/17–11/10	11/10–12/4	12/4–12/27	12/27–1/20/78		1/4–2/2
8/6–9/7	9/7–1/7			1/20–2/13	2/13–3/9
9/17–10/11	10/11–11/4	1/7–2/5	2/5–3/3	3/3–3/29	3/29–4/23
		11/4–11/28	11/28–12/22	12/22–1/16/80	
10/30–11/24	11/24–12/18	12/18–1/11/81			1/16–2/9
8/18–9/12	9/12–10/9	10/9–11/5	1/11–2/4	2/4–2/28	2/28–3/24
			11/5–12/8	12/8–1/23/82	
10/2–10/26	10/26–11/18	11/18–12/12	1/23–3/2	3/2–4/6	4/6–5/4
			12/12–1/5/83		
11/9–12/6	12/6–1/1/84			1/5–1/29	1/29–2/22
9/1–9/25	9/25–10/20	1/1–1/25	1/25–2/19	2/19–3/14	3/14–4/7
		10/20–11/13	11/13–12/9	12/10–1/4	
10/16–11/9	11/9–12/3	12/3–12/27	12/28–1/19		1/4–2/2
8/7–9/7	9/7–1/7			1/20–2/13	2/13–3/9
9/16–10/10	10/10–11/3	1/7–2/5	2/5–3/3	3/3–3/28	3/28–4/22
		11/3–11/28	11/28–12/22	12/22–1/15	
10/29–11/23	11/23–12/17	12/17–1/10			1/15–2/9
8/18–9/12	9/12–10/8	10/8–11/5	1/10–2/3	2/3–2/27	2/27–3/23
			11/5–12/10	12/10–1/16/90	
10/1–10/25	10/25–11/18	11/18–12/12	1/16–3/3	3/3–4/6	4/6–5/4
			12/12–1/5		
11/9–12/6	12/6–12/31	12/31–1/25/92		1/5–1/29	1/29–2/22
8/31–9/25	9/25–10/19	10/19–11/13	1/25–2/18	2/18–3/13	3/13–4/7
			11/13–12/8	12/8–1/3/93	
10/16–11/9	11/9–12/2	12/2–12/26	12/26–1/19		1/3–2/2
8/7–9/7	9/7–1/7			1/19–2/12	2/12–3/8
9/16–10/10	10/10–11/13	1/7–2/4	2/4–3/2	3/2–3/28	3/28–4/22
		11/3–11/27	11/27–12/21	12/21–1/15	
10/29–11/23	11/23–12/17	12/17–1/10/97			1/15–2/9
8/17–9/12	9/12–10/8	10/8–11/5	1/10–2/3	2/3–2/27	2/27–3/23
			11/5–12/12	12/12–1/9	
9/30–10/24	10/24–11/17	11/17–12/11	1/9–3/4	3/4–4/6	4/6–5/3
11/9–12/5	12/5–12/31	12/31–1/24		1/4–1/28	1/28–2/21
8/31–9/24	9/24–10/19	10/19–11/13	1/24–2/18	2/18–3/12	3/13–4/6
			11/13–12/8	12/8	
10/15–11/8	11/8–12/2	12/2–12/26	12/26/01–1/18/02	12/8/00–1/3/01	1/3–2/2
8/7–9/7	9/7–1/7/03		12/26/01–1/18	1/18–2/11	2/11–3/7
9/15–10/9	10/9–11/2	1/7–2/4	2/4–3/2	3/2–3/27	3/27–4/21
		11/2–11/26	11/26–12/21	12/21–1/14/04	
10/28–11/22	11/22–12/16	12/16–1/9/05		1/1–1/14	1/14–2/8
8/17–9/11	9/11–10/8	10/8–11/15	1/9–2/2	2/2–2/26	2/26–3/22
			11/5–12/15	12/15–1/1/06	
9/30–10/24	10/24–11/17	11/17–12/11	1/1–3/5	3/5–4/6	4/6–5/3

How to Use the Mars, Jupiter, and Saturn Tables

Find the year of your birth on the left side of each column. The dates when the planet entered each sign are listed on the right side of each column. (Signs are abbreviated to three letters.) Your birthday should fall on or between each date listed, and your planetary placement should correspond to the earlier sign of that period.

All planet changes are calculated for the Greenwich Mean Time zone.

MARS SIGNS 1901–2006

1901	MAR	1	Leo		OCT	1	Vir
	MAY	11	Vir		NOV	20	Lib
	JUL	13	Lib	1905	JAN	13	Scp
	AUG	31	Scp		AUG	21	Sag
	OCT	14	Sag		OCT	8	Cap
	NOV	24	Cap		NOV	18	Aqu
1902	JAN	1	Aqu		DEC	27	Pic
	FEB	8	Pic	1906	FEB	4	Ari
	MAR	19	Ari		MAR	17	Tau
	APR	27	Tau		APR	28	Gem
	JUN	7	Gem		JUN	11	Can
	JUL	20	Can		JUL	27	Leo
	SEP	4	Leo		SEP	12	Vir
	OCT	23	Vir		OCT	30	Lib
	DEC	20	Lib		DEC	17	Scp
1903	APR	19	Vir	1907	FEB	5	Sag
	MAY	30	Lib		APR	1	Cap
	AUG	6	Scp		OCT	13	Aqu
	SEP	22	Sag		NOV	29	Pic
	NOV	3	Cap	1908	JAN	11	Ari
	DEC	12	Aqu		FEB	23	Tau
1904	JAN	19	Pic		APR	7	Gem
	FEB	27	Ari		MAY	22	Can
	APR	6	Tau		JUL	8	Leo
	MAY	18	Gem		AUG	24	Vir
	JUN	30	Can		OCT	10	Lib
	AUG	15	Leo		NOV	25	Scp

1909	JAN	10	Sag		MAR	9	Pic
	FEB	24	Cap		APR	16	Ari
	APR	9	Aqu		MAY	26	Tau
	MAY	25	Pic		JUL	6	Gem
	JUL	21	Ari		AUG	19	Can
	SEP	26	Pic		OCT	7	Leo
	NOV	20	Ari	1916	MAY	28	Vir
1910	JAN	23	Tau		JUL	23	Lib
	MAR	14	Gem		SEP	8	Scp
	MAY	1	Can		OCT	22	Sag
	JUN	19	Leo		DEC	1	Cap
	AUG	6	Vir	1917	JAN	9	Aqu
	SEP	22	Lib		FEB	16	Pic
	NOV	6	Scp		MAR	26	Ari
	DEC	20	Sag		MAY	4	Tau
1911	JAN	31	Cap		JUN	14	Gem
	MAR	14	Aqu		JUL	28	Can
	APR	23	Pic		SEP	12	Leo
	JUN	2	Ari		NOV	2	Vir
	JUL	15	Tau	1918	JAN	11	Lib
	SEP	5	Gem		FEB	25	Vir
	NOV	30	Tau		JUN	23	Lib
1912	JAN	30	Gem		AUG	17	Scp
	APR	5	Can		OCT	1	Sag
	MAY	28	Leo		NOV	11	Cap
	JUL	17	Vir		DEC	20	Aqu
	SEP	2	Lib	1919	JAN	27	Pic
	OCT	18	Scp		MAR	6	Ari
	NOV	30	Sag		APR	15	Tau
1913	JAN	10	Cap		MAY	26	Gem
	FEB	19	Aqu		JUL	8	Can
	MAR	30	Pic		AUG	23	Leo
	MAY	8	Ari		OCT	10	Vir
	JUN	17	Tau		NOV	30	Lib
	JUL	29	Gem	1920	JAN	31	Scp
	SEP	15	Can		APR	23	Lib
1914	MAY	1	Leo		JUL	10	Scp
	JUN	26	Vir		SEP	4	Sag
	AUG	14	Lib		OCT	18	Cap
	SEP	29	Scp		NOV	27	Aqu
	NOV	11	Sag	1921	JAN	5	Pic
	DEC	22	Cap		FEB	13	Ari
1915	JAN	30	Aqu		MAR	25	Tau

	MAY	6	Gem		OCT	26	Scp
	JUN	18	Can		DEC	8	Sag
	AUG	3	Leo	1928	JAN	19	Cap
	SEP	19	Vir		FEB	28	Aqu
	NOV	6	Lib		APR	7	Pic
	DEC	26	Scp		MAY	16	Ari
1922	FEB	18	Sag		JUN	26	Tau
	SEP	13	Cap		AUG	9	Gem
	OCT	30	Aqu		OCT	3	Can
	DEC	11	Pic		DEC	20	Gem
1923	JAN	21	Ari	1929	MAR	10	Can
	MAR	4	Tau		MAY	13	Leo
	APR	16	Gem		JUL	4	Vir
	MAY	30	Can		AUG	21	Lib
	JUL	16	Leo		OCT	6	Scp
	SEP	1	Vir		NOV	18	Sag
	OCT	18	Lib		DEC	29	Cap
	DEC	4	Scp	1930	FEB	6	Aqu
1924	JAN	19	Sag		MAR	17	Pic
	MAR	6	Cap		APR	24	Ari
	APR	24	Aqu		JUN	3	Tau
	JUN	24	Pic		JUL	14	Gem
	AUG	24	Aqu		AUG	28	Can
	OCT	19	Pic		OCT	20	Leo
	DEC	19	Ari	1931	FEB	16	Can
1925	FEB	5	Tau		MAR	30	Leo
	MAR	24	Gem		JUN	10	Vir
	MAY	9	Can		AUG	1	Lib
	JUN	26	Leo		SEP	17	Scp
	AUG	12	Vir		OCT	30	Sag
	SEP	28	Lib		DEC	10	Cap
	NOV	13	Scp	1932	JAN	18	Aqu
	DEC	28	Sag		FEB	25	Pic
1926	FEB	9	Cap		APR	3	Ari
	MAR	23	Aqu		MAY	12	Tau
	MAY	3	Pic		JUN	22	Gem
	JUN	15	Ari		AUG	4	Can
	AUG	1	Tau		SEP	20	Leo
1927	FEB	22	Gem		NOV	13	Vir
	APR	17	Can	1933	JUL	6	Lib
	JUN	6	Leo		AUG	26	Scp
	JUL	25	Vir		OCT	9	Sag
	SEP	10	Lib		NOV	19	Cap

	DEC	28	Aqu		FEB	17	Tau
1934	FEB	4	Pic		APR	1	Gem
	MAR	14	Ari		MAY	17	Can
	APR	22	Tau		JUL	3	Leo
	JUN	2	Gem		AUG	19	Vir
	JUL	15	Can		OCT	5	Lib
	AUG	30	Leo		NOV	20	Scp
	OCT	18	Vir	1941	JAN	4	Sag
	DEC	11	Lib		FEB	17	Cap
1935	JUL	29	Scp		APR	2	Aqu
	SEP	16	Sag		MAY	16	Pic
	OCT	28	Cap		JUL	2	Ari
	DEC	7	Aqu	1942	JAN	11	Tau
1936	JAN	14	Pic		MAR	7	Gem
	FEB	22	Ari		APR	26	Can
	APR	1	Tau		JUN	14	Leo
	MAY	13	Gem		AUG	1	Vir
	JUN	25	Can		SEP	17	Lib
	AUG	10	Leo		NOV	1	Scp
	SEP	26	Vir		DEC	15	Sag
	NOV	14	Lib	1943	JAN	26	Cap
1937	JAN	5	Scp		MAR	8	Aqu
	MAR	13	Sag		APR	17	Pic
	MAY	14	Scp		MAY	27	Ari
	AUG	8	Sag		JUL	7	Tau
	SEP	30	Cap		AUG	23	Gem
	NOV	11	Aqu	1944	MAR	28	Can
	DEC	21	Pic		MAY	22	Leo
1938	JAN	30	Ari		JUL	12	Vir
	MAR	12	Tau		AUG	29	Lib
	APR	23	Gem		OCT	13	Scp
	JUN	7	Can		NOV	25	Sag
	JUL	22	Leo	1945	JAN	5	Cap
	SEP	7	Vir		FEB	14	Aqu
	OCT	25	Lib		MAR	25	Pic
	DEC	11	Scp		MAY	2	Ari
1939	JAN	29	Sag		JUN	11	Tau
	MAR	21	Cap		JUL	23	Gem
	MAY	25	Aqu		SEP	7	Can
	JUL	21	Cap		NOV	11	Leo
	SEP	24	Aqu		DEC	26	Can
	NOV	19	Pic	1946	APR	22	Leo
1940	JAN	4	Ari		JUN	20	Vir

	AUG	9	Lib		OCT	12	Cap
	SEP	24	Scp		NOV	21	Aqu
	NOV	6	Sag		DEC	30	Pic
	DEC	17	Cap	1953	FEB	8	Ari
1947	JAN	25	Aqu		MAR	20	Tau
	MAR	4	Pic		MAY	1	Gem
	APR	11	Ari		JUN	14	Can
	MAY	21	Tau		JUL	29	Leo
	JUL	1	Gem		SEP	14	Vir
	AUG	13	Can		NOV	1	Lib
	OCT	1	Leo		DEC	20	Scp
	DEC	1	Vir	1954	FEB	9	Sag
1948	FEB	12	Leo		APR	12	Cap
	MAY	18	Vir		JUL	3	Sag
	JUL	17	Lib		AUG	24	Cap
	SEP	3	Scp		OCT	21	Aqu
	OCT	17	Sag		DEC	4	Pic
	NOV	26	Cap	1955	JAN	15	Ari
1949	JAN	4	Aqu		FEB	26	Tau
	FEB	11	Pic		APR	10	Gem
	MAR	21	Ari		MAY	26	Can
	APR	30	Tau		JUL	11	Leo
	JUN	10	Gem		AUG	27	Vir
	JUL	23	Can		OCT	13	Lib
	SEP	7	Leo		NOV	29	Scp
	OCT	27	Vir	1956	JAN	14	Sag
	DEC	26	Lib		FEB	28	Cap
1950	MAR	28	Vir		APR	14	Aqu
	JUN	11	Lib		JUN	3	Pic
	AUG	10	Scp		DEC	6	Ari
	SEP	25	Sag	1957	JAN	28	Tau
	NOV	6	Cap		MAR	17	Gem
	DEC	15	Aqu		MAY	4	Can
1951	JAN	22	Pic		JUN	21	Leo
	MAR	1	Ari		AUG	8	Vir
	APR	10	Tau		SEP	24	Lib
	MAY	21	Gem		NOV	8	Scp
	JUL	3	Can		DEC	23	Sag
	AUG	18	Leo	1958	FEB	3	Cap
	OCT	5	Vir		MAR	17	Aqu
	NOV	24	Lib		APR	27	Pic
1952	JAN	20	Scp		JUN	7	Ari
	AUG	27	Sag		JUL	21	Tau

	SEP	21	Gem		NOV	6	Vir
	OCT	29	Tau	1965	JUN	29	Lib
1959	FEB	10	Gem		AUG	20	Scp
	APR	10	Can		OCT	4	Sag
	JUN	1	Leo		NOV	14	Cap
	JUL	20	Vir		DEC	23	Aqu
	SEP	5	Lib	1966	JAN	30	Pic
	OCT	21	Scp		MAR	9	Ari
	DEC	3	Sag		APR	17	Tau
1960	JAN	14	Cap		MAY	28	Gem
	FEB	23	Aqu		JUL	11	Can
	APR	2	Pic		AUG	25	Leo
	MAY	11	Ari		OCT	12	Vir
	JUN	20	Tau		DEC	4	Lib
	AUG	2	Gem	1967	FEB	12	Scp
	SEP	21	Can		MAR	31	Lib
1961	FEB	5	Gem		JUL	19	Scp
	FEB	7	Can		SEP	10	Sag
	MAY	6	Leo		OCT	23	Cap
	JUN	28	Vir		DEC	1	Aqu
	AUG	17	Lib	1968	JAN	9	Pic
	OCT	1	Scp		FEB	17	Ari
	NOV	13	Sag		MAR	27	Tau
	DEC	24	Cap		MAY	8	Gem
1962	FEB	1	Aqu		JUN	21	Can
	MAR	12	Pic		AUG	5	Leo
	APR	19	Ari		SEP	21	Vir
	MAY	28	Tau		NOV	9	Lib
	JUL	9	Gem		DEC	29	Scp
	AUG	22	Can	1969	FEB	25	Sag
	OCT	11	Leo		SEP	21	Cap
1963	JUN	3	Vir		NOV	4	Aqu
	JUL	27	Lib		DEC	15	Pic
	SEP	12	Scp	1970	JAN	24	Ari
	OCT	25	Sag		MAR	7	Tau
	DEC	5	Cap		APR	18	Gem
1964	JAN	13	Aqu		JUN	2	Can
	FEB	20	Pic		JUL	18	Leo
	MAR	29	Ari		SEP	3	Vir
	MAY	7	Tau		OCT	20	Lib
	JUN	17	Gem		DEC	6	Scp
	JUL	30	Can	1971	JAN	23	Sag
	SEP	15	Leo		MAR	12	Cap

	MAY	3	Aqu		JUN	6	Tau
	NOV	6	Pic		JUL	17	Gem
	DEC	26	Ari		SEP	1	Can
1972	FEB	10	Tau		OCT	26	Leo
	MAR	27	Gem	1978	JAN	26	Can
	MAY	12	Can		APR	10	Leo
	JUN	28	Leo		JUN	14	Vir
	AUG	15	Vir		AUG	4	Lib
	SEP	30	Lib		SEP	19	Scp
	NOV	15	Scp		NOV	2	Sag
	DEC	30	Sag		DEC	12	Cap
1973	FEB	12	Cap	1979	JAN	20	Aqu
	MAR	26	Aqu		FEB	27	Pic
	MAY	8	Pic		APR	7	Ari
	JUN	20	Ari		MAY	16	Tau
	AUG	12	Tau		JUN	26	Gem
	OCT	29	Ari		AUG	8	Can
	DEC	24	Tau		SEP	24	Leo
1974	FEB	27	Gem		NOV	19	Vir
	APR	20	Can	1980	MAR	11	Leo
	JUN	9	Leo		MAY	4	Vir
	JUL	27	Vir		JUL	10	Lib
	SEP	12	Lib		AUG	29	Scp
	OCT	28	Scp		OCT	12	Sag
	DEC	10	Sag		NOV	22	Cap
1975	JAN	21	Cap		DEC	30	Aqu
	MAR	3	Aqu	1981	FEB	6	Pic
	APR	11	Pic		MAR	17	Ari
	MAY	21	Ari		APR	25	Tau
	JUL	1	Tau		JUN	5	Gem
	AUG	14	Gem		JUL	18	Can
	OCT	17	Can		SEP	2	Leo
	NOV	25	Gem		OCT	21	Vir
1976	MAR	18	Can		DEC	16	Lib
	MAY	16	Leo	1982	AUG	3	Scp
	JUL	6	Vir		SEP	20	Sag
	AUG	24	Lib		OCT	31	Cap
	OCT	8	Scp		DEC	10	Aqu
	NOV	20	Sag	1983	JAN	17	Pic
1977	JAN	1	Cap		FEB	25	Ari
	FEB	9	Aqu		APR	5	Tau
	MAR	20	Pic		MAY	16	Gem
	APR	27	Ari		JUN	29	Can

	AUG	13	Leo	1990	JAN	29	Cap
	SEP	30	Vir		MAR	11	Aqu
	NOV	18	Lib		APR	20	Pic
1984	JAN	11	Scp		MAY	31	Ari
	AUG	17	Sag		JUL	12	Tau
	OCT	5	Cap		AUG	31	Gem
	NOV	15	Aqu		DEC	14	Tau
	DEC	25	Pic	1991	JAN	21	Gem
1985	FEB	2	Ari		APR	3	Can
	MAR	15	Tau		MAY	26	Leo
	APR	26	Gem		JUL	15	Vir
	JUN	9	Can		SEP	1	Lib
	JUL	25	Leo		OCT	16	Scp
	SEP	10	Vir		NOV	29	Sag
	OCT	27	Lib	1992	JAN	9	Cap
	DEC	14	Scp		FEB	18	Aqu
1986	FEB	2	Sag		MAR	28	Pic
	MAR	28	Cap		MAY	5	Ari
	OCT	9	Aqu		JUN	14	Tau
	NOV	26	Pic		JUL	26	Gem
1987	JAN	8	Ari		SEP	12	Can
	FEB	20	Tau	1993	APR	27	Leo
	APR	5	Gem		JUN	23	Vir
	MAY	21	Can		AUG	12	Lib
	JUL	6	Leo		SEP	27	Scp
	AUG	22	Vir		NOV	9	Sag
	OCT	8	Lib		DEC	20	Cap
	NOV	24	Scp	1994	JAN	28	Aqu
1988	JAN	8	Sag		MAR	7	Pic
	FEB	22	Cap		APR	14	Ari
	APR	6	Aqu		MAY	23	Tau
	MAY	22	Pic		JUL	3	Gem
	JUL	13	Ari		AUG	16	Can
	OCT	23	Pic		OCT	4	Leo
	NOV	1	Ari		DEC	12	Vir
1989	JAN	19	Tau	1995	JAN	22	Leo
	MAR	11	Gem		MAY	25	Vir
	APR	29	Can		JUL	21	Lib
	JUN	16	Leo		SEP	7	Scp
	AUG	3	Vir		OCT	20	Sag
	SEP	19	Lib		NOV	30	Cap
	NOV	4	Scp	1996	JAN	8	Aqu
	DEC	18	Sag		FEB	15	Pic

	MAR	24	Ari		SEP	8	Cap
	MAY	2	Tau		OCT	27	Aqu
	JUN	12	Gem		DEC	8	Pic
	JUL	25	Can	2002	JAN	18	Ari
	SEP	9	Leo		MAR	1	Tau
	OCT	30	Vir		APR	13	Gem
1997	JAN	3	Lib		MAY	28	Can
	MAR	8	Vir		JUL	13	Leo
	JUN	19	Lib		AUG	29	Vir
	AUG	14	Scp		OCT	15	Lib
	SEP	28	Sag		DEC	1	Scp
	NOV	9	Cap	2003	JAN	17	Sag
	DEC	18	Aqu		MAR	4	Cap
1998	JAN	25	Pic		APR	21	Aqu
	MAR	4	Ari		JUN	17	Pic
	APR	13	Tau		DEC	16	Ari
	MAY	24	Gem	2004	FEB	3	Tau
	JUL	6	Can		MAR	21	Gem
	AUG	20	Leo		MAY	7	Can
	OCT	7	Vir		JUN	23	Leo
	NOV	27	Lib		AUG	10	Vir
1999	JAN	26	Scp		SEP	26	Lib
	MAY	5	Lib		NOV	11	Sep
	JUL	5	Scp		DEC	25	Sag
	SEP	2	Sag	2005	FEB	6	Cap
	OCT	17	Cap		MAR	20	Aqu
	NOV	26	Aqu		MAY	1	Pic
2000	JAN	4	Pic		JUN	12	Ari
	FEB	12	Ari		JUL	28	Tau
	MAR	23	Tau	2006	FEB	17	Gem
	MAY	3	Gem		APR	14	Can
	JUN	16	Can		JUN	3	Leo
	AUG	1	Leo		JUL	22	Vir
	SEP	17	Vir		SEP	8	Lib
	NOV	4	Lib		OCT	23	Scp
	DEC	23	Scp		DEC	6	Sag
2001	FEB	14	Sag				

JUPITER SIGNS 1901–2006

1901	JAN	19	Cap
1902	FEB	6	Aqu
1903	FEB	20	Pic
1904	MAR	1	Ari
	AUG	8	Tau
	AUG	31	Ari
1905	MAR	7	Tau
	JUL	21	Gem
	DEC	4	Tau
1906	MAR	9	Gem
	JUL	30	Can
1907	AUG	18	Leo
1908	SEP	12	Vir
1909	OCT	11	Lib
1910	NOV	11	Scp
1911	DEC	10	Sag
1913	JAN	2	Cap
1914	JAN	21	Aqu
1915	FEB	4	Pic
1916	FEB	12	Ari
	JUN	26	Tau
	OCT	26	Ari
1917	FEB	12	Tau
	JUN	29	Gem
1918	JUL	13	Can
1919	AUG	2	Leo
1920	AUG	27	Vir
1921	SEP	25	Lib
1922	OCT	26	Scp
1923	NOV	24	Sag
1924	DEC	18	Cap
1926	JAN	6	Aqu
1927	JAN	18	Pic
	JUN	6	Ari
	SEP	11	Pic
1928	JAN	23	Ari
	JUN	4	Tau
1929	JUN	12	Gem
1930	JUN	26	Can
1931	JUL	17	Leo
1932	AUG	11	Vir
1933	SEP	10	Lib
1934	OCT	11	Scp
1935	NOV	9	Sag
1936	DEC	2	Cap
1937	DEC	20	Aqu
1938	MAY	14	Pic
	JUL	30	Aqu
	DEC	29	Pic
1939	MAY	11	Ari
	OCT	30	Pic
	DEC	20	Ari
1940	MAY	16	Tau
1941	MAY	26	Gem
1942	JUN	10	Can
1943	JUN	30	Leo
1944	JUL	26	Vir
1945	AUG	25	Lib
1946	SEP	25	Scp
1947	OCT	24	Sag
1948	NOV	15	Cap
1949	APR	12	Aqu
	JUN	27	Cap
	NOV	30	Aqu
1950	APR	15	Pic
	SEP	15	Aqu
	DEC	1	Pic
1951	APR	21	Ari
1952	APR	28	Tau
1953	MAY	9	Gem
1954	MAY	24	Can
1955	JUN	13	Leo
	NOV	17	Vir
1956	JAN	18	Leo
	JUL	7	Vir
	DEC	13	Lib

109

1957	FEB	19	Vir
	AUG	7	Lib
1958	JAN	13	Scp
	MAR	20	Lib
	SEP	7	Scp
1959	FEB	10	Sag
	APR	24	Scp
	OCT	5	Sag
1960	MAR	1	Cap
	JUN	10	Sag
	OCT	26	Cap
1961	MAR	15	Aqu
	AUG	12	Cap
	NOV	4	Aqu
1962	MAR	25	Pic
1963	APR	4	Ari
1964	APR	12	Tau
1965	APR	22	Gem
	SEP	21	Can
	NOV	17	Gem
1966	MAY	5	Can
	SEP	27	Leo
1967	JAN	16	Can
	MAY	23	Leo
	OCT	19	Vir
1968	FEB	27	Leo
	JUN	15	Vir
	NOV	15	Lib
1969	MAR	30	Vir
	JUL	15	Lib
	DEC	16	Scp
1970	APR	30	Lib
	AUG	15	Scp
1971	JAN	14	Sag
	JUN	5	Scp
	SEP	11	Sag
1972	FEB	6	Cap
	JUL	24	Sag
	SEP	25	Cap
1973	FEB	23	Aqu
1974	MAR	8	Pic
1975	MAR	18	Ari
1976	MAR	26	Tau
	AUG	23	Gem
	OCT	16	Tau
1977	APR	3	Gem
	AUG	20	Can
	DEC	30	Gem
1978	APR	12	Can
	SEP	5	Leo
1979	FEB	28	Can
	APR	20	Leo
	SEP	29	Vir
1980	OCT	27	Lib
1981	NOV	27	Scp
1982	DEC	26	Sag
1984	JAN	19	Cap
1985	FEB	6	Aqu
1986	FEB	20	Pic
1987	MAR	2	Ari
1988	MAR	8	Tau
	JUL	22	Gem
	NOV	30	Tau
1989	MAR	11	Gem
	JUL	30	Can
1990	AUG	18	Leo
1991	SEP	12	Vir
1992	OCT	10	Lib
1993	NOV	10	Scp
1994	DEC	9	Sag
1996	JAN	3	Cap
1997	JAN	21	Aqu
1998	FEB	4	Pic
1999	FEB	13	Ari
	JUN	28	Tau
	OCT	23	Ari
2000	FEB	14	Tau
	JUN	30	Gem
2001	JUL	14	Can
2002	AUG	1	Leo

2003	AUG	27	Vir	2005	OCT	26	Scp
2004	SEP	24	Lib	2006	NOV	24	Sag

SATURN SIGNS 1903–2006

1903	JAN	19	Aqu		SEP	22	Ari
1905	APR	13	Pic	1940	MAR	20	Tau
	AUG	17	Aqu	1942	MAY	8	Gem
1906	JAN	8	Pic	1944	JUN	20	Can
1908	MAR	19	Ari	1946	AUG	2	Leo
1910	MAY	17	Tau	1948	SEP	19	Vir
	DEC	14	Ari	1949	APR	3	Leo
1911	JAN	20	Tau		MAY	29	Vir
1912	JUL	7	Gem	1950	NOV	20	Lib
	NOV	30	Tau	1951	MAR	7	Vir
1913	MAR	26	Gem		AUG	13	Lib
1914	AUG	24	Can	1953	OCT	22	Scp
	DEC	7	Gem	1956	JAN	12	Sag
1915	MAY	11	Can		MAY	14	Scp
1916	OCT	17	Leo		OCT	10	Sag
	DEC	7	Can	1959	JAN	5	Cap
1917	JUN	24	Leo	1962	JAN	3	Aqu
1919	AUG	12	Vir	1964	MAR	24	Pic
1921	OCT	7	Lib		SEP	16	Aqu
1923	DEC	20	Scp		DEC	16	Pic
1924	APR	6	Lib	1967	MAR	3	Ari
	SEP	13	Scp	1969	APR	29	Tau
1926	DEC	2	Sag	1971	JUN	18	Gem
1929	MAR	15	Cap	1972	JAN	10	Tau
	MAY	5	Sag		FEB	21	Gem
	NOV	30	Cap	1973	AUG	1	Can
1932	FEB	24	Aqu	1974	JAN	7	Gem
	AUG	13	Cap		APR	18	Can
	NOV	20	Aqu	1975	SEP	17	Leo
1935	FEB	14	Pic	1976	JAN	14	Can
1937	APR	25	Ari		JUN	5	Leo
	OCT	18	Pic	1977	NOV	17	Vir
1938	JAN	14	Ari	1978	JAN	5	Leo
1939	JUL	6	Tau		JUL	26	Vir

1980	SEP	21	Lib		1994	JAN	28	Pic
1982	NOV	29	Scp		1996	APR	7	Ari
1983	MAY	6	Lib		1998	JUN	9	Tau
	AUG	24	Scp			OCT	25	Ari
1985	NOV	17	Sag		1999	MAR	1	Tau
1988	FEB	13	Cap		2000	AUG	10	Gem
	JUN	10	Sag			OCT	16	Tau
	NOV	12	Cap		2001	APR	21	Gem
1991	FEB	6	Aqu		2003	JUN	3	Can
1993	MAY	21	Pic		2005	JUL	16	Leo
	JUN	30	Aqu					

CHAPTER 7

The Astrology Code: The History and Mystery of Those Symbols on Your Chart

If you're about to meet your horoscope chart for the first time, the scene may resemble a blind date with someone from a distant culture who doesn't speak your language. Your first reaction is to throw up your hands. This is as complicated as Chinese or Egyptian! Do I have to learn a whole new language to read and understand the chart?

Before you put the chart away, or turn off your new astrology computer program, or click off the free chart you've downloaded from the Internet, read this chapter. Learning the glyphs is not a big deal. Each little symbol has built-in clues to help you not only decipher which sign or planet it represents, but what the object means in a deeper, more esoteric sense. Actually the physical act of writing the symbol is a mystical experience in itself, a way to invoke the deeper meaning of the sign or planet through age-old visual elements that have been with us since time began.

The glyphs are a language that is used by astrologers around the globe. Once you understand them, you can begin to find your way around the chart, beginning your journey to deeper understanding.

Since there are only twelve signs and ten planets (not counting a few asteroids and other space objects some astrologers use), it's a lot easier than learning to read a foreign language. Here's a code cracker for the glyphs, beginning with the glyphs for the planets. To those who already know their glyphs, don't just skim over the chapter. These familiar graphics have hidden meanings you will discover!

The Glyphs for the Planets

The glyphs for the planets are easy to learn. They're simple combinations of the most basic visual elements: the circle, the semicircle or arc, and the cross. However, each component of a glyph has a special meaning in relation to the other parts of the symbol.

The circle, which has no beginning or end, is one of the oldest symbols of spirit or spiritual forces. Early diagrams of the heavens—spiritual territory—are shown in circular form. The never-ending line of the circle is the perfect symbol for eternity. The semicircle or arc is an incomplete circle, symbolizing the receptive, finite soul, which contains spiritual potential in the curving line.

The vertical line of the cross symbolizes movement from heaven to earth. The horizontal line describes temporal movement, here and now, in time and space. Combined in a cross, the vertical and horizontal planes symbolize manifestation in the material world.

The Sun Glyph ☉

The sun is always shown by this powerful solar symbol, a circle with a point in the center. The center point is you, your spiritual center, and the symbol represents your infinite personality incarnating (the point) into the finite cycles of birth and death.

The sun has been represented by a circle or disk since ancient Egyptian times when the solar disk represented the sun god, Ra. Some archaeologists believe the great stone circles found in England were centers of sun worship. This particular version of the symbol was brought into common use in the sixteenth century after German occultist and scholar Cornelius Agrippa (1486–1535) wrote a book called the *Die Occulta Philosophia,* which became accepted as the authority in the field. Agrippa collected many medieval astrological and magical symbols in this book, which have been used by astrologers since then.

The Moon Glyph ☽

The moon glyph is the most recognizable symbol on a chart, a left-facing arc stylized into the crescent moon. As part of a circle, the arc symbolizes the potential fulfillment of the entire circle, the life force that is still incomplete. Therefore, it is the ideal representation of the reactive, receptive, emotional nature of the moon.

The Mercury Glyph ☿

Mercury contains all three elemental symbols: the crescent, the circle, and the cross in vertical order. This is the "Venus with a hat" glyph (compare with the symbol of Venus). With another stretch of the imagination, can't you see the winged cap of Mercury the messenger? Think of the upturned crescent as antennae that tune in and transmit messages from the sun, reminding you that Mercury is the way you communicate, the way your mind works. The upturned arc is receiving energy into the spirit or solar circle, which will later be translated into action on the material plane, symbolized by the cross. All the elements are equally sized because Mercury is neutral; it doesn't play favorites! This planet symbolizes objective, detached, unemotional thinking.

The Venus Glyph ♀

Here the relationship is between two components: the circle of spirit and the cross of matter. Spirit is elevated over matter, pulling it upward. Venus asks, "What is beautiful? What do you like best? What do you love to have done to you?" Consequently, Venus determines both your ideal of beauty and what feels good sensually. It governs your own allure and power to attract, as well as what attracts and pleases you.

The Mars Glyph ♂

In this glyph, the cross of matter is stylized into an arrowhead pointed up and outward, propelled by the circle of spirit. With a little imagination, you can visualize it as the shield and spear of Mars, the ancient god of war. You can deduce that Mars embodies your spiritual energy projected into the outer world. It's your assertiveness, your initiative, your aggressive drive, what you like to do to others, your temper. If you know someone's Mars, you know whether they'll blow up when angry or do a slow burn. Your task is to use your outgoing Mars energy wisely and well.

The Jupiter Glyph ♃

Jupiter is the basic cross of matter, with a large stylized crescent perched on the left side of the horizontal, temporal plane. You might think of the crescent as an open hand, because one meaning of Jupiter is "luck," what's handed to you. You don't have to work for what you get from Jupiter; it comes to you, if you're open to it.

The Jupiter glyph might also remind you of a jumbo jet plane, with a huge tail fin, about to take off. This is the planet of travel, mental and spiritual, of expanding your horizons via new ideas, new spiritual dimensions, and new places. Jupiter embodies the optimism and enthusiasm of the traveler about to embark on an exciting adventure.

The Saturn Glyph ♄

Flip Jupiter over, and you've got Saturn. This might not be immediately apparent because Saturn is usually stylized into an "h" form like the one shown here. The principle it expresses is the opposite of Jupiter's expansive tendencies.

Saturn pulls you back to earth: the receptive arc is pushed down underneath the cross of matter. Before there are any rewards or expansion, the duties and obligations of the material world must be considered. Saturn says, "Stop, wait, finish your chores before you take off!"

Saturn's glyph also resembles the sickle of old "Father Time." Saturn was first known as Chronos, the Greek god of time, for time brings all matter to an end. When it was the most distant planet (before the discovery of Uranus), Saturn was believed to be the place where time stopped. After the soul departed from earth, it journeyed back to the outer reaches of the universe and finally stopped at Saturn, or at "the end of time."

The Uranus Glyph ♅

The glyph for Uranus is often stylized to form a capital *H* after Sir William Herschel who discovered the planet. But the more esoteric version curves the two pillars of the H into crescent antennae, or "ears," like satellite disks receiving signals from space. These are perched on the horizontal material line of the cross of matter and pushed from below by the circle of the spirit. To many sci-fi fans, Uranus looks like an orbiting satellite.

Uranus channels the highest energy of all, the white electrical light of the universal spiritual force that holds the cosmos together. This pure electrical energy is gathered from all over the universe. Because Uranus energy doesn't follow any ordinary celestial drumbeat, it can't be controlled or predicted (which is also true of those who are strongly influenced by this eccentric planet). In the symbol, this energy is manifested through the balance of polarities (the two opposite arms of the glyph) like the two polarized wires of a lightbulb.

The Neptune Glyph ♆

Neptune's glyph is usually stylized to look like a trident, the weapon of the Roman god Neptune. However, on a more esoteric level, it shows the large upturned crescent of the soul pierced through by the cross of matter. Neptune nails down, or materializes, soul energy, bringing impulses from the soul level into manifestation. That is why Neptune is associated with imagination or "imagining in," making an image of the soul. Neptune works through feelings, sensitivity, and mystical capacity to bring the divine into the earthly realm.

The Pluto Glyph ♀

Pluto is written two ways. One is a composite of the letters *PL,* the first two letters of the word Pluto and coincidentally the initials of Percival Lowell, one of the planet's discoverers. The other, more esoteric symbol is a small circle above a large open crescent that surmounts the cross of matter. This depicts Pluto's power to regenerate. Imagine a new little spirit emerging from the sheltering cup of the soul. Pluto rules the forces of life and death. After this planet has passed a sensitive point in your chart, you are transformed, reborn in some way.

Sci-fi fans might visualize this glyph as a small satellite (the circle) being launched. It was shortly after Pluto's discovery that we learned how to harness the nuclear forces that made space exploration possible. Pluto rules the transformative power of atomic energy, which totally changed our lives and from which there is no turning back.

The Glyphs for the Signs

On an astrology chart, the glyph for the sign will appear after that of the planet. For example, when you see the moon glyph followed first by a number and then by another glyph representing the sign, this means that the moon was passing over a certain degree of that astrological sign at the time of the chart. On the dividing lines between the houses on your chart, you'll find the symbol for the sign that rules the house.

Because sun sign symbols do not contain the same basic geometric components of the planetary glyphs, we must look elsewhere for clues to their meanings. Many have been passed down from ancient Egyptian and Chaldean civilizations with few modifications. Others have been adapted over the centuries.

In deciphering many of the glyphs, you'll often find that the symbols reveal a dual nature of the sign, which is not always apparent in the usual sun sign descriptions. For instance, the Gemini glyph is similar to the Roman numeral for two, and reveals this sign's longing to discover a twin soul. The Cancer glyph may be interpreted as resembling either the nurturing breasts or the self-protective claws of a crab, both symbols associated with the contrasting qualities of this sign. Libra's glyph embodies the duality of the spirit balanced with material reality. The Sagittarius glyph shows that the aspirant must also carry along the earthly animal nature in his quest. The Capricorn sea goat is another symbol with dual emphasis. The goat climbs high, yet is always pulled back by the deep waters of the unconscious. Aquarius embodies the double waves of mental detachment, balanced by the desire for connection with others in a friendly way. Finally, the two fishes of Pisces, which are forever tied together, show the duality of the soul and the spirit that must be reconciled.

The Aries Glyph ♈

Since the symbol for Aries is the Ram, this glyph is obviously associated with a ram's horns, which characterize one aspect of the Aries personality—an aggressive, me-first, leaping-headfirst attitude. But the symbol can be interpreted in other ways as well. Some astrologers liken it to a fountain of energy, which Aries people also embody. The first sign of the zodiac bursts on the scene eagerly, ready to go. Another analogy is to the eyebrows and nose of the human head, which Aries rules, and the thinking power that is initiated by the brain.

One theory of this symbol links it to the Egyptian god Amun, represented by a ram in ancient times. As Amun-Ra, this god was believed to embody the creator of the universe, the leader of all the other gods. This relates easily to the position of Aries as the leader (or first sign) of the zodiac, which begins at the spring equinox, a time of the year when nature is renewed.

The Taurus Glyph ♉

This is another easy glyph to draw and identify. It takes little imagination to decipher the bull's head with long curving horns. Like its symbol the Bull, the archetypal Taurus is slow to anger but ferocious when provoked, as well as stubborn, steady, and sensual. Another association is the larynx (and thyroid) of the throat area (ruled by Taurus) and the eustachian tubes running up to the ears, which coincides with the relationship of Taurus to the voice, song, and music. Many famous singers, musicians, and composers have prominent Taurus influences.

Many ancient religions involved a bull as the central figure in fertility rites or initiations, usually symbolizing the victory of man over his animal nature. Another possible origin is in the sacred bull of Egypt, who embodied the incarnate form of Osiris, god of death and resurrection. In early Christian imagery, the Taurus Bull represented St. Luke.

The Gemini Glyph ♊

The standard glyph immediately calls to mind the Roman numeral for two (II) and the Twins symbol, as it is called, for Gemini. In almost all drawings and images used for this sign, the relationship between two persons is emphasized. Usually one twin will be touching the other, which signifies communication, human contact, the desire to share.

The top line of the Gemini glyph indicates mental communication, while the bottom line indicates shared physical space.

The most famous Gemini legend is that of the twin sons, Castor and Pollux, one of whom had a mortal father while the other was the son of Zeus, king of the gods. When it came time for the mortal twin to die, his grief-stricken brother pleaded with Zeus, who agreed to let them spend half the year on earth in mortal form and half in immortal life, with the gods on Mount Olympus. This reflects a basic duality of humankind, which possesses an immortal soul yet is also subject to the limits of mortality.

The Cancer Glyph ♋

Two convenient images relate to the Cancer glyph. It is easiest to decode the curving claws of the Cancer symbol, the Crab. Like the crab, Cancer's element is water. This sensitive sign also has a hard protective shell to protect its tender interior. The crab must be wily to escape predators, scampering sideways and hiding under rocks. The crab also responds to the cycles of the moon, as do all shellfish. The other image is that of two female breasts, which Cancer rules, showing that this is a sign that nurtures and protects others as well as itself.

In ancient Egypt, Cancer was also represented by the scarab beetle, a symbol of regeneration and eternal life.

The Leo Glyph ♌

Notice that the Leo glyph seems to be an extension of Cancer's glyph, with a significant difference. In the Cancer glyph, the lines curve inward protectively. The Leo glyph expresses energy outwardly. And there is no duality in the symbol, the Lion, or in Leo, the sign.

Lions have belonged to the sign of Leo since earliest times. It is not difficult to imagine the king of beasts with his sweeping mane and curling tail from this glyph. The upward sweep of the glyph easily describes the positive energy of Leo: the flourishing tail, their flamboyant qualities. Another analogy, perhaps a stretch of the imagination, is that of a heart leaping up with joy and enthusiasm, also very typical of Leo, which also rules the heart. In early Christian imagery, the Leo Lion represented St. Mark.

The Virgo Glyph ♍

You can read much into this mysterious glyph. For instance, it could represent the initials of "Mary Virgin," or a young woman holding a staff of wheat, or stylized female genitalia, all common interpretations. The M shape might also remind you that Virgo is ruled by Mercury. The cross beneath the symbol reveals the grounded, practical nature of this earth sign.

The earliest zodiacs link Virgo with the Egyptian goddess Isis who gave birth to the god Horus, after her husband Osiris had been killed, in the archetype of a miraculous conception. There are many ancient statues of Isis nursing her baby son, which are reminiscent of medieval Virgin and Child motifs. This sign has also been associated with the image of the Holy Grail, when the Virgo symbol was substituted with a chalice.

The Libra Glyph ♎

It is not difficult to read the standard image for Libra, the Scales, into this glyph. There is another meaning, however, that is equally relevant: the setting sun as it descends over the horizon. Libra's natural position on the zodiac wheel is the descendant, or sunset position (as the Aries natural position is the ascendant, or rising sign). Both images relate to Libra's personality. Libra is always weighing pros and cons for a balanced decision. In the sunset image, the sun (male) hovers over the horizontal earth (female) before setting. Libra is the space between these lines, harmonizing yin and yang, spiritual and material, male and female, ideal and real worlds. The glyph has also been linked to the kidneys, which are ruled by Libra.

The Scorpio Glyph ♏

With its barbed tail, this glyph is easy to identify as the Scorpion for the sign of Scorpio. It also represents the male sexual parts, over which the sign rules. From the arrowhead, you can draw the conclusion that Mars was once its ruler. Some earlier Egyptian glyphs for Scorpio represent it as an erect serpent, so the Serpent is an alternate symbol.

Another symbol for Scorpio, which is not identifiable in this glyph, is the Eagle. Scorpios can go to extremes, either in soaring like the eagle or self-destructing like the scorpion. In early Christian imagery, which often used zodiacal symbols, the Scorpio Eagle was chosen to symbolize the intense apostle St. John the Evangelist.

The Sagittarius Glyph ♐

This is one of the easiest to spot and draw: an upward pointing arrow lifting up a cross. The arrow is pointing skyward, while the cross represents the four elements of the material world, which the arrow must convey. Elevating materiality into spirituality is an important Sagittarius quality, which explains why this sign is associated with higher learning, religion, philosophy, travel—the aspiring professions. Sagittarius can also send barbed arrows of frankness in the pursuit of truth, so the Archer symbol for Sagittarius is apt. (Sagittarius is also the sign of the supersalesman.)

Sagittarius is symbolically represented by the centaur, a mythological creature who is half man, half horse, aiming his arrow toward the skies. Though Sagittarius is motivated by spiritual aspiration, it also must balance the powerful appetites of the animal nature. The centaur Chiron, a figure in Greek mythology, became a wise teacher who, after many adventures and world travels, was killed by a poisoned arrow.

The Capricorn Glyph ♑

One of the most difficult symbols to draw, this glyph may take some practice. It is a representation of the sea goat:

a mythical animal that is a goat with a curving fish's tail. The goat part of Capricorn wants to leave the waters of the emotions and climb to the elevated areas of life. But the fish tail is the unconscious, the deep chaotic psychic level that draws the goat back. Capricorn is often trying to escape the deep, feeling part of life by submerging himself in work, steadily ascending to the top. To some people, the glyph represents a seated figure with a bent knee, a reminder that Capricorn governs the knee area of the body.

An interesting aspect of this glyph is the contrast of the sharp pointed horns—which represent the penetrating, shrewd, conscious side of Capricorn—with the swishing tail—which represents its serpentine, unconscious, emotional force. One Capricorn legend, which dates from Roman times, tells of the earthy fertility god, Pan, who tried to save himself from uncontrollable sexual desires by jumping into the Nile. His upper body then turned into a goat, while the lower part became a fish. Later, Jupiter gave him a safe haven as a constellation in the skies.

The Aquarius Glyph ≋

This ancient water symbol can be traced back to an Egyptian hieroglyph representing streams of life force. Symbolized by the Water Bearer, Aquarius is distributor of the waters of life—the magic liquid of regeneration. The two waves can also be linked to the positive and negative charges of the electrical energy that Aquarius rules, a sort of universal wavelength. Aquarius is tuned in intuitively to higher forces via this electrical force. The duality of the glyph could also refer to the dual nature of Aquarius, a sign that runs hot and cold and that is friendly but also detached in the mental world of air signs.

In Greek legends, Aquarius is represented by Ganymede, who was carried to heaven by an eagle in order to become the cupbearer of Zeus and to supervise the annual flooding of the Nile. The sign later became associated with aviation and notions of flight.

The Pisces Glyph ♓

Here is an abstraction of the familiar image of Pisces, two Fishes swimming in opposite directions yet bound together by a cord. The Fishes represent the spirit—which yearns for the freedom of heaven—and the soul—which remains attached to the desires of the temporal world. During life on earth, the spirit and the soul are bound together. When they complement each other, instead of pulling in opposite directions, they facilitate the Pisces creativity. The ancient version of this glyph, taken from the Egyptians, had no connecting line, which was added in the fourteenth century.

In another interpretation, it is said that the left fish indicates the direction of involution or the beginning of a cycle, while the right fish signifies the direction of evolution, the way to completion of a cycle. It's an appropriate grand finale for Pisces, the last sign of the zodiac.

CHAPTER 8

Your Rising Sign Makes Your Horoscope Unique

Have you wondered why your horoscope is different from that of anyone else born on your birthday? Yes, other babies who may have been born later or earlier on the same day will be sure to have most planets in the same signs as you do. Most of your high school class, in fact, will have several planets in the same signs as your planets, especially the slow-moving planets (Uranus, Neptune, Pluto) and very possibly Jupiter and Saturn, which usually spend a year or more in each sign.

What makes a horoscope truly yours is the rising sign (often referred to as the ascendant), the sign that was coming up over the eastern horizon at the moment you were born. This sign changes every two hours, as the earth moves. It is so important because the degree of the rising sign establishes the exact horoscope of your birth time—in other words, it sets up your special moment in time.

In the horoscope chart, your rising sign marks the beginning of the first house, one of twelve stationary divisions of the horoscope that represent different areas of your life. The first house represents your first presentation to the world, your physical body, and how you come across to the world. It is where you say, "Here I am!" It has been called your shop window, the first impression you give to others.

Once the rising sign is established, it becomes possible to analyze a chart accurately because the astrologer knows in which area of life (house) the planets will operate. For instance, if Mars is in Gemini and your rising sign is Taurus,

Mars will most likely be active in the second or financial house of your chart. If you were born later in the day when the rising sign is Virgo, Mars will be positioned at the top of your chart, energizing your tenth house of career. That is why many astrologers insist on knowing the exact time of a client's birth before they analyze a chart. The more accurate your birth time, the more accurately an astrologer can position the planets in your chart. Without a valid rising sign, your collection of planets would have no homes. One would have no idea which area of your life would be influenced by a particular planet.

Your rising sign has an important relationship with your sun sign. Some will complement the sun sign; others hide it under a totally different mask, as if playing an entirely different role, making it difficult to guess the person's sun sign from outer appearances. This may be the reason why you might not look or act like your sun sign's archetype. For example, a Leo with a conservative Capricorn ascendant would come across as much more serious than a Leo with a fiery Aries or Sagittarius ascendant.

Though the rising sign usually creates the first impression you make, there are exceptions. When the sun sign is reinforced by other planets in the same sign, this might overpower the impression of the rising sign. For instance, a Leo sun plus a Leo Venus and Leo Jupiter would counteract the more conservative image that would otherwise be conveyed by the person's Capricorn ascendant.

Those born early in the morning when the sun was on the horizon will be most likely to project the image of their sun sign. These people are often called a "double Aries" or a "double Virgo" because the same sun sign and ascendant reinforce each other.

Look up your rising sign from the chart at the end of this chapter. Since rising signs change every two hours, it is important to know your birth time as close to the minute as possible. Even a few minutes' difference could change the rising sign and therefore the setup of your chart. If you are unsure about the exact time, but know within a few hours, check the following descriptions to see which is most like the personality you project.

Aries Rising: High Energy

You are the most aggressive version of your sun sign, with boundless energy that can be used productively if it's channeled in the right direction. Watch a tendency to overreact emotionally and blow your top. You come across as openly competitive, a positive asset in business or sports. Be on guard against impatience, which could lead to head injuries. Your walk and bearing could have the telltale head-forward Aries posture. You may wear more bright colors, especially red, than others of your sign. You may also have a tendency to drive your car faster.

Can you see the alpha Aries tendency in Barbra Streisand (a sun-sign Taurus) and Bette Midler (a sun-sign Sagittarius)?

Taurus Rising: Earthbound

You're slow-moving, with a beautiful (or distinctive) speaking or singing voice that can be especially soothing or melodious. You probably surround yourself with comfort, good food, luxurious environments, and other sensual pleasures. You prefer welcoming others into your home to gadding about. You may have a talent for business, especially in trading, appraising, and real estate. A Taurus ascendant gives a well-padded physique that gains weight easily, like Liza Minnelli. This ascendant can also endow females with a curvaceous beauty.

Gemini Rising: The Communicator

You're naturally sociable, with lighter, more ethereal mannerisms than others of your sign, especially if you're female. You love to communicate with people, and express your ideas and feelings easily, like British prime minister Tony Blair. You may have a talent for writing or public speaking. You thrive on variety, a constantly changing scene, and a lively social life. However, you may relate to others at a deeper level than might be suspected. And you will be far more sympathetic and caring than you project. You will probably travel widely, changing partners and jobs several times (or juggle two at once). Physically, your nerves are quite sensitive. Occasionally, you would benefit from a calm, tranquil atmosphere away from your usual social scene.

Cancer Rising: Nurturing

You are naturally acquisitive, possessive, private, a moneymaker, like Bill Gates or Michael Bloomberg. You easily pick up on others' needs and feelings—a great gift in business, the arts, and personal relationships. But you must guard against overreacting or taking things too personally, especially during full moon periods. Find creative outlets for your natural nurturing gifts, such as helping the less fortunate, particularly children. Your insights would be helpful in psychology. Your desire to feed and care for others would be useful in the restaurant, hotel, or child-care industries. You may be especially fond of wearing romantic old clothes, collecting antiques, and, of course, dining on exquisite food. Since your body may retain fluids, pay attention to your diet. To relax, escape to places near water.

Leo Rising: Scene Player

You may come across as more poised than you really feel. However, you play it to the hilt, projecting a proud royal presence. A Leo ascendant gives you a natural flair for drama, like Marilyn Monroe, and you might be accused of stealing the spotlight. You'll also project a much more outgoing, optimistic, sunny personality than others of your sign. You take care to please your public by always projecting your best star quality, probably tossing a luxuriant mane of hair, sporting a striking hairstyle, or dressing to impress. Females often dazzle with spectacular jewelry. Since you may have a strong parental nature, you could well be the regal family matriarch or patriarch, like George W. Bush.

Virgo Rising: Discriminating

Virgo rising masks your inner nature with a practical, analytical outer image. You seem neat, orderly, more particular than others of your sign. Others in your life may feel they must live up to your high standards. Though at times you may be openly critical, this masks a well-meaning desire to have only the best for loved ones. Your sharp eye for details could be used in the financial world, or your literary skills could draw you to teaching or publishing. The healing arts, health care, and service-oriented professions attract many with a Virgo ascendant. You're likely to take good care of yourself, with great attention to health, diet, and exercise, like Madonna. You might even show some hypochondriac tendencies, like Woody Allen. Physically, you may have a very sensitive digestive system.

Libra Rising: Charming and Social

Libra rising gives you a charming, social public persona, like Bill Clinton. You tend to avoid confrontations in relationships, preferring to smooth the way or negotiate diplomatically rather than give in to an emotional reaction. Because you are interested in all aspects of a situation, you may be slow to reach decisions. Physically, you'll have good proportions and symmetry. You will move with natural grace and balance. You're likely to have pleasing, if not beautiful, facial features, with a winning smile, like Cary Grant. You'll show natural good taste and harmony in your clothes and home decor. Legal, diplomatic, or public relations professions could draw your interest.

Scorpio Rising: Mysterious Charisma

You project an intriguing air of mystery with this ascendant, as the Scorpio secretiveness and sense of underlying power combines with your sun sign. As with Jackie O, there's more to you than meets the eye. You seem like someone who is always in control and who can move comfortably in the world of power. Your physical look comes across as intense. Many of you have remarkable eyes, with a direct, penetrating gaze. But you'll never reveal your private agenda, and you tend to keep your true feelings under wraps (watch a tendency toward paranoia). You may have an interesting romantic history with secret love affairs, like Grace Kelly. Many of you heighten your air of mystery by wearing black. You're happiest near water and should provide yourself with a seaside retreat.

Sagittarius Rising: The Wanderer

You travel with this ascendant. You may also be a more outdoor, sportive type, with an athletic, casual, outgoing air. Your moods are camouflaged with cheerful optimism or a philosophical attitude. Though you don't hesitate to speak your mind, like Ted Turner, who was called the Mouth of the South, you can also laugh at your troubles or crack a joke more easily than others of your sign. A Sagittarius ascendant can also draw you to the field of higher education or to spiritual life. You'll seem to have less attachment to things and people, and may travel widely. Your strong, fast legs are a physical bonus.

Capricorn Rising: Serious Business

This rising sign makes you come across as serious, goal-oriented, disciplined, and careful with cash. You are not one of the zodiac's big spenders, though you might splurge occasionally on items with good investment value. You're the traditional, conservative type in dress and environment, and you might come across as quite normal and businesslike, like Rupert Murdoch. You'll function well in a structured or corporate environment where you can climb to the top. (You are always aware of who's the boss.) In your personal life, you could be a loner or a single parent who is "father and mother" to your children.

Aquarius Rising: One of a Kind

You come across as less concerned about what others think and could even be a bit eccentric. You're more at ease with groups of people than others in your sign, and you may be attracted to public life, like Jay Leno. Your appearance may be unique, either unconventional or unimportant to you. Those of you whose sun is in a water sign (Cancer, Scorpio, Pisces) may exercise your nurturing qualities with a large group, an extended family, or a day-care or community center.

Pisces Rising: Romantic Roles

Your creative, nurturing talents are heightened and so is your ability to project emotional drama. And, like Antonio Banderas, your dreamy eyes and poetic air bring out the protective instinct in others. You could be attracted to the arts, especially theater, dance, film, and photography, or to psychology, spiritual practice, and charity work. You are happiest when you are using your creative ability to help others. Since you are vulnerable to mood swings, it is especially important for you to find interesting, creative work where you can express your talents and heighten your self-esteem. Accentuate the positive. Be wary of escapist tendencies, particularly involving alcohol or drugs to which you are supersensitive, like Whitney Houston.

RISING SIGNS—A.M. BIRTHS

	1 AM	2 AM	3 AM	4 AM	5 AM	6 AM	7 AM	8 AM	9 AM	10 AM	11 AM	12 NOON
Jan 1	Lib	Sc	Sc	Sc	Sag	Sag	Cap	Cap	Aq	Aq	Pis	Ar
Jan 9	Lib	Sc	Sc	Sag	Sag	Cap	Cap	Aq	Pis	Ar	Tau
Jan 17	Sc	Sc	Sc	Sag	Sag	Cap	Cap	Aq	Aq	Pis	Ar	Tau
Jan 25	Sc	Sc	Sag	Sag	Sag	Cap	Cap	Aq	Pis	Ar	Tau	Tau
Feb 2	Sc	Sc	Sag	Sag	Cap	Cap	Aq	Pis	Pis	Ar	Tau	Gem
Feb 10	Sc	Sag	Sag	Sag	Cap	Cap	Aq	Pis	Ar	Tau	Tau	Gem
Feb 18	Sc	Sag	Sag	Cap	Cap	Aq	Aq	Pis	Pis	Ar	Tau	Gem	Gem
Feb 26	Sag	Sag	Sag	Cap	Aq	Aq	Pis	Ar	Tau	Tau	Gem	Gem
Mar 6	Sag	Sag	Cap	Cap	Aq	Pis	Pis	Ar	Tau	Gem	Gem	Can
Mar 14	Sag	Cap	Cap	Aq	Aq	Pis	Ar	Tau	Tau	Gem	Gem	Can
Mar 22	Sag	Cap	Cap	Aq	Pis	Ar	Ar	Tau	Gem	Gem	Can	Can
Mar 30	Cap	Cap	Aq	Pis	Pis	Ar	Tau	Tau	Gem	Can	Can	Can
Apr 7	Cap	Cap	Aq	Pis	Ar	Ar	Tau	Gem	Gem	Can	Can	Leo
Apr 14	Cap	Aq	Aq	Pis	Ar	Tau	Tau	Gem	Can	Can	Can	Leo
Apr 22	Cap	Aq	Pis	Ar	Ar	Tau	Gem	Gem	Can	Can	Leo	Leo
Apr 30	Aq	Aq	Pis	Ar	Tau	Tau	Gem	Can	Can	Can	Leo	Leo
May 8	Aq	Pis	Ar	Ar	Tau	Gem	Gem	Can	Can	Leo	Leo	Leo
May 16	Aq	Pis	Ar	Tau	Gem	Gem	Can	Can	Can	Leo	Leo	Vir
May 24	Pis	Ar	Ar	Tau	Gem	Gem	Can	Leo	Leo	Leo	Vir
June 1	Pis	Ar	Tau	Gem	Gem	Can	Can	Leo	Leo	Vir	Vir
June 9	Ar	Ar	Tau	Gem	Gem	Can	Leo	Leo	Leo	Vir	Vir
June 17	Ar	Tau	Gem	Gem	Can	Can	Leo	Leo	Vir	Vir	Vir
June 25	Tau	Tau	Gem	Gem	Can	Can	Leo	Leo	Leo	Vir	Vir	Lib
July 3	Tau	Gem	Gem	Can	Can	Can	Leo	Leo	Vir	Vir	Vir	Lib
July 11	Tau	Gem	Gem	Can	Can	Leo	Leo	Leo	Vir	Vir	Lib	Lib
July 18	Gem	Gem	Can	Can	Can	Leo	Leo	Vir	Vir	Vir	Lib	Lib
July 26	Gem	Gem	Can	Can	Leo	Leo	Vir	Vir	Vir	Lib	Lib	Lib
Aug 3	Gem	Can	Can	Can	Leo	Leo	Vir	Vir	Vir	Lib	Lib	Sc
Aug 11	Gem	Can	Can	Leo	Leo	Leo	Vir	Vir	Lib	Lib	Lib	Sc
Aug 18	Can	Can	Can	Leo	Leo	Vir	Vir	Vir	Lib	Lib	Sc	Sc
Aug 27	Can	Can	Leo	Leo	Leo	Vir	Vir	Lib	Lib	Lib	Sc	Sc
Sept 4	Can	Can	Leo	Leo	Leo	Vir	Vir	Vir	Lib	Lib	Sc	Sc
Sept 12	Can	Leo	Leo	Leo	Vir	Vir	Lib	Lib	Lib	Sc	Sc	Sag
Sept 20	Leo	Leo	Leo	Vir	Vir	Vir	Lib	Lib	Sc	Sc	Sc	Sag
Sept 28	Leo	Leo	Vir	Vir	Lib	Lib	Lib	Sc	Sc	Sc	Sag	Sag
Oct 6	Leo	Leo	Vir	Vir	Lib	Lib	Sc	Sc	Sc	Sag	Sag
Oct 14	Leo	Vir	Vir	Vir	Lib	Lib	Lib	Sc	Sc	Sag	Sag	Cap
Oct 22	Leo	Vir	Vir	Lib	Lib	Lib	Sc	Sc	Sc	Sag	Sag	Cap
Oct 30	Vir	Vir	Vir	Lib	Lib	Sc	Sc	Sc	Sag	Sag	Cap	Cap
Nov 7	Vir	Vir	Lib	Lib	Lib	Sc	Sc	Sc	Sag	Sag	Cap	Cap
Nov 15	Vir	Vir	Lib	Lib	Sc	Sc	Sc	Sag	Sag	Cap	Cap	Aq
Nov 23	Vir	Lib	Lib	Lib	Sc	Sc	Sag	Sag	Sag	Cap	Cap	Aq
Dec 1	Vir	Lib	Lib	Sc	Sc	Sc	Sag	Sag	Cap	Cap	Aq	Aq
Dec 9	Lib	Lib	Lib	Sc	Sc	Sag	Sag	Cap	Cap	Aq	Aq	Pis
Dec 18	Lib	Lib	Sc	Sc	Sc	Sag	Sag	Cap	Cap	Aq	Aq	Pis
Dec 28	Lib	Lib	Sc	Sc	Sag	Sag	Sag	Cap	Aq	Aq	Pis	Ar

RISING SIGNS—P.M. BIRTHS

	1 PM	2 PM	3 PM	4 PM	5 PM	6 PM	7 PM	8 PM	9 PM	10 PM	11 PM	12 MIDNIGHT
Jan 1	Tau	Gem	Gem	Can	Can	Can	Leo	Leo	Vir	Vir	Vir	Lib
Jan 9	Tau	Gem	Gem	Can	Can	Leo	Leo	Leo	Vir	Vir	Vir	Lib
Jan 17	Gem	Gem	Can	Can	Can	Leo	Leo	Vir	Vir	Vir	Lib	Lib
Jan 25	Gem	Gem	Can	Can	Leo	Leo	Leo	Vir	Vir	Lib	Lib	Lib
Feb 2	Gem	Can	Can	Can	Leo	Leo	Vir	Vir	Vir	Lib	Lib	Sc
Feb 10	Gem	Can	Can	Leo	Leo	Leo	Vir	Vir	Lib	Lib	Lib	Sc
Feb 18	Can	Can	Can	Leo	Leo	Vir	Vir	Vir	Lib	Lib	Sc	Sc
Feb 26	Can	Can	Leo	Leo	Leo	Vir	Vir	Lib	Lib	Lib	Sc	Sc
Mar 6	Can	Leo	Leo	Leo	Vir	Vir	Vir	Lib	Lib	Sc	Sc	Sc
Mar 14	Leo	Leo	Leo	Vir	Vir	Vir	Lib	Lib	Lib	Sc	Sc	Sag
Mar 22	Leo	Leo	Leo	Vir	Vir	Lib	Lib	Lib	Sc	Sc	Sc	Sag
Mar 30	Leo	Leo	Vir	Vir	Vir	Lib	Lib	Sc	Sc	Sc	Sag	Sag
Apr 7	Leo	Leo	Vir	Vir	Lib	Lib	Lib	Sc	Sc	Sc	Sag	Sag
Apr 14	Leo	Vir	Vir	Vir	Lib	Lib	Sc	Sc	Sc	Sag	Sag	Cap
Apr 22	Leo	Vir	Vir	Lib	Lib	Lib	Sc	Sc	Sc	Sag	Sag	Cap
Apr 30	Vir	Vir	Vir	Lib	Lib	Sc	Sc	Sc	Sag	Sag	Cap	Cap
May 8	Vir	Vir	Lib	Lib	Lib	Sc	Sc	Sag	Sag	Sag	Cap	Cap
May 16	Vir	Vir	Lib	Lib	Sc	Sc	Sc	Sag	Sag	Cap	Cap	Cap
May 24	Vir	Lib	Lib	Lib	Sc	Sc	Sag	Sag	Sag	Cap	Cap	Aq
June 1	Vir	Lib	Lib	Sc	Sc	Sc	Sag	Sag	Cap	Cap	Aq	Aq
June 9	Lib	Lib	Lib	Sc	Sc	Sag	Sag	Sag	Cap	Cap	Aq	Pis
June 17	Lib	Lib	Sc	Sc	Sc	Sag	Sag	Cap	Cap	Aq	Aq	Pis
June 25	Lib	Lib	Sc	Sc	Sag	Sag	Sag	Cap	Cap	Aq	Pis	Ar
July 3	Lib	Sc	Sc	Sc	Sag	Sag	Cap	Cap	Aq	Aq	Pis	Ar
July 11	Lib	Sc	Sc	Sag	Sag	Sag	Cap	Cap	Aq	Pis	Ar	Tau
July 18	Sc	Sc	Sc	Sag	Sag	Cap	Cap	Aq	Aq	Pis	Ar	Tau
July 26	Sc	Sc	Sag	Sag	Sag	Cap	Cap	Aq	Pis	Ar	Tau	Tau
Aug 3	Sc	Sc	Sag	Sag	Cap	Cap	Aq	Aq	Pis	Ar	Tau	Gem
Aug 11	Sc	Sag	Sag	Sag	Cap	Cap	Aq	Pis	Ar	Tau	Tau	Gem
Aug 18	Sc	Sag	Sag	Cap	Cap	Aq	Pis	Pis	Ar	Tau	Gem	Gem
Aug 27	Sag	Sag	Sag	Cap	Cap	Aq	Pis	Ar	Tau	Tau	Gem	Gem
Sept 4	Sag	Sag	Cap	Cap	Aq	Pis	Pis	Ar	Tau	Gem	Gem	Can
Sept 12	Sag	Sag	Cap	Aq	Aq	Pis	Ar	Tau	Tau	Gem	Gem	Can
Sept 20	Sag	Cap	Cap	Aq	Pis	Pis	Ar	Tau	Gem	Gem	Can	Can
Sept 28	Cap	Cap	Aq	Aq	Pis	Ar	Tau	Tau	Gem	Gem	Can	Can
Oct 6	Cap	Cap	Aq	Pis	Ar	Ar	Tau	Gem	Gem	Can	Can	Leo
Oct 14	Cap	Aq	Aq	Pis	Ar	Tau	Tau	Gem	Gem	Can	Can	Leo
Oct 22	Cap	Aq	Pis	Ar	Ar	Tau	Gem	Gem	Can	Can	Leo	Leo
Oct 30	Aq	Aq	Pis	Ar	Tau	Tau	Gem	Can	Can	Can	Leo	Leo
Nov 7	Aq	Aq	Pis	Ar	Tau	Tau	Gem	Can	Can	Can	Leo	Leo
Nov 15	Aq	Pis	Ar	Tau	Gem	Gem	Can	Can	Can	Leo	Leo	Vir
Nov 23	Pis	Ar	Ar	Tau	Gem	Gem	Can	Can	Leo	Leo	Leo	Vir
Dec 1	Pis	Ar	Tau	Gem	Gem	Can	Can	Can	Leo	Leo	Vir	Vir
Dec 9	Ar	Tau	Tau	Gem	Gem	Can	Can	Leo	Leo	Leo	Vir	Vir
Dec 18	Ar	Tau	Gem	Gem	Can	Can	Can	Leo	Leo	Vir	Vir	Vir
Dec 28	Tau	Tau	Gem	Gem	Can	Can	Leo	Leo	Vir	Vir	Vir	Lib

CHAPTER 9

Join Astrology Fans Around the World

Would you like a free copy of your chart, some sophisticated software to perform all the astrological calculations and give you a beautiful printout, or a screensaver of a spectacular scene from outer space? There's a global community of astrologers online with sites that offer everything from chart services to chat rooms to individual readings. Even better, many of the best sites offer free charts sent to your e-mail address, free software, and fascinating articles to download. You can get an education in astrology from your computer screen, create a network of astrology-minded friends around the world, and then meet in person at one of the many local meetings and international conferences. There's a vast community of astrology fans ready to welcome you.

You need only type the word *astrology* into any Internet search engine and watch hundreds of listings of astrology-related sites pop up. To help you sort out the variety of options available, here are our top picks of the Internet and the astrological community at large. Since the Internet is constantly changing, some of these sites may have changed address or content, even though this selection was chosen with an eye to longevity.

Nationwide Astrology Organizations and Conferences

National Council for Geocosmic Research (NCGR)

Whether you'd like to know more about such specialties as financial astrology or techniques for timing events, or if you'd prefer the psychological or mythological approach, you'll meet the top astrologers at conferences sponsored by the National Council for Geocosmic Research. NCGR is dedicated to providing quality education, bringing astrologers and astrology fans together at conferences, and promoting fellowship. Their course structure provides a systematized study of the many facets of astrology. The organization sponsors educational workshops, taped lectures, conferences, and a directory of professional astrologers. For an annual membership fee, you get their excellent publications and newsletters, plus the opportunity to network with other astrology buffs at local chapter events. (At this writing there are forty-two chapters in twenty-six states and four countries.)

To join NCGR for the latest information on upcoming events and chapters in your city, consult their Web site: www.geocosmic.org.

American Federation of Astrologers (AFA)

Established in 1938, this is one of the oldest astrological organizations in the United States. AFA offers conferences, conventions, and a thorough correspondence course. If you are looking for a reading, their interesting Web site will refer you to an accredited AFA astrologer.

AFA
6535 South Rural Road
Tempe, AZ 85283-3746

Phone: (888) 301-7630 or (480) 838-1751
Fax: (480) 838-8293
Web site: www.astrologers.com

Association for Astrological Networking (AFAN)

Did you know that astrologers are still being harassed for practicing astrology? AFAN provides support and legal information and works toward improving the public image of astrology. AFAN's network of local astrologers links with the international astrological community. Here are the people who will go to bat for astrology when it is attacked in the media. Everyone who cares about astrology should join!

AFAN
8306 Wilshire Boulevard
PMB 537
Beverly Hills, CA 90211
Phone: (800) 578-2326
E-mail: info@afan.org
Web site: www.afan.org

International Society for Astrology Research (ISAR)

An international organization of professional astrologers dedicated to encouraging the highest standards of quality in the field of astrology with an emphasis on research. Among ISAR's benefits are a quarterly journal, a weekly e-mail newsletter, frequent conferences, and a free membership directory.

ISAR
P.O. Box 38613
Los Angeles, CA 90038
Fax: (805) 933–0301
Web site: www.isarastrology.com

Astrology Software

Astrolabe

One of the top astrology software resources. Check out the latest version of their powerful Solar Fire software for Windows. It's a breeze to use and will grow with your increasing knowledge of astrology to the most sophisticated levels. This company also markets a variety of programs for all levels of expertise and a wide selection of computer-generated astrology readings. A good resource for innovative software as well as applications for older computers.

The Astrolabe Web site is a great place to start your astrology tour of the Internet. Visitors to the site are greeted with a chart of the time you log on. You can download a free demo sample of their Solar Fire program. And you can get your chart calculated, also free, with a short interpretation e-mailed to you.

Astrolabe
P.O. Box 1750-R
Brewster, MA 02631
Phone: (800) 843-6682
Web site: www.alabe.com

Matrix Software

A wide variety of software in all price ranges, demo disks (student and advanced levels), and interesting readings. Check out Winstar Express, a powerful but reasonably priced program suitable for all skill levels. The Matrix Web site offers lots of fun activities for Web surfers, such as free readings from the *I Ching,* the runes, and the tarot. There are many free desktop backgrounds with astrology themes. Here's where to connect with news groups and online discussions. Their online almanac helps you schedule the best day to sign on the dotted line, ask for a raise, or plant your tomatoes.

Matrix Software
126 S. Michigan Avenue
Big Rapids, MI 49307
Phone: (800) 416-3924
Web site: www.astrologysoftware.com

Astro Communications Services (ACS)

Books, software for Mac and IBM compatibles, individual charts, and telephone readings are offered by this California company. Their freebies include astrology greeting cards and new moon reports. Find technical astrology materials here such as the American Ephemeris and PC atlases. ACS will calculate and send charts to you, a valuable service if you do not have a computer.

ACS Publications
5521 Ruffin Road
San Diego, CA 92123
Phone: (800) 888-9983
Fax: (858) 492-9917
Web site: www.astrocom.com

Air Software

Here you'll find powerful, creative astrology software, plus current stock market analysis. Financial astrology programs for stock market traders are a specialty.

Air Software
115 Caya Avenue
West Hartford, CT 06110
Phone: (800) 659-1247
Web site: www.alphee.com

Time Cycles Research (for Mac Users)

Here's where Mac users can find astrology software that's as sophisticated as it gets. If you have a Mac, you'll love their beautiful graphic IO Series programs.

Time Cycles Research
P.O. Box 797
Waterford, CT 06385
Web site: www.timecycles.com

Halloran Software (A Super Shareware Program)

Check out Halloran Software's Web site (www.halloran.com), which offers several levels of Windows astrology software. Beginners should consider their Astrology for Windows shareware program, which is available in unregistered demo form as a free download and in registered form for a very reasonable price.

Astrolog

If you're computer-savvy, you can't go wrong with Walter Pullen's amazingly complete astrology program, which is offered absolutely free at the site. The Web address is www.astrolog.org/astrolog.htm.

Astrolog is an ultrasophisticated program with all the features of much more expensive programs. It comes in versions for all formats—DOS, Windows, Mac, UNIX—and has some cool features such as a revolving globe and a constellation map. If you are looking for astrology software with bells and whistles that doesn't cost big bucks, this program has it all!

Astroscan

Surf to www.astroscan.ca for a free program called Astroscan. Stunning graphics and ease of use make this basic program a winner. Astroscan has a fun list of celebrity charts you can call up with a few clicks.

Programs for the Pocket PDA and Palm Pilot

Take astrology with you on your Palm Pilot or pocket PDA to check the chart of the moment (or of someone you've met). There are programs now available for each format. You will need to know the astrological symbols, in order to read the charts.

For the pocket PC that has the Microsoft Pocket PC 2002 or Microsoft Windows Mobile 2003 operating system, there is the versatile Astracadabra, which can interchange charts with the popular Solar Fire software. (At this writing, the software is not available for Palm Pilots.) It can be ordered at www.leelehman.com.

Astropocket is free software for the Palm OS5 and compatible handheld devices. You can download it on www.yves.robert.org/features.html. The only thing it won't do is save charts until you pay the 28 dollar registration fee.

Another program for the Palm Pilot is 1horoscope. It is available at www.1horoscope.com.

Astrology Magazines

In addition to articles by top astrologers, most have listings of astrology conferences, events, and local happenings.

Horoscope Guide
Kappa Publishing Group
Dept. 4
P.O. Box 2085
Marion, OH 43306-8121

Dell Horoscope
P.O. Box 54097
Boulder, CO 80322-4907

The Mountain Astrologer

A favorite magazine of astrology fans! *The Mountain Astrologer* also has an interesting Web site featuring the latest news from an astrological point of view, plus feature articles from the magazine.

The Mountain Astrologer
P.O. Box 970
Cedar Ridge, CA 95924
Phone: (800) 247-4828
Web site: www.mountainastrologer.com

Astrology College

Kepler College of Astrological Arts and Sciences

A degree-granting college, which is also a center of astrology, has long been the dream of the astrological community and is a giant step forward in providing credibility to the profession. Therefore, the opening of Kepler College in 2000 was a historical event for astrology. It is the only college in the western hemisphere authorized to issue B.A. and M.A. degrees in Astrological Studies. Here is where to study with the best scholars, teachers, and communicators in the field. A long-distance study program is available for those interested.

For more information, contact:

Kepler College of Astrological Arts and Sciences
4630 200th Street SW
Suite A-1
Lynnwood, WA 98036
Phone: (425) 673-4292
Fax: (425) 673-4983
Web site: www.kepler.edu

Our Favorite Web Sites

It's a daunting task to choose from the thousands of astrological Web sites that come and go on the Internet. Here are some favorites which have stood the test of time and are likely to still be operating when this book is published.

Astrodienst (www.astro.com)

Don't miss this fabulous international site that has long been one of the best astrology resources on the Internet. It's also a great place to view and download your own astrology chart. The world atlas on this site will give you the accurate longitude and latitude of your birthplace for setting up your horoscope. Then you can print out your free chart in a range of easy-to-read formats. Other attractions: a list of famous people born on your birth date, a feature that helps you choose the best vacation spot, plus articles by world-famous astrologers.

AstroDatabank (www.astrodatabank.com)

When the news is breaking, you can bet this site will be the first to get accurate birthdays of the headliners. The late astrologer Lois Rodden was a stickler for factual information and her meticulous research is being continued, much to the benefit of the astrological community. The Web site specializes in charts of current newsmakers, political figures, and international celebrities. You can also participate in discussions and analysis of the charts and see what some of the world's best astrologers have to say about them. Their AstroDatabank program, which you can purchase at the site, provides thousands of verified birthdays sorted into categories. It's an excellent research tool.

StarIQ (www.stariq.com)

Find out how top astrologers view the latest headlines at the must-see StarIQ site. Many of the best minds in astrology comment on the latest news, stock market ups and downs, political contenders. You can sign up to receive e-mail forecasts at the most important times keyed to your individual chart. (This is one of the best of the many online forecasts.)

Astrology Books (www.astroamerica.com)

The Astrology Center of America sells a wide selection of books on all aspects of astrology, from the basics to the most advanced, at this online bookstore. Also available are many hard-to-find and recycled books.

Weather Forecasting by the Stars (www.weathersage.com)

How about using astrology to forecast the weather? Visit this fascinating Web site and learn how Carolyn Egan, a pioneer in astrometeorology, uses astrology to predict weather patterns across the globe. (And she's usually more accurate than your local TV station.)

Astrology Scholars' Sites

See what one of astrology's great teachers, Robert Hand, has to offer on his site: www.robhand.com. A leading expert on the history of astrology, he's on the cutting edge of the latest research.

The Project Hindsight group of astrologers is devoted to restoring the astrology of the Hellenistic period, the primary source for all later Western astrology. There are fascinating articles for astrology fans on this site, www.projecthindsight.com.

Financial Astrology Sites

Financial astrology is a hot specialty, with many tipsters, players, and theorists. There are online columns, newsletters, specialized financial astrology software, and mutual funds run by astrology seers. One of the more respected financial astrologers is Ray Merriman, whose column on www.stariq.com is a must read for those following the bulls and bears. Other top financial astrologers offer tips and forecasts at the www.afund.com and www.alphee.com sites.

CHAPTER 10

Empower Yourself with a Personal Reading

Though you can learn much about yourself and others by studying astrology on your own, there comes a time when you might benefit from the opinion of a professional astrologer. Perhaps an important occasion is coming up—a wedding or the start of a new business—and you're wondering if an astrologically picked date could influence the outcome. You've fallen in love and must know if this is the One. Your business partnership is not going well, and you're not sure if you can continue to work together. You need to figure out some complicated family dynamics or deal with problems that seem insurmountable. Or you simply want to have your chart interpreted by an expert.

But what kind of reading should you have? There are so many options for readings that sorting through them can be a daunting task. Besides individual one-on-one readings with a professional astrologer, there are personal readings by mail, telephone, Internet, and tape. Then there are well-advertised computer-generated reports and celebrity-sponsored readings. Here's what to look for and some cautionary notes.

Done by a qualified astrologer, the personal reading can be an empowering experience if you want to reach your full potential, size up a lover or business situation, or find out what the future has in store. There are astrologers who are specialists in certain areas such as finance or medical astrology. And, unfortunately, there are many questionable practitioners who range from streetwise gypsy fortune-tellers to unscrupulous scam artists.

The following basic guidelines can help you sort out your options to find the reading that's right for you.

One-on-One Consultations with a Professional Astrologer

Nothing compares to a one-on-one consultation with a professional astrologer who has analyzed thousands of charts and can pinpoint the potential in yours. During your reading, you can get your specific questions answered. For instance, how to get along better with your mate or coworker. There are many astrologers who now combine their skills with training in psychology and are well-suited to help you examine your alternatives.

To give you an accurate reading, an astrologer needs certain information from you: the date, time, and place where you were born. (A horoscope can be cast about anyone or anything that has a specific time and place.) Most astrologers will then enter this information into a computer, which will calculate a chart in seconds. From the resulting chart, the astrologer will do an interpretation.

If you don't know your exact birth time, you can usually locate it at the Bureau of Vital Statistics at the city hall or county seat of the state where you were born. If you still have no success in getting your time of birth, some astrologers can estimate an approximate birth time by using past events in your life to determine the chart. This technique is called *rectification*.

How to Find an Astrologer

Choose your astrologer with the same care as any trusted adviser such as a doctor, lawyer, or banker. Unfortunately, anyone can claim to be an astrologer—to date, there is no licensing of astrologers or universally established professional criteria. However, there are nationwide organizations of serious, committed astrologers that can help you in your search.

Good places to start your investigation are organizations such as the American Federation of Astrologers (AFA) or the National Council for Geocosmic Research (NCGR), which offer a program of study and certification. If you live near a major city, there is sure to be an active NCGR chapter or astrology club in your area; many are listed in astrology magazines available at your local newsstand. In response to many requests for referrals, both the AFA and the NCGR have directories of professional astrologers listed on their Web sites; these directories include a glossary of terms and an explanation of specialties within the astrological field. Contact the NCGR and AFA headquarters for information (see chapter 9 in this book).

Warning Signals

As a potentially lucrative freelance business, astrology has always attracted self-styled experts who may not have the knowledge or the counseling experience to give a helpful reading. These astrologers can range from the well-meaning amateur to the charlatan or street-corner gypsy who has for many years given astrology a bad name. Be very wary of astrologers who claim to have occult powers or who make pretentious claims of celebrated clients or miraculous achievements. You can often tell from the initial phone conversation if the astrologer is legitimate. He or she should ask for your birthday time and place, then conduct the conversation in a professional manner. Any astrologer who gives a reading based only on your sun sign is highly suspect.

When you arrive at the reading, the astrologer should be prepared. The consultation should be conducted in a private, quiet place. The astrologer should be interested in your problems of the moment. A good reading involves feedback on your part. So if the reading is not relating to your concerns, you should let the astrologer know. You should feel free to ask questions and get clarifications of technical terms. The more you actively participate, rather than expecting the astrologer to carry the reading or come forth with oracular predictions, the more meaningful your experience will be. An astrologer should help you validate your current experience and be frank about possible negative happenings, but also suggest a positive course of action.

In their approach to a reading, some astrologers may be more literal, others more intuitive. Those who have had counseling training may take a more psychological approach. Though some astrologers may seem to have an almost psychic ability, extrasensory perception or any other parapsychological talent is not essential. A very accurate picture can be drawn from the data in your horoscope chart.

An astrologer may do several charts for each client, including one for the time of birth and a *progressed chart*, showing the evolution from birth to the present time. According to your individual needs, there are many other possibilities, such as a chart for a different location if you are contemplating a change of place. Relationships between any two people, things, or events can be interpreted with a chart that compares one partner's horoscope with the other's. A composite chart, which uses the midpoint between planets in two individual charts to describe the relationship, is another commonly used device.

An astrologer will be particularly interested in transits, those times when cycling planets activate the planets or sensitive points in your birth chart. These indicate important events in your life.

Many astrologers offer tape-recorded readings, another option to consider, especially if the astrologer you choose lives at a distance. In this case, you'll be mailed a taped reading based on your birth chart. This type of reading is more personal than a computer printout and can give you valuable insights, though it is not equivalent to a live dialogue with the astrologer when you can discuss your specific interests and issues of the moment.

The Telephone Reading

Telephone readings come in two varieties: a dial-in taped reading, usually recorded in advance by an astrologer, or a live consultation with an "astrologer" on the other end of the line. The taped readings are general daily or weekly forecasts, applied to all members of your sign and charged by the minute. The quality depends on the astrologer. One caution: Be aware that these readings can run up quite a telephone bill, especially if you get into the habit of calling every day. Be sure that you are aware of the per-minute cost of each call beforehand.

Live telephone readings also vary with the expertise of the astrologer. Ideally, the astrologer at the other end of the line enters your birth data into a computer, which then quickly calculates your chart. This chart will be referred to during the consultation. The advantage of a live telephone reading is that your individual chart is used and you can ask about a specific problem. However, before you invest in any reading, be sure that your astrologer is qualified and that you fully understand in advance how much you will be charged. There should be no unpleasant financial surprises later.

Computer-Generated Reports

Companies that offer computer programs (such as ACS, Matrix, Astrolabe) also offer a variety of computer-generated horoscope readings. These can be quite comprehensive, offering a beautiful printout of the chart plus many pages of detailed information about each planet and aspect of the chart. You can then study it at your convenience. Of course, the interpretations will be general, since there is no personal input from you, and may not cover your immediate concerns. Since computer-generated horoscopes are much lower in cost than live consultations, you might consider them as either a supplement or a preparation for an eventual live reading. You'll then be more familiar with your chart and able to plan specific questions in advance. They also make a terrific gift for astrology fans. There are several companies, listed in chapter 9, that offer computerized readings prepared by reputable astrologers.

Whichever option you decide to pursue, may your reading be an empowering one!

CHAPTER 11

Are You Having a Baby This Year? An Astrological Portrait of Children Born This Year

Children born this year will belong to one of the most spiritual generations in history. The three outer planets—Uranus, Neptune, and Pluto, which stay in a sign for at least seven years—are the ones that most affect each generation. These outer planets are now passing through Pisces, Aquarius, and Sagittarius respectively, the three most visionary signs, and they are sure to imprint the children of 2006.

In the past century, Uranus in Pisces coincided with enormous creativity, which should impact this year's children. Neptune in Aquarius and Pluto in Sagittarius are continuing in these signs, bringing a time of dissolving barriers, of globalization, of interest in religion and spirituality . . . breaking away from the materialism of the last century. In contrast, the members of this generation will truly be children of the world, searching for deeper meanings to existence.

Astrology can be an especially helpful tool that can be used to design an environment that will enhance and encourage each child's positive qualities. Some parents start from before conception, planning the birth of their child as far as possible to harmonize with the signs of other family members. However, each baby has its own schedule so if yours arrives a week early or late, or elects a different sign than you'd planned, recognize that the new sign may be more in line with the mission your child is here to accomplish. In other words, if you were hoping for a Libra child and he arrives during Virgo, that Virgo energy may be just what is needed to stimulate or complement your family. Remember that there are many astrological elements besides the sun sign that indicate strong family ties. Usually each child will share a particular planetary placement, an emphasis on a particular sign or house, or a certain chart configuration with his parents and other family members. Often there is a significant planetary angle that will define the parent-child relationship, such as family sun signs that form a T-square or a triangle.

One important thing you can do is to be sure the exact moment of birth is recorded. This will be essential in calculating an accurate astrological chart. The following descriptions can be applied to the sun or moon sign (if known) of a child—the sun sign will describe basic personality and the moon sign indicates the child's emotional needs.

The Aries Child

Baby Aries is quite a handful! This energetic child will walk—and run—as soon as possible and perform daring feats of exploration. Caregivers should be vigilant. Little Aries seems to know no fear (and is especially vulnerable to head injuries). Many Aries children, in their rush to get on with life, seem hyperactive and are easily frustrated when they can't get their own way. Violent temper tantrums and dramatic physical displays are par for the course with these children.

The very young Aries should be monitored carefully, since he is prone to take risks and may injure himself. An Aries loves to take things apart and may break toys easily, but with encouragement, the child will develop formidable coordination. Aries's bossy tendencies should be molded into leadership qualities, rather than bullying. Otherwise, the me-first Aries will have many clashes with other strong-willed youngsters. Encourage this child to take out aggressions and frustrations in active, competitive sports. When a young Aries learns to focus his energies long enough to master a subject and learns consideration for others, the indomitable Aries spirit will rise to the head of the class.

Aries born in 2006 will benefit from Mars, their planetary ruler, in Gemini until April 15, giving the children sharp minds and sociable outlooks. Those born after the 15th will have a strong water-sign influence with Mars in Cancer, Mercury and Venus in Pisces, and Jupiter in Scorpio, making this a much more reactive, emotional, intuitive version of Aries.

The Taurus Child

This is a cuddly, affectionate child who eagerly explores the world of the senses, especially the senses of taste and touch. The Taurus child can be a big eater and will put on weight easily if not encouraged to exercise. Since this child likes comfort and gravitates to beauty, try coaxing little Taurus to exercise to music or take him outdoors for hikes or long walks. Though Taurus may be a slow learner, those born under this sign have excellent retentive memory and generally master a subject thoroughly. Taurus is interested in results and will see each project patiently through to completion, continuing long after others have given up.

Choose Taurus toys carefully to help develop innate talents. Construction toys, such as blocks or erector sets, appeal to their love of building. Paints or crayons develop their sense of color. Many Taurus have musical talents and love to sing, which is apparent at a young age.

This year's Taurus will want a pet or two and a few plants of his own. Give little Taurus a minigarden and watch the natural green thumb develop. This child has a strong sense of acquisition and an early grasp of material value. After filling a piggy bank, Taurus graduates to a savings account, before other children have started to learn the value of money.

With Jupiter in their house of relationship, this year's Taurus children should have many friends and successful partnerships. These children are sure to have at least one best friend and will love to do things with a partner.

The Gemini Child

Little Gemini will talk as soon as possible, filling the air with questions and chatter. This is a friendly child who enjoys social contact, seems to require company, and adapts quickly to different surroundings. Geminis have quick minds that easily grasp the use of words, books, and telephones and will probably learn to talk and read at an earlier age than most. Though they are fast learners, Gemini may have a short attention span, darting from subject to subject. Projects and games that help focus the mind could be used to help them concentrate. Musical instruments, typewriters, and computers help older Gemini children combine mental with manual dexterity. Geminis should be encouraged to finish what they start before they go on to another project. Otherwise, they can become jack-of-all-trade types who have trouble completing anything they do. Their dispositions are usually cheerful and witty, making these children popular with their peers and delightful company at home.

This year's Gemini baby should go to the head of the class. Uranus in Pisces could inspire Gemini to make an unusual career choice, perhaps in a high-tech field. When he grows up, this year's Gemini may change fields several times before he finds a job that satisfies his need for stimulation and variety.

The Cancer Child

This emotional, sensitive child is especially influenced by patterns set early in life. Young Cancers cling to their first memories as well as their childhood possessions. They thrive in calm emotional waters, with a loving, protective mother and usually remain close to her (even if their relationship with her was difficult) throughout their lives. Divorce, death—anything that disturbs the safe family unit—are devastating to Cancers, who may need extra support and reassurance during a family crisis.

They sometimes need a firm hand to push the positive, creative side of their personality and discourage them from getting swept away by emotional moods or resorting to emotional manipulation to get their way. Praised and encouraged to find creative expression, Cancer will be able to express his positive side consistently on a firm, secure foundation.

This year's Cancer child should be especially creative, thanks to Jupiter in Scorpio. Encourage this child to express himself and develop artistic talents to the fullest.

The Leo Child

Leo children love the limelight and will plot to get the lion's share of attention. These children assert themselves with flair and drama and can behave like tiny tyrants to get their way. But in general, they have sunny, positive dispositions and are rarely subject to blue moods. At school, they're the ones who are voted most popular, head cheerleader, or homecoming queen. Leo is sure to be noticed for personality, if not for stunning looks or academic work; the homely Leo will be a class clown and the unhappy Leo can be the class bully.

Above all, a Leo child cannot tolerate being ignored for long. Drama or performing-arts classes, sports and school politics are healthy ways for Leo to be a star. But Leos must learn to take lesser roles occasionally, or they will have some painful put-downs in store. Usually, the popularity of Leos is well earned; they are hard workers who try to measure up to their own high standards—and usually succeed.

The Leo of 2006 is likely to be more serious than the

typical Leo, thanks to Saturn in Leo this year. This endows the child with self-discipline and the ability to function well in structured situations. With enhanced focusing ability, little Leo can be a high achiever.

The Virgo Child

The young Virgo can be a quiet, rather serious child, with a quick, intelligent mind. Early on, little Virgo shows far more attention to detail and concern with small things than other children. Little Virgo has a built-in sense of order and a fascination with how things work. It is important for these children to have a place of their own, which they can order as they wish and where they can read or busy themselves with crafts and hobbies.

This child's personality can be very sensitive. Little Virgo may get hyper and overreact to seemingly small irritations, which can take the form of stomach upsets or delicate digestive systems. But this child will flourish where there is mental stimulation and a sense of order. Virgos thrive in school, especially in writing or language skills, and seem truly happy when buried in books. Chances are, young Virgo will learn to read ahead of classmates. Hobbies that involve detail work or that develop fine craftsmanship are especially suited to young Virgos.

Little Virgo of 2006 is a quick study with the ability to focus his attention on a subject and learn it thoroughly. Virgos born before September 9 will be especially likely to manifest Virgo characteristics, since they will have Mercury and Mars backing up their Virgo sun. After September 6, Venus enters the scene gracing this child with charm and good looks.

The Libra Child

The Libra child learns early about the power of charm and appearance. This is often a very physically appealing child with an enchanting dimpled smile who is naturally sociable and enjoys the company of both children and adults. It is a rare Libra child who is a discipline problem, but when their behavior is unacceptable, they respond better to calm discussion than displays of emotion, especially if the discussion revolves around fairness. Because young Libras without a strong direction tend to drift with the mood of the group, these children should be encouraged to develop their unique talents and powers of discrimination so they can later stand on their own.

In school, this child is usually popular and will often have to choose between social invitations and studies. In the teen years, social pressures mount as the young Libra begins to look for a partner. This is the sign of best friends, so Libra's choice of companions can have a strong effect on his future direction. Beautiful Libra girls may be tempted to go steady or have an unwise early marriage. Chances are, both sexes will fall in and out of love several times in their search for the ideal partner.

Little Libra of 2006 gets a double dose of charm from both Venus (after October 1) and Mars. This is sure to be a good-looking and appealing child. Later in life, Libra could choose a legal career.

The Scorpio Child

The Scorpio child may seem quiet and shy, but will surprise others with intense feelings and formidable willpower. Scorpio children are single-minded when they want something and intensely passionate about whatever they do. One of a caregiver's tasks is to teach this child to balance activities and emotions, yet at the same time to make the most of their great concentration and intense commitment.

Since young Scorpios do not show their depth of feelings easily, parents will have to learn to read almost imperceptible signs that troubles are brewing beneath the surface. Both Scorpio boys and girls enjoy games of power and control on or off the playground. Scorpio girls may take an early interest in the opposite sex, masquerading as a tomboy, while Scorpio boys may be intensely competitive and loner. When their powerful energies are directed into work, sports, or challenging studies, Scorpio is a superachiever, focused on a goal. With trusted friends, young Scorpio is devoted and caring—the proverbial friend through thick and thin, loyal for life.

Jupiter in Scorpio guarantees lucky vibrations for this year's little Scorpio, especially since it is accompanied by Mars, which endows the child with energy, and Venus, good looks and charm. This is a winner in the zodiac sweepstakes this year!

The Sagittarius Child

This restless, athletic child will be out of the playpen and off on adventures as soon as possible. Little Sagittarius is remarkably well-coordinated, attempting daredevil feats on any wheeled vehicle from scooters to skateboards. These natural athletes need little encouragement to channel their energies into sports. Their cheerful, friendly dispositions earn them popularity in school, and once they have found a subject where their talent and imagination can soar, they will do well academically. They love animals, especially horses, and will be sure to have a pet or two, if not a home zoo. When they are old enough to take care of themselves, they'll clamor to be off on adventures of their own, away from home, if possible.

This child loves to travel, will not get homesick at summer camp, and may sign up to be a foreign-exchange student or spend summers abroad. Outdoor adventure appeals to little Sagittarius, especially if it involves an active sport, such as skiing, cycling, or mountain climbing. Give them enough space and encouragement, and their fiery spirit will propel them to achieve high goals.

The Sagittarius of 2006 has charisma and power, thanks to potent Pluto in Sagittarius. This year's Sagittarius could be quieter than others, with a lot going on beneath the surface. There's plenty of imagination and creativity to be developed in this visionary child.

The Capricorn Child

These purposeful, goal-oriented children will work to capacity if they feel this will bring results. They're not ones who enjoy work for its own sake—there must be an end in sight. Authority figures can do much to motivate these children, but once set on an upward path, young Capricorns will mobilize energy and talent and work harder, and with more perseverance, than any other sign. Capricorn has built-in self-discipline that can achieve remarkable results, even if lacking the flashy personality, quick brain power, or penetrating insight of others. Once involved, young Capricorn will stick to a task until it is mastered. These children also know how to use others to their advantage and may well become team captains or class presidents.

A wise parent will set realistic goals for the Capricorn child, paving the way for the early thrill of achievement. Youngsters should be encouraged to express their caring, feeling side to others, as well as their natural aptitude for leadership. Capricorn children may be especially fond of grandparents and older relatives and will enjoy spending time with them and learning from them. It is not uncommon for young Capricorns to have an older mentor or teacher who guides them. With their great respect for authority, Capricorn children will take this influence very much to heart.

The Capricorn born in 2006 will have serious and responsible alliances, thanks to Saturn in the house of mutual ventures. This placement also hints at financial savvy—so give the child a savings account early on. Jupiter in Scorpio promises a stellar social life and influential friends.

The Aquarius Child

The Aquarius child has an innovative, well-focused mind that often streaks so far ahead of those of peers that this child seems like an oddball. Routine studies never hold the restless youngster for long; he will look for another, more experimental place to try out his ideas and develop his inventions. Life is a laboratory to the inquiring Aquarius mind. School politics, sports, science, and the arts offer scope for such talents. But if there is no room for expression within approved social limits, Aquarius is sure to rebel. Questioning institutions and religions comes naturally, so these children may find an outlet elsewhere, becoming rebels with a cause. It is better not to force this child to conform, but rather to channel forward-thinking young minds into constructive group activities.

This year's Aquarius will have far-out glamour as well as charisma, thanks to his ruler, Uranus, in a friendly bond with Neptune. This child could be a rock star, a statesman, or a scientist.

The Pisces Child

Give young Pisces praise, applause, and a gentle, but firm, push in the right direction. Lovable Pisces children may be abundantly talented, but may be hesitant to express themselves, because they are quite sensitive and easily hurt. It is a parent's challenge to help them gain self-esteem and self-confidence. However, this same sensitivity makes them trusted friends who'll have many confidants as they develop socially. It also endows many Pisces with spectacular creative talent.

Pisces adores drama and theatrics of all sorts; therefore, encourage them to channel their creativity into art forms rather than indulging in emotional dramas. Understand that they may need more solitude than other children, as they develop their creative ideas. But though daydreaming can be creative, it is important that these natural dreamers not dwell too long in the world of fantasy. Teach them practical coping skills for the real world. Since Pisces are physically sensitive, parents should help them build strong bodies with proper diet and regular exercise. Young Pisces may gravitate to more individual sports, such as swimming, sailing, and skiing, rather than to team sports. Or they may prefer more artistic physical activities like dance or ice skating.

Born givers, these children are often drawn to the underdog (they fall quickly for sob stories) and attract those who might take advantage of their empathic nature. Teach them to choose friends wisely and to set boundaries in relationships, to protect their emotional vulnerability—invaluable lessons in later life.

With the planet Uranus now in Pisces, this generation of Pisces will be full of movers and shakers. This child may have a rebellious streak that rattles the status quo, with a visionary nature, much concerned with the welfare of the world at large.

CHAPTER 12

The Love Detective: Your Star Guide for Finding the Most Compatible Partner

True astrology offers no partnership insurance, but it does offer you enough clues to navigate even the stormiest relationship safely, whether it's an emotion-packed love affair or a pressurized business partnership.

The key is learning how to detect the trouble spots ahead of time, when you must expect to compromise, and when you will have an easy flow of communication. Then you can work toward maintaining balance and harmony. Since we are all a configuration of planetary energies, there are no truly incompatible horoscopes. However, there are signs whose energy flows together easily. On the other hand, when communication is too easy, some couples may become bored and look for stimulation elsewhere. In other combinations, there is so much excitement that the people involved have to split up or blow their circuits.

When we analyze a relationship astrologically, we are really dealing with the chemical interactions of the planets closest to the earth: the sun, moon, Mercury, Venus, and Mars. The sun signs of each partner can give us the basic character of the relationship, while the four other planets add specific dimensions, which can explain how two people who have a very difficult aspect between their sun signs can be very happy together. For instance, a Scorpio with a moon in Gemini might be much more compatible with a Gemini partner than with another

Scorpio who has a moon in Capricorn. So it is important to take those personal planets into account when speculating on whether a relationship will last.

Look for Signs of Love

Successful partners often say, "We have great chemistry," to describe their immediate compatibility, while others complain, "I don't know why we couldn't get together. We had everything going for us, but the chemistry was off." Astrology takes this comment quite literally. By now you know that each sign is described by an element (earth, air, fire, or water) and a quality (cardinal, fixed, mutable) that tells how the sign operates. Signs of the same element have a natural ease of communication. You've heard the saying "He's in his element" to describe someone who is able to use his energy easily and productively. When you are in your element with someone else, the same is likely to hold true.

You must also consider the quality of the signs, which really influences whether a couple will be on the same wavelength. If you remember, the quality of a sign is the way that sign operates. It is either a cardinal doer or a stable, fixed sign or a changeable mutable sign. But signs of the same quality are of different elements (unless both partners are the same sign), and therein lies the problem. For instance, Aries and Capricorn partners, both cardinal signs, will often have competing points of view. Impatient fiery Aries is idealistic and courageous, always in a hurry, while earthy Capricorn is more calculating, organized, and focused on achievement. So these two signs could tend to grate on each other. A mutable earth sign, Virgo has a constant need to analyze and edit that could irritate other mutable signs, such as the freewheeling fiery Sagittarius or sensitive Pisces. Two stubborn fixed signs such as Taurus and Leo might tune each other out or have a Mexican standoff.

For quick reference, the general rules are:

1. Signs of the same element get along most easily, as follows:
   Earth: Taurus, Virgo, Capricorn
   Air: Gemini, Libra, Aquarius
   Fire: Aries, Leo, Sagittarius
   Water: Cancer, Scorpio, Pisces

2. Signs of the same quality will have to make compromises to resolve their differing points of view:
   Cardinal signs: Aries, Cancer, Libra, Capricorn
   Fixed: Taurus, Leo, Scorpio, Aquarius
   Mutable: Gemini, Virgo, Sagittarius, Pisces

3. Some elements mix together more successfully than others. If you go back to your very first chemistry lessons, remember what fire does to water. The analogy generally holds true for signs of these elements when the partnership is under stress. Fire sign energy will evaporate water. An excess of water sign emotion will dampen fire's enthusiasm. Earth signs generally work much better with water signs and fire signs are more compatible with air.

If this is an air sign, does this mean that you should associate with only fire or other air signs who do not have the same quality? Not necessarily. Your horoscope is really a balance of many planets in different signs. And too much of any sign can easily tip the scales in a relationship.

Pair Up the Love Planets

The planets closest to the earth (Mercury, Venus, Mars and the Moon) each play a different role in your love relationships. Mercury placements will show how well you each communicate and how your mind works. If you want constant mental stimulation, your partner's Mercury in the same quality will give you a good debate, but you may have to constantly explain and justify your point of view. Your partner's Mercury in the same sign as your Mercury will help you to read each other's thoughts, though you may not have such lively dinner conversations.

Mars indicates sexual drive, your different tempers, your ambition. A hot Mars in Aries, impatient and impulsive, might be driven to distraction by the cooler, more critical Mars in Virgo. That same Mars could find much better chemistry with a fun-loving Sagittarius Mars.

The moon will show your emotional nature and what kind of atmosphere makes you happiest. The moon is such a strong factor that it can offset more stressful forces between two people, especially if one person's moon is in the other person's sun sign. Sometimes the moon sign of a compatible partner will echo the moon sign of your own family members. For instance if several members of your immediate family have moon in Leo, your mate might also have that moon sign.

So-called stressful aspects can often stimulate a love relationship, generating sparks and excitement or a slightly dangerous edge. Many passionate love affairs have Venus or Mars in the same cardinal, fixed or mutable quality. The interaction between these signs can produce the opposites-attract syndrome, where one partner provides what the other partner lacks. Or there will be a sense of competition that turns the love light on. There is usually never a dull moment with these couples, at least in the beginning of the relationship. Later on, the tension might become more exhausting than stimulating.

Success in love, as in so many other things, depends on the matter of balance. Too much emphasis on any one element or quality usually tips the relationship to the extreme and unless there are other people in the scenario to provide what is missing, the relationship dissipates. A combination with no love planets in earth signs, for example, might get bogged down with financial or practical problems. One with no water signs might lack feeling or creativity.

Your Best Love Partner

The most romantic affairs are those between partners whose Mars and Venus are in the same element or quality. The same element will produce soul mates; the same quality will produce sparks.

Long-term relationships usually fare well if the sun and moon are in the same element. It is better here if the moons are not in the same quality. You'll want emotional harmony, rather than stimulation, over the long haul.

Make a chart similar to the one below to compare potential partners using the Venus and Mars tables in this book. The Mercury and moon placements will have to be estimated, however. For best results, have an accurate chart calculated by one of the online services recommended in this book.

PARTNER A: ROMEO—ARIES SUN SIGN
    Sign/Quality/Element
MOON: Scorpio/fixed/water
VENUS: Taurus/fixed/earth
MARS: Leo/fixed/fire
MERCURY: Pisces/mutable/water

PARTNER B: JULIET—CANCER SUN SIGN
MOON: Taurus/fixed/earth
VENUS: Leo/fixed/fire
MARS: Pisces/mutable/water
MERCURY: Cancer/mutable/water

Look for Love in the Right Places

If you have a sign in mind, here are places where they are likely to be (and like to go):

ARIES:
Where there's news and plenty of activity, Aries will be on hand. Try a sports event, martial arts display, action

movie, cooking school, adventure sports vacation, the exciting, trendy hot spot in town, the jogging or bike path.

TAURUS:
Taurus loves beautiful things and places, so go where they'll be bought, sold, or traded. Meet them at a gourmet restaurant, auction house, farm or place where there are animals, flower show, garden shop, art classes, stores—especially food or jewelry stores. Take a gourmet cooking class. Shop at a farmer's market or the best grocery store in town. Trade recipes online. Learn to be an art or antiques appraiser. Take a real estate course.

GEMINI:
Meet them working for a newspaper or radio station, at parties or social events, writing courses, lectures, sociable watering holes where there's good talk. Join a club and help plan social activities. Throw a party and invite the most interesting people you know. Gemini will hear about it!

CANCER:
Family dinners, boating or boat shows, cruises, at the beach, at seafood dinners, fishing, cooking schools, gourmet food stores, photography classes, art exhibits. Hang out at your local camera store. Learn to make sophisticated home movies. Take a course in interior design or home renovation. Collect antiques or silver.

LEO:
Think big to lure the lion. Look glamorous, rich, and regal. Find them at big parties, country clubs, golfing, tanning salons, acting classes, theatrical events, movie showings, dancing, night clubs, fine department stores, classy restaurants, VIP lounges at the airport, first-class hotels and travel, anywhere the elite meet.

VIRGO:
Engage the mind and you might engage a Virgo. Craft stores, craft shows, and flea markets, adult-education courses, your local college, libraries, bookstores, health food stores, doctor's offices, volunteering at your local hospital or medical center, lectures, concerts, fine art events.

LIBRA:
Libras like beauty and justice. Art shows, fine restaurants, shopping centers, tennis, glamorous social events, parties and entertainment, the most fashionable stores, exhibits of beautiful objects, antique shows, decorating centers, ballet, and the theater. Places where lawmakers gather and debate attract Libra.

SCORPIO:
Scorpios are often loners, so you might have to work harder to find them. Dress in seductive black, especially black leather. Look in banks, tax preparation offices, police stations, sports events, motorcycle rallies, at the beach or swimming pool, doing water sports, at the gym, at action or mystery movies, psychic fairs, ghostbusting.

SAGITTARIUS:
These gregarious fun lovers gather at comedy clubs, laugh-a-minute films, at horse races or horse shows, pet stores or animal breeders. You could meet one while walking your dog, taking night courses at your local college, at a political debate, traveling to an exotic place, at a car show, mountain climbing, jogging, skiing, discussion group.

CAPRICORN:
Capricorns enjoy status places and fine dining and tend to be conservative, so mind your manners. Find them at a country music show, decorator show house, investment seminar, prestigious country club, exclusive resort, moun-

tain climbing, party for a worthy cause, self-improvement course.

AQUARIUS:
This sign is usually out there, active in the community, crusading for a cause. Find them at a political rally, sci-fi convention, restaurant off the beaten path, union meeting, working for a worthy cause, campaigning for your candidate, fund-raising, taking flying lessons or at the airport en route to a meeting.

PISCES:
Be creative and think out of the box—Pisces loves the imaginative approach. The Fish are happy to hang out at any waterside place, at the theater or acting class, art museum, dance club or performance, swimming pool, fishing spot, seafood restaurant, psychic event, church or other spiritual gathering, visiting at a hospital, at your local watering hole.

CHAPTER 13

Hot Careers for 2006: Where Are the Future Billionaires?

If you're considering a career that's not only going to survive, but thrive in the next few years, why not get some astrological help in making your choice? There are big changes in the stars ahead, so projecting astrologically a few years down the line could point your career in the most profitable direction.

For long-term trends, look to the outer planets, which effect major changes as they move into a different sign. Soon there will be a shift in the atmosphere as Pluto, the planet of transformation, moves into Capricorn in 2008 for a long stay until 2024. (You'll notice a different kind of energy starting a few months in advance.) What's more, Jupiter, the planet of luck and expansion, also moves through Capricorn during 2008, accelerating changes and bringing luck to Capricorn, so expect many of that sign to surge into prominence. Bet on the Sea Goat (Capricorn's symbol) and areas associated with it. Capricorns should prepare to move into the limelight. ("It's about time," you Capricorns may well say!)

If you're headed for the fast track, set your sights on Capricorn fields, which will be going through radical changes. This will affect Capricorn-associated corporations, big business, government, institutions of all kinds, mining, land speculation, property owners and dealers, builders and building trades, contractors and engineers, civil service, providers of status products. Capricorn-influenced fields are known for function, structure, discipline, and order, so consider careers that have these qualities or can provide them to others.

Everything Old Is New

Want to cash in on a much-neglected market? Services and care for the aging should be booming with career opportunities, thanks to our elder population explosion. Remember that the generation now entering the aging population was born with Pluto in Leo; it's the rock-and-roll generation who will resist the idea of aging and retirement as long as possible.

This particular elder population will be highly visible and financially viable. They are big spenders who will be remaining much longer in the work force. Those who do retire may begin second careers, so the workplace will be rethinking its relationship to Grandma and Grandpa and changing to accommodate them. Since America has been a youth-oriented culture, expect a major transformation in advertising, retailing, fashion, housing and health care.

Cater to Horatio Alger

Capricorn is the Horatio Alger sign of rising through one's own volition and ambition. Self-improvement courses will be booming as we search for more fulfilling careers and try to keep up with new technology.

Do you enjoy helping others fulfill their potential? Career coaching, in fact, coaching in all aspects of life, is a hot field. In the corporate area, human resources is a much-touted area of job growth in the nineties. You'll need skills in training and in helping other people find jobs. Get involved with helping people adapt to the times and retrain themselves for new careers. Leos, Sagittarians, Virgos, and Aquarians make excellent trainers and teachers. Aries are the supermotivators.

Education, especially higher education, will be in for a whole new approach, as gray-haired students decide to complete their education or simply enjoy expanding their knowledge. College towns will become hot retirement destinations, which provide intellectual stimulation plus an elder-compatible atmosphere.

The demand for teachers increases and will provide a steady stream of jobs. Look into special education, private education of all kinds, and unusual approaches to teaching. The natural teaching signs—Virgo, Leo, Sagittarius, and Aquarius—are winners here.

Since the world has become a smaller place and the trend toward international involvement is escalating, demand for language skills has also increased. Americans may need to speak several languages, including some once considered exotic for the average American, such as Chinese or Arabic. Language teachers, translators and linguists, especially those with a Gemini emphasis in their charts, should find many opportunities.

Waste Not, Want Not

Capricorn is an intensely practical sign that dislikes waste of any kind, so consider careers in recycling and waste management, antiques, renovation, preserving old buildings, land conservation and teaching history.

Environment-related careers are hot options, since there will be so much cleaning up of toxic wastes, rebuilding after cataclysmic natural events, and redesigning of equipment. Engineers, attorneys, designers, bankers, and researchers should slant their career search in this direction. Taurus, Scorpio, Libra, Pisces, and Aquarius could make their fortune here.

Keep Treasured Traditions Alive

It looks like a conservative time, when people will be concerned with traditional values. Hospitality businesses can capitalize on this trend by promoting the beloved holidays of all cultures, reviving the old customs and memories. Holiday vacations for the whole family to share, reunions, and celebrations could revitalize the resort and cruise businesses. Tourism that caters to the needs of the aging, but still adventurous, traveler should thrive.

Head for the Hills

If you're thinking about a change of scene, consider relocating to a Capricorn-influenced place, which should have growth potential now. If you're adventurous, head for Central Europe, especially mountainous regions. The Balkans, Bosnia, Bulgaria, Lithuania, Macedonia, Albania are Capricorn places. India, Belgium, Hesse and Constance in Germany, Mexico, and New Zealand are also on the Capricorn wavelength.

Health Care for the Antiaging Population

Have you considered the health care field? Careers in medical services are among the hottest prospects as the nation begins to reform its health care systems. Physical therapists, nurses, physicians' assistants and pharmacists, as well as health services administrators, will all be in demand to service the aging population. If you have strong Virgo, Scorpio, or Capricorn placements, which give you a flair for the health field and excellent organizational skills, you should consider this area. Compassionate signs such as Pisces and Cancer make excellent health caregivers.

Consider the Capricorn fields of knee surgery and therapy, bone and joint diseases, chiropractic care, dermatology. New techniques in self-enhancement, such as plastic surgery, dental work and hair replacement, should also do well, for this aging generation who'd love to look and feel forever young.

Therapists specializing in treatment of disabling conditions, optometrists, nursing home operators and managers and home care for the aged should be thriving.

The Talent Finder

Designers and manufacturers of clothing, furniture and equipment suited to the over-sixty consumer should also do well. Look into this area if you have planets in Capricorn (ruler of old age), Pisces (creativity, compassion), Taurus and Cancer (associated with the home environment and of nurturing), and Aries (pioneering ventures).

Do you thrive on life in the fast lane? Sports and special events are high-visibility careers where salesmanship and flair count, so they're especially suited to fire signs Aries, Leo, and Sagittarius. Good communicators like Gemini and Libra do well in public relations in this market.

Capricorn-favored sports require great discipline and endurance and are luckiest when they take place in the mountains. Rock and mountain climbing, hiking, and skiing are especially favored.

There will be a continuing boom in fitness careers, with the emphasis on well-run health clubs, personal attention, and social atmosphere. As the population ages, there will be more emphasis on weight training and rehabilitation aimed at elder bodies. Virgos, Sagittarius, Leos, and Aries are especially suited to the high-energy demands of this field, while Libras, Geminis, and Pisces provide good communication, diplomacy, and compassion.

We'll be eating more consciously as America slims down (Capricorn is the sign of discipline). Diet-specific restaurants, vegetarian restaurants, diet consultants and organic food farmers and gardeners should be expanding. We'll be especially concerned with the quality of our meat and seafood. This is a fertile area for Taurus, Virgo, Cancer, Pisces, and Leos with skills in working with agriculture, diet counseling, cooking, restaurant management, organizing farmers' markets, and managing health food stores.

High-Tech Options

Though computer fields should continue to grow, the outsourcing of high-tech service jobs is also likely to continue. The good news is that there will still be a need for software designers, trainers, salespersons and local repair staff, as computers have become an integral part of our lives. Aquarians are natural in all areas of computer work. Sagittarius and Geminis do well in teaching and sales, while Capricorns excel in organization, Pisces in creative software design, and Cancers in applying high tech to industry.

Video-related careers can only get bigger in 2010 as Neptune, ruler of film, moves into Pisces, its strongest position. Video stores, cameras, and viewing equipment, new uses of video for education and entertainment, technical experts production and performing—all should be booming. Pisces, Leo, Sagittarius, and Gemini should find plenty of opportunities in performance, sales, and marketing.

Take these tips from the stars and do your career planning with the planets!

CHAPTER 14

Your Capricorn Sign Power: Your Capricorn Potential, Possibilities, and Passion!

Discover new possibilities for your life, make better decisions, and share your starlight with others by using your Capricorn sun sign as a guide.

You may wonder why we describe Capricorn in a certain way. The recipe for your sun sign is a blend of several ingredients. Your Capricorn element: earth. The way Capricorn operates: cardinal—a doer. Your sign's polarity: negative, feminine, yin, reactive. And your planetary ruler: Saturn, the planet of discipline, structure, order. Add your sign's place in the zodiac: tenth, the place of career, prestige, public life. Finally, stir in your symbol, the Sea Goat, half climbing goat, half fish, with his tail in the waters of the emotions.

This cosmic mix influences everything we say about Capricorn. Is a disciplined earth sign with career emphasis likely to be ambitious, to try to rise to the top of your profession? Naturally. Do you have traditional values? Very likely. But remember that your total astrological personality contains a blend of many other planets colored by the signs they occupy, plus factors such as the sign coming over the horizon at the exact moment of your birth. The more Capricorn planets in your horoscope, the more likely you'll follow your sun sign's prototype. However, if many planets are grouped together in another sign, they will color your horoscope accordingly, sometimes making a low-key, mellow sun sign come on much stronger. So if the Capricorn traits mentioned here don't describe you, there could be other factors flavoring your cosmic stew. (Look up your other planets in the tables in this book to find out what they might be!)

The Capricorn Man: A High Achiever

The Capricorn man is an ambitious achiever, a hard methodical worker who is most comfortable in a male-run world. Sometimes the young Capricorn man may appear to be a drifter, but this is usually just a phase where you are learning how the world works and setting serious goals. Later in life, the dignified Capricorn manner takes over. Like Cary Grant, Robert Stack, or Humphrey Bogart, you'll embody the elegant tough guy, wise in the ways of the world.

While focused on the top job, you may discount anything or anyone who is not related to your goals. Your personal life is sure to be second to your pursuit of success, at least in the early part of your career. Many Capricorns hold down two jobs at once in a desire to get ahead, or work overtime to move up the ladder of a corporation. Once established, you may decide to make up for lost time and to enjoy the fruits of your labors, allowing your hidden romantic, dreamy side to be revealed.

The Capricorn man generally has an earthy, chauvinistic view of women. You are usually more interested in the physical side of a relationship, and may dismiss women as serious companions or competitors. A woman who can help you in your career or create the right public image is most likely to appeal to you. Though you may experiment sexually with women of a lower class, your wire is usually chosen for her ability to support your cause or elevate your position in some way.

The Capricorn man usually ages very well and is more appealing after forty than before. Then your natural dignity and dry sense of humor shin through. Gray hair or baldness looks distinguished on you. By then you have established yourself financially and feel free to enjoy life. Cary Grant and Humphrey Bogart portrayed the sexy middle-aged Capricorn, the tough guy with a heart and a dry sense of humor.

As a family man, you also improve as you get older, especially when you become the family rock of Gibraltar, a source of paternal help and wisdom. Family security means a great deal to you. When you are ready to settle down, you'll look for a traditional family relationship.

In a Relationship

The Capricorn man's way of showing love is to share your goals with your mate, and you'll expect her to do everything in her power to help you achieve them. Career comes first, and your wife is expected to adjust to your plans, not vice versa. You won't commit to anyone who doesn't support your goals. Often you'll marry someone who can help you up the mountain with good contacts. You usually don't go for a liberated woman because you need to be the strong figure. It is no surprise that there is often a considerable May–September (or even May–December) generation gap between the Capricorn man and his wife.

The bonus of being with a Capricorn is that this sign gets better as you get older. Many of these older man—younger woman relationships last because the Capricorn mate mellow with age, becoming more fun-loving and easier to live with.

The Capricorn Woman: Upwardly Mobile

Capricorn women seem to be born competent, well-organized, and ambitious—on the fast track to success. Elegantly dressed, beautifully groomed, in classic, feminine clothes, the typical Capricorn, like Diane Sawyer, presents a cool, calm image, with everything under control. You give the impression of someone who takes life very seriously. Even those who run counter to type, such as Dolly Parton, are, beneath the glittery facade, shrewd businesswomen who understand the commercial value of their image.

Many Capricorns have followed a rocky road through life, starting out with disadvantages. Yet, with enormous self-discipline, you can muster all your resources for the road ahead and overcome many obstacles to reach a high position. You often have entrepreneurial talent, as you are able to recognize workable projects, follow through on your ideas, and make them happen. Your focus on the path upward puts great value on quality, power, and prestige—and those who have it. But though you'll carefully cultivate contacts with VIPs, you'll remain loyal to anyone who helps you, and you always repay favors in full.

You are most fulfilled when you are using your energy to manage someone or something. You understand how to use and profit from the talents of others, which makes you an excellent manager or supervisor who enjoys directing other lives. On the negative side, Capricorn can also be the stage mother who, when you feel you cannot accomplish goals on your own, will do it vicariously through others in your life. This attitude can cause problems dealing with independent people who have different values or less ambition. However, you are usually a very astute mentor and teacher who can offer valuable practical advice to those who would like to get ahead.

Family relationships mean a great deal to Capricorn women. You are very caring and solicitous of elders, often taking personal care of older relatives. You are proud of your family background, and will make special efforts to keep up appearances and promote traditional family gatherings. You can always be counted on to attend important family-related events and ceremonies.

You are also dedicated to your work. You're the first to arrive in the office and the last to leave, always delivering what you promise. Though you may have conflicts juggling work and family, you'll work hard to assure that your family is well provided for.

In a Relationship

Capricorn often works out a very complex past relationship with her father and lives out her desire for personal power through a man. You rarely marry impulsively for grand passion. If your husband produces the expected lifestyle, you'll fulfill your responsibilities. And once you learn to stand alone and feel totally secure inside, you make a wise, realistic, and helpful mate. As you mature, you may indulge more in affairs of the heart, allowing yourself more spontaneous pleasure as your earthly, sensual side finally emerges.

But you will not commit yourself until you feel totally secure inside (or until you have established yourself at the top of your profession). Many Capricorn women, once they have a successful career, will marry a much younger husband and be able to keep up with him easily.

Capricorn in the Family

The Capricorn Parent

Your sign of Capricorn is regarded as the father figure of the Zodiac just as Cancer, your opposite sign, is regarded as the mother figure. Even female Capricorns have the paternal, responsible, dutiful outlook of the family provider. An ambitious, hard worker yourself, you'll want your children to rise to the top in life, and you'll try to give them the best tools to get there. That includes education, good manners, and knowledge of how to handle finances. You are especially good at teaching your children the perseverance and organizational skills they'll need to achieve their goals. Your children will probably be given an allowance at an early age and taught how to budget their money wisely. As they grow up, you'll provide your children with steady support, though never spoiling or indulging them. For the artistic child who may seem unfocused, you'll provide a sense of direction and a strong dose of reality. Even the more flamboyant Capricorns are solidly rooted in family ties. As a parent, you will impart this sense of lineage and tradition to your children.

The Capricorn Stepparent

Stepchildren can be a big challenge. Your goal as stepparent will be to reestablish a stable family structure, with rules to be followed and lines of authority clarified. (Remember that rules are made to be bent, if not broken, from time to time.) Though you may seem cool and calculating to your stepchildren at first, they will come to respect your strictness and gradual approach to intimacy. Later, they will come to trust you as a mentor and adviser—you're the one who knows what works. Let your stepchildren see your creative side and your delightful dry sense of humor. You're *not* all work, no play! When they get to know you, they will appreciate your sense of values, your realistic outlook, and your sincere support.

The Capricorn Grandparent

Your grandchildren catch you at the mellowest time of your life—you've aged well and lightened up after putting the workaholic days far behind. You're more relaxed and free now that you have reached the top of the mountain, where the air is clear and rarefied. As a grandparent, you'll kick up your heels; you'll enjoy your grandchildren, play with them, and probably be much more openly affectionate than you were with your own children. You welcome your grandchildren's youthful energy; it's like an injection of vitamins. You are the grandparent who goes out dancing (often with a much younger mate). You'll stay in great shape and look terrific—silver hair is sensational on you.

CHAPTER 15

Capricorn at Home and Away: Home Decor, Music, Color, Vacation Getaways

Does your home atmosphere express who you really are? If not, you probably don't feel as comfortable as you should in your environment, which could adversely affect your health and well-being.

Astrology offers you many ways to attune your environment to your natural tendencies. There are colors, styles, places, and music that will help you create the setting that complements your sun sign, one where you're sure to feel truly relaxed and at home.

Your choice of vacation spots might also benefit from some sun-sign input. Should you head for the mountains or for the seashore? Would a cruise be fun or would you enjoy a solitary swim in a tropical cove? There are places that resonate with Capricorn, as well as types of activities that might suit you best. A pampering spa vacation could be a yawn if you groove by dancing all night or sparkle with the bright lights and excitement of a casino resort. Let the astrological travel tips in this chapter help you plan a dream vacation.

Capricorn Home Decor

The "House in Good Taste" is the Capricorn ideal. Good taste to a Capricorn generally means a traditional look inspired by classic designs from many ports of call, from the Far East to American folk art.

Capricorn takes home decor seriously and usually has a strong sense of the "right" and proper way to do things. Your trademarks are high ceilings, beautiful dark woods, and the look of old money. Monograms, crests, heraldic motifs, fine antiques, Oriental rugs, and rich colors suit you. Capricorns from the South like columns in front of their house and a "country club" look (Elvis Presley's Graceland and Dolly Parton's home, for example). In the North, Capricorns love the traditional look of Ivy League Gothic. If the decor is modern, it should still feature fine woods, cabinetry, cathedral ceilings, and a solid, structured look.

Since many of you take work home, space should be set aside fro a home office with computer equipment housed in beautiful wood cabinets. Later in life, you may be able to afford a vacation home and may indulge in more escapist fantasy in your decor, like rock star David Bowie, who once built an elaborate Indonesian-style hide-away in the Caribbean.

The woman who created the profession of interior decorating, the legendary Elsie de Wolfe Mendl, was an archetypal Capricorn, with striking silver hair. Lady Mendl's key word was "suitability," which is the perfect description of the typical Capricorn home. Lady Mendl also swept out the overpowering Victorian look and swept in fine French furniture, uncluttered rooms, and a lively use of color. Lady Mendl conveyed such an atmosphere of prestige and "class" that Cole Porter mentioned her in the lyrics of his song "You're the Top."

Capricorn Music

Capricorn has eclectic musical tastes. You like classical music, string quartets, and medieval sounds. But earthy country and western also appeals, particularly Capricorn singers Dolly Parton, Barbara Mandrell, and Crystal Gayle. The cool tones of Sade set a romantic mood. As the sign of rock, you kick up your heels to rockers Kid Rock, Rod Stewart and David Bowie, and the nostalgic records of Elvis Presley. But it is Latin music that really lights your fire.

Capricorn Color

In decor, Capricorn favors classic colors and fabrics. Lady Mendl was noted for her use of dark green and white, in stripes and lattice patterns. Warm earth tones paired with winter white are another Capricorn decorating look. Capricorns resonated to the jewel tones of Spanish tapestry tones and deep garnet reds. Designer Carolina Herrera's rooms done in an elegant toile fabric are a perfect example of Capricorn elegance.

Capricorn Vacation Getaways

Work-oriented Capricorns need to make time for regular vacations. If you are typical of your sign, you like traditional, clubby places with an organized social life and superb service. Capricorn-friendly resorts are where the rich and famous congregate: Newport, Rhode Island; Southampton, Long Island; Washington, D.C.; Bar Harbor, Maine; Palm Beach, Florida; Monte Carlo; the Caribbean. Both South America and Spain speak to your wild side and could lure you away from business. India, Iowa, Georgia, and Utah are other Capricorn places.

Head for the mountains when you need to be uplifted. High-altitude sports such as mountain hikes, climbing, and skiing can help you leave the workday world far behind and gain perspective.

Or try a yoga retreat where you can stretch mind and body in a beautiful natural setting. Yoga is a very effective way to relax and take your mind off work.

Spa vacations are another Capricorn specialty, appealing to those who enjoy the structure of a well-planned fitness schedule. Early-morning hikes along mountain and canyon trails, sessions with a personal trainer, and a spa's antiaging therapies could help you get back on the fast track.

Organized Capricorns travel with ease, packing exactly what you need. You tend to take work along with you, so a portable computer with a modem might be a good travel investment. Nothing's wasted with Capricorn, and that includes time—you always have something to do during flight delays. You're the one who has change for the telephone, knows where the executive services are in each airport, and is busily doing paperwork while others impatiently pace the waiting room.

Since you're budget-minded (you spend where it counts the most), you may skimp on luxuries while you travel. Remember to pamper yourself once in a while with an in-room movie, a massage, room service, beauty treatments at a local salon, or perhaps a car service waiting to speed you to your destination stress-free and with energy to spare.

CHAPTER 16

Your Capricorn Fashion Stylist

Most celebrities these days hire high-priced stylists to dress them for red-carpet appearances, but you've already got a built-in fashion adviser in your sun sign. Styling your wardrobe by the stars is one of the secrets to projecting the most positive side of your Capricorn personality.

There's a current look that has the name of your sign on it—just follow what Capricorn designers and celebrities are doing this year and you won't go wrong.

Wear Your Capricorn Colors

The colors of deep winter belong to Capricorn. The red of holly berries, black-and-white contrasts, the green of spruce trees. Rich browns, medieval tapestry tones, and earthy hunter greens also complement Capricorn.

Follow Your Capricorn Fashion Stars

Capricorn is concerned with maintaining a specific and appropriate image—and you usually find the one that works for you early in life. It can be as extreme as Dolly Parton's or Diane Keaton's or as elegant as supermodel Christy Turlington's. Capricorns stay true to this image, rarely varying their basic style throughout life. Consider the eternal glamour of the late Capricorn legends: Marlene Dietrich, Loretta Young, and Ava Gardner. Each had a specific and unforgettable fashion look.

You take a no-nonsense approach to fashion. Your clothes have to project the look that is appropriate for your job or social requirements and be of the highest quality possible. You're a disciplined shopper who'll shop sales and buy wholesale whenever possible. And you'll rarely make a fashion mistake, with your discriminating eye. Your wardrobe contains styles you can wear forever.

Clever Capricorns buy separates that stretch your wardrobe and span the seasons. (Years ago, Marlene Dietrich once counseled women on a budget to stick to black, white, and gray—advice that is still right on target today.) You'll accessorize with real, often antique, jewelry; an elegant bag or briefcase; and beautiful, expensive shoes. Your hair and makeup also work for your strong bone structure and busy lifestyle. Capricorn is always in perfect order and projects the best image for the career she chooses.

Designer Carolina Herrera is the summit of Capricorn high-fashion style, with her elegant suits and ladylike dresses. Diane von Furstenburg creates sensual, but practical, clothing that is ideally suited to the working woman. It is interesting that neither of these designers had formal fashion training. Like the mother of interior decorating, Elsie de Wolfe Mendl, they rose to the top through becoming known for their own personal taste and style, as well as their contacts in the right places. The design team of Badgley and Mishka, both Capricorns, interpret the newest trends for you.

On the fashion runway, Capricorn models such as Kate Moss, Vendela, and Helena Christiansen are known for their beautiful bone structure and longevity in the fickle fashion business. Former supermodel Christy Turlington now designs a successful collection of stylish yoga wear.

Capricorn men have been equally influential in setting fashion trends. (Nobody wears a business suit like Capricorn!) Think of how many men would love to look like Cary Grant or Humphrey Bogart, and who still imitate their impeccable style. Singers Elvis Presley, David Bowie, and Ricky Martin have defined the way a rock star should look. Trust your own taste, Capricorn. It's probably just right.

CHAPTER 17

Stay Healthy and Slim the Capricorn Way

This year, the stars say we'll be taking a more focused approach to our health. This means taking control of our eating habits and resolving to become as healthy as possible. Some signs naturally have an easier time than others committing to a health and diet regimen. (And lucky Capricorn, a naturally disciplined active sign, is one of them.) Astrology can clue you in to the Capricorn tendencies that contribute to good or ill health (especially when it comes to controlling your appetite). So follow these sun-sign tips on how best to lose those extra pounds. Then help yourself to become the healthiest Capricorn possible.

Capricorn: Disciplined Dieting

It was a Capricorn hostess and decorator, Lady Elsie de Wolfe Mendl, who introduced dieting to America, via the 1920s health guru Gayelord Hauser. Lady Mendl served very small portions of exquisitely prepared health food at her elegant dinner parties, a good tip for you who may need to downsize your portions. Another one of the skinny signs, Capricorn has amazing self-discipline, a big help in maintaining weight loss. Exercise or active sports should help you keep the pounds off without strenuous dieting. Food and mood are linked with Capricorn, so avoid eating to console or comfort yourself; instead, choose upbeat, relaxed companions. Since you are likely mix business with pleasure, plan your work-related lunches and dinners in advance, so you won't be led astray by the dessert tray.

The Healthy Capricorn

As a Capricorn you naturally take good care of yourself, getting regular medical checkups and tending toward moderation in your lifestyle. You're one of the signs that ages well and remains physically active in your senior years. But Capricorn's fast-paced, action-packed life can be stressful, so here are some ways to unwind and put the spring back into your step.

Since Capricorn is associated with the bone structure, you need to watch for signs of osteoporosis and take preventive measures. Good posture and stretching exercises are essential to remain flexible. You might try yoga, as Christy Turlington does. Another way to counteract osteoporosis is by adding weight-bearing exercise to your routine. If your knees or joints are showing signs of arthritis, calcium supplements may be helpful. For those who enjoy strenuous sports, remember to protect your knees by doing special exercises to strengthen this area, and always warm up beforehand.

Capricorn's natural self-discipline is a big help in maintaining good health. Keep a steady, even pace for lasting results. Remember to balance workouts with pleasurable activities in your self-care program. Grim determination can be counterproductive, especially if one of your exercise goals is to relieve tension. Take up a sport for pure enjoyment, not necessarily to become a champion.

Since you probably spend much of your life in an office, check your working environment for hidden health saboteurs like poor air quality, bad lighting, and uncomfortable seating. Get an ergonomically designed chair to protect your back, or buy a specially designed back support cushion if your chair is uncomfortable. If you work at a computer, adjust your keyboard and the height of the computer screen for ergonomic comfort.

Capricorn, the sign of Father Time, brings up the subject of aging. If sags and wrinkles are keeping you from looking as young as you feel, investigate plastic surgery to give you a younger look and psychological lift. Teeth are also associated with your sign, a reminder to have regular cleanings and dental checkups.

CHAPTER 18

Your Capricorn Career Coach

The Capricorn archetype is the original Horatio Alger story, someone who starts out in the mailroom and winds up in the boardroom. You are highly motivated and usually have a clear strategy for reaching the top. You move deliberately, according to plan, with focus and discipline. By using your instinct for spotting potential business opportunities, you often get in on the ground floor of a very profitable venture.

Any job with a power structure, a status product, an organization (a mountain to climb) is foil for Capricorn talents. Banks, publishing houses, large corporations, politics, and big business of every kind have the terrain you need to climb. Your conservative, high-status tastes could lead you to a career in haute couture, status retailing, or interior design. Orthopedic medicine, chiropractic work, and dentistry are possible health-care careers that treat Capricorn-ruled parts of the body, the bones and teeth.

Because Capricorn is the sign of age and maturity, you may find a career working with the elderly in some way. You have a special talent for this age group, which could point you toward a fulfilling career. With the aging of the overall population, this is an excellent area for Capricorns who are staring out.

When You're Supervising Others

You are a rather formal boss who gives subordinates strong, definite directions. Your style is all business;

many of you literally live for your job. You drive a hard bargain with employees and clients alike, demanding full value for every dollar. You'll stick to the budget, often skipping many of your job's perks, and never stretching your expense account. Since you are very bottom-line oriented, you may undervalue creativity and have trouble understanding freedom-loving creative types. But you are an expert at delegating jobs and can make even the most disorganized worker produce. And you will retain your valued employees, rewarding them for first-class work.

When You're Working on a Team

You will be the hardest worker, as long as your job is a stepping-stone to advancement. Otherwise, you may just bide your time, doing the minimum necessary, until a prime opportunity arises. Few Capricorns are content to stay at a low-level job. Capricorn is practical, determined, and superorganized in pursuit of success. No one gets the job done as quickly and economically as you. You function best in a structured situation where you'll strive to be promoted from within. Though you'll take full advantage of any opportunities to develop your talents within the company, you'll never abuse your expense account. You pride yourself in coming in under budget.

How to Promote Yourself

Look for a company that promotes from within and stick with it. Play up these Capricorn attributes:
- Good judgment
- Managerial ability
- Organizational skills
- Reliability
- Concentration

- Persistence
- Ability to produce

Your Capricorn Sun-Sign Mentors

The Capricorn success story is the one who started at the bottom and worked his way to the top. You keep your eye on the top of the mountain all the way. And you have a great talent for spotting potential business opportunities. Diane von Furstenberg saw a little wrap dress as the perfect dress for the modern career woman and then made her fortune with it. Capricorn moves carefully, according to a plan, and often sees opportunity where others see none.

For more inspiration, there's the career of Capricorn Jeff Bezos, who took a loan from his parents to start Amazon.com, which became the paradigm of e-commerce. Bezos believed in the Internet and saw retailing possibilities far ahead of everyone else. He has weathered the ups and downs of the Internet to become an established success.

CHAPTER 19

Capricorn Celebrity Sightings: Look Who's Born on Your Birthday!

Do you have some favorite Capricorn celebrities in your sun-sign family? You'll find lots in common with other members of your sign, including the famous ones. You may even have a celebrity twin, born on the same day and year. Discover from their horoscopes how they made it big, and perhaps identify some of the stellar Capricorn qualities you share.

You'll recognize the ageless sex appeal of your sign in Cary Grant, Marlene Dietrich, Humphrey Bogart, and Ava Gardner. The classic style of Diane Sawyer and Faye Dunaway only gets better. The wilder side of Capricorn shows up in Elvis Presley, David Bowie, Rod Stewart, and Howard Stern. Armed with their birthday and birth year, you can look up the other planets of your favorite celebrity. Top the tabloids' bragging rights with the inside scoop on their Venus turn-ons and Mars temper, their Saturn panic button and Jupiter luck. It's a fun way to turn your brush with fame into an education in astrology.

Capricorn Celebrities

Lady Bird Johnson (12/22/12)
Hector Elizondo (12/22/36)
Diane Sawyer (12/22/45)
Maurice and Robin Gibb (12/22/49)
Ralph Fiennes (12/22/62)
Susan Lucci (12/23/49)
Carey Holm (12/23/71)
Howard Hughes (12/24/1905)
Ava Gardner (12/24/22)
Ricky Martin (12/24/71)
Humphrey Bogart (12/25/1899)
Tony Martin (12/25/13)
Hanna Schygylla (12/25/43)
Jimmy Buffett (12/25/46)
Barbara Mandrell (12/25/48)
Sissy Spacek (12/25/49)
Annie Lennox (12/25/54)
Tracy Nelson (12/25/63)
Steve Allen (12/26/21)
Jared Leto (12/26/71)
Marlene Dietrich (12/27/1901)
Mick Jones (12/27/44)
Gerard Depardièu (12/27/48)
Maggie Smith (12/28/34)
Denzel Washington (12/28/54)
Joe Diffie (12/28/58)
Mary Tyler Moore (12/29/36)
Jon Voight (12/29/38)
Ted Danson (12/29/47)
Jude Law (12/29/72)
Patti Smith (12/30/46)
Suzy Boggus (12/30/56)
Matt Lauer (12/30/57)
Tracey Ullman (12/30/59)
Tiger Woods (12/30/59)

Julianne Moore (12/30/60)
Heidi Fleiss (12/30/65)
Anthony Hopkins (12/31/37)
John Denver (12/31/43)
Ben Kingsley (12/31/43)
Diane von Furstenberg (12/31/46)
Val Kilmer (12/31/59)
Bebe Neuwirth (12/31/59)
Betsy Ross (1/1/1752)
J. Edgar Hoover (1/1/1895)
Frank Langella (1/1/40)
Famke Janssen (1/1/64)
Roger Miller (1/2/36)
Jim Bakker (1/2/40)
Joanna Pacula (1/2/57)
Christy Turlington (1/2/69)
Robert Loggia (1/3/30)
Dabney Coleman (1/3/32)
Victoria Principal (1/3/50)
Mel Gibson (1/3/56)
Jane Wyman (1/4/14)
Floyd Patterson (1/4/35)
Dyan Cannon (1/4/37)
Patty Loveless (1/4/57)
Paramahansa Yogananda (1/5/1893)
Robert Duvall (1/5/30)
Raisa Gorbachev (1/5/34)
Charlie Rose (1/5/42)
Diane Keaton (1/5/45)
Carl Sandburg (1/6/1878)
Loretta Young (1/6/13)
Katie Couric (1/7/57)
Nicolas Cage (1/7/64)
Nolan Miller (1/8/35)
Elvis Presley (1/8/35)
Stephen Hawking (1/8/42)
Yvette Mimieux (1/8/42)
David Bowie (1/8/47)

Simone de Beauvoir (1/9/1908)
Bob Denver (1/9/35)
Joan Baez (1/9/41)
David Johansen (1/9/50)
Crystal Gayle (1/9/51)
Joely Richardson (1/9/65)
Dave Matthews (1/9/67)
Maurice Sendak (1/10/28)
Sal Mineo (1/10/39)
Jim Croce (1/10/43)
Rod Stewart (1/10/45)
Pat Benatar (1/10/53)
Grant Tinker (1/11/26)
Naomi Judd (1/11/46)
Stanley Tucci (1/11/60)
Mary J. Blige (1/11/71)
Kirstie Alley (1/12/51)
Rush Limbaugh (1/12/51)
Howard Stern (1/12/54)
Olivier Martinez (1/12/66)
Vendela (1/12/67)
Horatio Alger (1/13/1834)
Robert Stack (1/13/19)
Julia Louis Dreyfus (1/13/61)
Penelope Ann Miller (1/13/64)
Orlando Bloom (1/13/77)
Cecil Beaton (1/14/1904)
Faye Dunaway (1/14/41)
Sydney Biddle Barrows (1/14/52)
Steven Soderburgh (1/14/63)
Emily Watson (1/14/67)
Jason Bateman (1/14/69)
Aristotle Onassis (1/15/1906)
Martin Luther King, Jr. (1/15/29)
Chad Lowe (1/15/68)
Sade (1/16/60)
Kate Moss (1/16/74)
Vidal Sassoon (1/17/28)

Maury Povich (1/17/39)
Muhammad Ali (1/17/42)
Mick Taylor (1/17/48)
David Caruso (1/17/56)
Jim Carrey (1/17/62)
Kid Rock (1/17/71)
Cary Grant (1/18/1904)
Kevin Costner (1/18/55)
Edgar Allan Poe (1/19/1809)
Janis Joplin (1/19/43)
Dolly Parton (1/19/46)

CHAPTER 20

The Capricorn Connections: Your Love, Lust, or Break-up Potential with Every Other Sign

Can a career-minded Capricorn motivate a creative Pisces? What's the appeal of a hot-tempered Aries ram? Will your attraction to a sensual Taurus stand the test of time? Say you're magnetized by a sexy Scorpio and want to turn the lusty chemistry into lasting love. Or you're interacting with a difficult boss at work and need to play your cards carefully.

Knowing what your Capricorn sun sign needs in a relationship and how your partner (or lover or workmate) is likely to react can give you stop signs and green lights. Your love could be written in the stars or star-crossed. So whether you're looking for a business partner or a life companion, use this chapter to help you evaluate each other's basic needs. Once you understand how your partner's sun sign is likely to view commitment and what each of you wants from a relationship, you'll be in a much better position to judge whether you'll connect or dis-connect. We've included some celebrity romances (current or past) and lifetime mates to help you visualize each sun-sign combination.

Capricorn/Aires

THE CONNECTIONS:

You're both high achievers and hard workers who respect each other's stamina. Capricorn provides the solid organizational skills. Aries provides the enthusiasm and pioneering ideas. The mature Capricorn outlook could offer the stable backup that Aries needs to get there first. In return, innovative Aries methods could pull Capricorn out of the ordinary.

THE DIS-CONNECTIONS:

Capricorn values the traditional; Aries, the trendy. Aries can seem like a self-centered baby; Capricorn, an old fuddy-duddy. Capricorn rules and structure might seem confining to Aries, whose headstrong methods seem foolhardy to Capricorn.

SIGN MATES:

Capricorn Michelle Williams and Aries Heath Ledger

Capricorn/Taurus

THE CONNECTIONS:

Your similar traditional values can make communication easy. This is a combination that works well on all levels. You find it easy to set goals, to organize, and to support each other. There are earthy passion and instinctive understanding.

THE DIS-CONNECTIONS:

There may be too much earth here, which could make your relationship too dutiful, practical, and unromantic.

You both need to expand your horizons occasionally, and may look for stimulation elsewhere. Taurus may resent Capricorn devotion to career.

SIGN MATES:

Costars Capricorn Marlene Dietrich and Taurus Gary Cooper

Capricorn/Gemini

THE CONNECTIONS:

Capricorn benefits from the Gemini abstract point of view and lighthearted sense of fun. Gemini shows Capricorn how to enjoy the rewards of hard work. Support and structure are Capricorn gifts to Gemini. (Taking that literally, Capricorn Howard Hughes designed the famous bra that supported Gemini Jane Russell's physical assets!)

THE DIS-CONNECTIONS:

Capricorn can be ultraconservative and tightfisted with money, which Gemini will not appreciate. Gemini will have to learn to take responsibility and to produce solid results, or Capricorn will tighten the bottom line.

SIGN MATES:

Capricorn Olivier Martinez and Gemini Kylie Minogue

Capricorn/Cancer

THE CONNECTIONS:

A serious sense of duty, family pride, and a basically traditional outlook bring you together. The zodiac mother

(Cancer) and father (Capricorn) establish a strong home base. Cancer tender devotion could bring out Capricorn earthy and sensual side. This couple gets closer over the years.

THE DIS-CONNECTIONS:

Melancholy moods could muddy this picture. Develop a strategy for coping if depression hits. Capricorn is a lone wolf who may isolate emotionally, or withdraw into work, or take on an overload of duties. Cancer could look elsewhere for comfort and consolation.

SIGN MATES:
Capricorn Kid Rock and Cancer Pamela Anderson

Capricorn/Leo

THE CONNECTIONS:

Here's the perfect mix of business and pleasure. Dignified, refined Capricorn has energy and discipline to match Leo passion. Leo comes to the rescue of your ambitious workaholic sign, adding confidence, poise, and joie de vivre. Capricorn reciprocates with the royal treatment.

THE DIS-CONNECTIONS:

Since Capricorn prefers underplayed elegance to glitter and glamour, Leo may have to tone down the flamboyant style. Capricorn cuts off the cash flow when Leo become extravagant, and may not pour out the megadoses of affection that Leo requires. Leo can't bear a partner who is stingy with love or money!

SIGN MATES:

Capricorn David Bowie and Leo supermodel Iman

Capricorn/Virgo

THE CONNECTIONS:

This looks like a sure thing between two signs who have so much in common. You're both good providers. You both have a strong sense of duty and respect for order, also similar conservative tastes and a basically traditional approach to relationships. You could accomplish much together.

THE DIS-CONNECTIONS:

You may be too similar! Cary Grant (Capricorn) and Sophia Loren (Virgo) had strong chemistry, but finally opted for other commitments. Romance needs challenges to keep the sparks flying.

SIGN MATES:

Capricorn Humphrey Bogart and Virgo Lauren Bacall

Capricorn/Libra

THE CONNECTIONS:

Capricorn is quick to spot Libra potential as a social asset as well as a romantic lead. Libra loves your dignified Capricorn demeanor and elegant taste. You can climb the heights together, helping each other get the lifestyle you want.

THE DIS-CONNECTIONS:

Capricorn is a loner and a home lover, while Libra is a party person who likes to do things in tandem. Expensive Libra tastes could create tension with your frugal Capricorn ways, unless Libra leans to consider the budget as well as the beauty.

SIGN MATES:

Capricorn Faye Dunaway and Libra Marcello Mastroianni

Capricorn/Scorpio

THE CONNECTIONS:

Sexy Scorpio takes your Capricorn mind off business. Though you could get wrapped up in each other, you are also turned on by power and position, and you'll join forces to scale the heights.

THE DIS-CONNECTIONS:

Capricorn has no patience for intrigue or hidden agendas. Scorpio will find you too focused on your own goals. As a Capricorn you won't be easily diverted, even if this means leaving Scorpio emotional needs and ego in the backseat.

SIGN MATES:

Capricorn Diane Sawyer and Scorpio Mike Nichols

Capricorn/Sagittarius

THE CONNECTIONS:

Capricorn has a built-in job organizing Sagittarius. But the challenge of doing something for the greater good could bring Capricorn status and recognition. Sagittarius encourages Capricorn to elevate goals beyond the material, and also brings out both the spiritual side and the humor of your sign.

THE DIS-CONNECTIONS:

Optimistic Sagittarius meets pessimistic Capricorn and you cancel each other out! Ultimately, you can't play it for laughs. Capricorn pushes Sagittarius to produce and commit. And Sagittarius runs off to do his or her own thing.

SIGN MATES:

Capricorn Carolyn Bessette Kennedy and Sagittarius JFK Jr.

Capricorn/Capricorn

THE CONNECTIONS:

You two mountain goats can climb to the top together. You'll share the same traditional values. You'll appreciate each other's thrifty, practical ways and excellent organization. You'll bring out each other's dry sense of humor and earthy sensuality.

THE DIS-CONNECTIONS:

Too much earth (sameness) could bury the romance. You both need the inspiration and stimulation of different kinds of energies to keep climbing. Otherwise, you two will be all work and no fun.

SIGN MATES:

Capricorns Jude Law and Sienna Miller

Capricorn/Aquarius

THE CONNECTIONS:

When the Capricorn lone wolf and the Aquarius oddball team up, the romantic route takes an unpredictable detour. Aquarius discovers that your Capricorn know-how and organizational skills can make wild dreams come true. Capricorn finds that an Aquarius shake-up can have productive results.

THE DIS-CONNECTIONS:

After the initial fascination, these two signs may go off in opposite directions unless there are shared goals or a project to get done. Capricorn may push for a traditional relationship, while Aquarius follows a different drummer.

SIGN MATES:

Capricorn Nicolas Cage and Aquarius Lisa Marie Presley

Capricorn/Pisces

THE CONNECTIONS:

Your Capricorn organizational abilities and worldly know-how impress Pisces. You can help this foggy, creative sign find a clear direction. The Pisces romance, tenderness, and knowledge of the art of love bring out the gypsy in you—a fair exchange.

THE DIS-CONNECTIONS:

You've got your work cut out for you with free-floating Pisces, who avoids nets of any kind. What spells security for Capricorn could look like a gilded cage to Pisces, who doesn't play by the same rules. If you can make allowances for radical differences, you'll go far together. Don't try to make each other over!

SIGN MATES:

Capricorn Jim Bakker and Pisces Tammy Faye Messner

CHAPTER 21

Astrological Outview for Capricorn in 2006

Your ruler, Saturn, continues its journey through the sign of Leo this year. Saturn, as the planet that rules physical reality and the rules by which we live, is transiting your eighth house of shared resources. You may experience delays or setbacks in obtaining mortgages, loans, or the use of other people's money. Your partner, spouse, or anyone else with whom you share finances may decide to change jobs or could get laid off, which impacts the money you have available to you.

However, as if to compensate for this, Jupiter is forming a harmonious angle to your sun for eleven months this year, expanding your network of friends and acquaintances. Jupiter's transit also expands your dreams and aspirations. Any work that you do before the public this year is well-received. You may also have publishing opportunities, if that's one of your interests, or opportunities to travel abroad.

Uranus continues its journey through Pisces in your third house. This planet, which rules sudden, unexpected change as well as your individuality, shakes up your relationships with siblings, relatives, and perhaps even neighbors, but does this only to rouse you from comfortable habits. Uranus also changes the way you communicate. You could make a move this year or, at the very least, be looking for a more suitable community for yourself or your family.

Neptune continues its transit through the sign of Aquarius and your second house. One thing this transit indicates is the ability to earn money through the arts. Perhaps you sell your poetry, your fiction, or your screenplay. But on the downside, Neptune can blind you to the truth concerning your income-earning abilities or you may need to watch your spending and your money more carefully. You may not be very interested in making money just for the sake of money; you'll be seeking deeper, spiritual compensations.

Pluto continues its transit through Sagittarius and your twelfth house. This transit began in 1995 and over the past several years has transformed your relationship with power. Perhaps you are reclaiming power you have disowned over the course of your life or are discovering the depths of your personal power. One thing is certain with this transit. Once you walk through the doors that it opens, you never look back.

In 1995, in terms of romance—the kind of romance when sparks fly—the best times this year are likely to fall from mid-December and into the new year. During this time period, Venus is in your sign, adding zest and charm to your personality and making you attractive to everyone. Another good period for romance—as well as anything you do for pleasure—falls from May 29 to June 22, when Venus is in Taurus and transiting your fifth house.

There are four eclipses this year, two in March and two in September. Three of them are harmonious for you, so check out 2006 annual for information on how these eclipses will affect you.

Mercury turns retrograde three times this year. During these periods, it's vital that you check and recheck travel plans, since plans can go awry. It's best not to sign contracts, but if you have to, read the fine print. Try to communicate as clearly as possible during these periods.

The dates are: March 2–March 25, Mercury retrograde in Pisces impacts your siblings, neighbors, short-distance travel, and communication; July 4–July 28, Mercury retrograde in Leo impacts shared resources; October 28–November 17, Mercury retrograde in Scorpio impacts your wishes, dreams, and networks.

CHAPTER 22

Eighteen Months of Day-by-Day Predictions—July 2005 to December 2006

Moon sign times are calculated for Eastern Standard Time and Eastern Daylight Time. Please adjust for your local time zone.

JULY 2005

Friday, July 1 (Moon in Taurus) It's great to start a month with the moon in sensuous Taurus. Today you need Taurus's strength to take on additional responsibilities because someone in the office or in your environment isn't fulfilling his promises. Some things are slowed down and seem tedious, but it's Friday and you're anticipating a good weekend.

Saturday, July 2 (Moon in Taurus to Gemini 4:27 p.m.) You wake up today with specific goals in mind. All of them are within your reach today. Check out that property you've been eyeing as a potential investment. Update your Web site. Answer e-mail. Stay in touch and make sure you're on top of your financial statements. If you're having guests for the weekend, take care of whatever needs to be done beforehand.

Sunday, July 3 (Moon in Gemini) You have a lot of nervous energy; it's best to use that energy to complete projects and tasks so that you can take tomorrow off and celebrate the Fourth of July without feeling pressured. Few signs are as wrapped up in a sense of responsibility as Capricorn, and the only way you folks can enjoy yourselves is to have all your bases covered.

Monday, July 4 (Moon in Gemini) Happy Independence Day! You're in a high mood and your communication skills are sharp. You hold an audience captive with your stories and everyone is impressed with your clear, concise opinions and beliefs.

Tuesday, July 5 (Moon in Gemini to Cancer 3:08 a.m.) If you've taken the week off, you and your partner should get away together and enjoy the amorous feelings that rise with the moon moving into your seventh house. Security issues are the focus and the specific issues depend on what you construe to be security.

Wednesday, July 6 (Moon in Cancer) You're more nurturing when the moon is in Cancer and your children and pets play a larger role in your affairs. Your significant other may need some nurturing; while you're at it, don't forget to nurture yourself. The new moon in your seventh house suggests a new chapter in your partnerships.

Thursday, July 7 (Moon in Cancer to Leo 3:11 p.m.) As the moon moves into your eighth house, the focus is on resources that you share with others or that they share with you. This can run the gamut from taxes, insurance, and jointly held properties to your spouse's income to joint contracts and metaphysical beliefs.

Friday, July 8 (Moon in Leo) News about joint finances. You're thrust into the limelight for some reason and rise to the occasion with grace and style. You get off work early and head to another town for dinner and a show—a change of scenery that you need.

Saturday, July 9 (Moon in Leo) Your sexuality is heightened today and you're definitely in the mood for love. Your partner or a new love interest showers you with shows of affection.

Sunday, July 10 (Moon in Leo to Virgo 3:57 a.m.) It's an ideal time to break a habit that is affecting your health. Smoking, drinking, drugs, not enough sleep—whatever it is, tackle the problem yourself or enlist the aid of a professional.

Monday, July 11 (Moon in Virgo) You join a gym or sign up for a weekly aerobic or yoga class. The group activity will keep you focused and you'll be more likely to attend the class regularly.

Tuesday, July 12 (Moon in Virgo to Libra 4:09 p.m.) Your professional relationships are highlighted today and for the next two days. The moon joins Jupiter in your tenth house, expanding your intuitive sensitivity and your professional opportunities.

Wednesday, July 13 (Moon in Libra) Your artistic and mediation abilities are strong today; you may be called upon to use one or both in your profession. You do the job perfectly and your bosses take note. Several weeks down the road, this will pay off.

Thursday, July 14 (Moon in Libra) The moon and Mars face off across 180 degrees of opposition today. You may feel more impatient and short-tempered than usual. Think before you speak and take nothing for granted.

Friday, July 15 (Moon in Libra to Scorpio 1:51 a.m.) The moon moves into your eleventh house very early this morning, highlighting intense emotional or psychic experiences. Your dreams should be especially vivid and may provide information or insight that you need at this time. Pay attention to them.

Saturday, July 16 (Moon in Scorpio) You're looking for the absolute bottom about a mystery you've encountered. You investigate the issue thoroughly, and by the time the moon goes into Sagittarius tomorrow, you've found the answer to what has puzzled you.

Sunday, July 17 (Moon in Scorpio to Sagittarius 7:35 a.m.) News today concerning publishing, advertising, the law, education, or your worldview. You may sign up for a workshop or seminar or be called upon to give your opinion about politics or spiritual beliefs. Your mood is more buoyant and optimistic.

Monday, July 18 (Moon in Sagittarius) You're looking for the bigger picture related to a previously hidden issue in your own life. Where did the issue begin? What does it mean in the long run for you and your family? Is it the direction in which you want to proceed?

Tuesday, July 19 (Moon in Sagittarius to Capricorn 9:27 a.m.) Yesterday's questions snap into greater clarity when the moon goes into your sign this morning. You suddenly feel more grounded and solid. It's reflected in the way you approach your work, your relationships, and your goals.

Wednesday, July 20 (Moon in Capricorn) Finances, ambition, and career are highlighted today. What's the thread that ties them together? You don't have time to figure it out until later this evening, when you've got everything right in front of you.

Thursday, July 21 (Moon in Capricorn to Aquarius 8:56 a.m.) You come up with a new business plan, a visionary strategy, or some other cutting-edge idea that can be applied to your home business. Your partners love it.

Friday, July 22 (Moon in Aquarius) Mercury turns retrograde today in your eighth house and Venus moves into Virgo, into your ninth house. You know the drill by now with retrograde Mercury; communications and travel are affected. The Venus transit spells luck with health, publishing, and education.

Saturday, July 23 (Moon in Aquarius to Pisces 8:13 a.m.) As the moon moves into Pisces, your spiritual beliefs and your compassion are highlighted. Your creativity is also deepened, with your imagination running overtime. Record all these great ideas for future use. Communication is highlighted.

Sunday, July 24 (Moon in Pisces) The Pisces moon slows down the pace of your life and offers a welcome reprieve from your left-brain pursuits. Enjoy it while it lasts. Let your creativity shine.

Monday, July 25 (Moon in Pisces to Aries 9:24 a.m.) Home and family are your focus today. Tempers may flare, so proceed with patience, kindness, and gentleness.

Tuesday, July 26 (Moon in Aries) You're feeling restless and decide to get out and do something different. You're searching for new ideas, new perspectives, new seeds. Brainstorm with friends and family.

Wednesday, July 27 (Moon in Aries to Taurus 1:55 p.m.) Your creativity and your children are your focus. Your sensuality is also heightened; it's important that you do what you love and enjoy. It's a pleasure day, Capricorn.

Thursday, July 28 (Moon in Taurus) Mars moves into Taurus, joining the moon in your fifth house. This boosts your sensuality and creativity and highlights your children.

Friday, July 29 (Moon in Taurus to Gemini 10:03 p.m.) The moon moves into your sixth house, focusing your energy on work and daily routines. Your communication skills are sharper, and whatever you talk or write about is well-received.

Saturday, July 30 (Moon in Gemini) You may do a lot of carpooling and running around this weekend, with the moon in Gemini both Saturday and Sunday. But it's also likely that if you have a novel, screenplay, or nonfiction book that you've been working on, this is the weekend you'll really dive into it.

Sunday, July 31 (Moon in Gemini) A surprise visit from a sibling or another relative is likely. This person has an agenda, so be alert and aware that things may not be exactly as they seem.

AUGUST 2005

Monday, August 1 (Moon in Gemini to Cancer 8:53 a.m.) With Mars continuing to move through your fifth house, your focus is on creative and pleasurable pursuits. Mars definitely lends itself to heightened sexuality and sexual encounters purely for pleasure. You generally aren't the type to indulge in casual affairs, but you may change your mind while Mars, which symbolizes your sexual and physical energy, transits this house.

Tuesday, August 2 (Moon in Cancer) You and your partners complete a project that you've been working on and get it in under deadline. Your new romantic interest stops by this evening, and the two of you hang out at your place—an evening that feels just about perfect to you.

Wednesday, August 3 (Moon in Cancer to Leo 9:10 p.m.) You're on center stage today. If you give presentations or do any public speaking, you are well-received. It's a good idea to dress for success today. Even if you don't feel that way, it behooves you to play the part.

Thursday, August 4 (Moon in Leo) With the new moon occurring in your eighth house, anything that you initiate this month in the area of joint resources bears fruit at the full moon later this month. So be sure that the seeds you plant are positive and concern what you want rather than what you think you want. There's a difference and you, Capricorn, know that better than most of us.

Friday, August 5 (Moon in Leo) This is a good weekend to travel for business, particularly if that business involves promoting yourself, your product, or your company. Possibilities include a trade show or a publicity tour.

Saturday, August 6 (Moon in Leo to Virgo 9:54 a.m.) Today you're in a major organizing mood. You may decide to clean out your desk drawers and organize tax forms, medical forms, or insurance forms. It's also a good day to file forms for anything related to health.

Sunday, August 7 (Moon in Virgo) In your exercise class, you meet someone to whom you're attracted. The chemistry is mutual, and over the next few weeks, the relationship heats up.

Monday, August 8 (Moon in Virgo to Libra 10:09 p.m.) Professional relationships and the arts are highlighted. You strive to maintain balance in your life, or you're seeking to balance two facets of your life, perhaps home and career. It's sometimes difficult to make decisions under a Libra moon; wait until Thursday or Friday before making an important decision related to your profession.

Tuesday, August 9 (Moon in Libra) You fall back on a familiar habit or frame of mind. There's nothing wrong with this, but it's possible the habit or frame of mind is holding you back in some way. Scrutinize it, understand it—and then release it.

Wednesday, August 10 (Moon in Libra) You initiate something professionally or find a different way of doing something familiar. This innovation is applauded by your superiors because they believe it will turn a profit for the company.

Thursday, August 11 (Moon in Libra to Scorpio 8:35 a.m.) Put your energy into fulfilling your obligations today and completing whatever is unfinished. Whether your unfinished projects relate to work or home, get them cleared up today so that tomorrow you can get off to a fresh start.

Friday, August 12 (Moon in Scorpio) Your intuition is right on the money. But if you don't listen to it, what good is it? Keep your senses open wide today and heal all inner guidance. This will help you to make the correct decision regarding a wish or hope that you have.

Saturday, August 13 (Moon in Scorpio to Sagittarius 3:48 p.m.) You have spectacular success today in something you do behind the scenes. It's related to an odd set of circumstances that begins to evolve early this morning.

Sunday, August 14 (Moon in Sagittarius) Focus on advertising and distribution, as well as volunteer work, perhaps with animals. A warm reunion with old friends is possible. Later this evening, you explore astrology, tarot, or some other divinatory system.

Monday, August 15 (Moon in Sagittarius to Capricorn 7:14 p.m.) When the moon moves into your sign, the pace of your life is more to your liking. Although your responsibilities may increase, you're able to plug along just fine on your own, with pragmatism as your highest priority. Mercury goes direct today, ending some frustrations in communication over the last few weeks.

Tuesday, August 16 (Moon in Capricorn) Now is the time to travel for business or pleasure. Or at the very least, start researching your travel plans for the fall.

Wednesday, August 17 (Moon in Capricorn to Aquarius 7:39 p.m.) A window of opportunity begins today and extends over the next three weeks. It concerns a stroke of luck in your profession and career and is the result of Venus moving into your tenth house. Women are supportive and helpful somehow in attaining your short-range goals.

Thursday, August 18 (Moon in Aquarius) Something you lost recently is found. Today you develop your inner resources and refine your values in some way. You won't feel like talking about your feelings, but you'll be eager to exchange your ideas and thoughts about new projects, finances, and emerging values.

Friday, August 19 (Moon in Aquarius to Pisces 6:53 p.m.) You explore the connection between money and power—and creativity. *Your* creativity. *Your* money and power. Can you separate your materialism from your creative urges?

Saturday, August 20 (Moon in Pisces) With the moon in the same house as Uranus, your ideas are highly original and intuitive. It's a great day to work on your creative projects or to get off with the kids and do something pleasurable and fun for everyone.

Sunday, August 21 (Moon in Pisces to Aries 7:02 p.m.) You take the lead and organize an outing for the family or for you and your partner. You go whitewater rafting, hiking, kayaking, camping, or all of the above. And the best news of all? You forget all about work!

Monday, August 22 (Moon in Aries) Your cooperation is required both at work and at home. Either situation calls for compromise, which may not be to your liking. But if you can compromise today, the end result benefits everyone.

Tuesday, August 23 (Moon in Aries to Taurus 9:58 p.m.) As the moon joins Mars in Taurus in your fifth house, your sexuality gears up. It's one of those days for sheer pleasure. Whether married or single, you take full advantage of it.

Wednesday, August 24 (Moon in Taurus) You feel especially stubborn about resisting something that your kids want. They are also very persistent about nagging you for whatever it is. Assess the cost, talk it over with your partner, and make a choice.

Thursday, August 25 (Moon in Taurus) You've skimped on sleep the last several days and now it's catching up to you. Early to bed may be the end result, or you may just take tomorrow off and make it a long weekend. Why not? You've earned it and summer is quickly drawing to a close.

Friday, August 26 (Moon in Taurus to Gemini 4:43 a.m.) It's one of those days when the energy at work is frantic and there's a lot to get done before five o'clock. If you can, strike the right balance between duty and need. Maybe a longer lunch hour is in order so you can sneak off to the gym.

Saturday, August 27 (Moon in Gemini) A lively debate may collapse into an argument with a sibling or relative. Keep your cool and back off. It isn't worth damaging a relationship just to prove who is right or wrong.

Sunday, August 28 (Moon in Gemini to Cancer 2:57 p.m.) With the moon moving into your seventh house, partnerships become your focus again. There really is a pattern to all this! Communication is easier now, so get talking.

Monday, August 29 (Moon in Cancer) Your intuitive abilities crank into high gear and help you understand what a partner or new love interest is actually trying to tell you. Even if you don't like the message, understanding it mitigates emotional turmoil.

Tuesday, August 30 (Moon in Cancer) You feel drawn to water or to water sports. There's something soul-soothing about water, and you may need to have your soul soothed.

Wednesday, August 31 (Moon in Cancer to Leo 3:15 a.m.) As you leave August to enter September, give thanks for all that you have and focus on what you would like to attain or have by the end of the year. It's never too late to dream!

SEPTEMBER 2005

Thursday, September 1 (Moon in Leo) This flashy moon marks the beginning of September and brings your focus on resources you share with others—or which others share with you. It may involve your spouse's income and earning capacity.

Friday, September 2 (Moon in Leo to Virgo 3:27 p.m.) Pluto finally turns direct again in your twelfth house. During this planet's long transit through your twelfth house (until 2008), it helps bring to light power that you have disowned. In a sense, it brings out the hidden aspects of your personality. You may do things you consider uncharacteristic.

Saturday, September 3 (Moon in Virgo) You and your partner may attend some type of health convention or workshop together. Or you may seek out the services of an alternative health practitioner—an acupuncturist, Rolfer, homeopath, or reconnective healer.

Sunday, September 4 (Moon in Virgo) With the moon moving through your ninth house, you're in an expansive, fun-loving mood. Someone around you may not be as buoyant, but don't let that person's mood change your own. Be precise and detailed. Mercury joins the moon in Virgo, in your ninth house. News is likely about publishing or publishers, publicity or advertising, or overseas travel plans.

Monday, September 5 (Moon in Virgo to Libra 3:53 a.m.) You may be dealing with temperamental artistic types today. They make demands that you aren't sure you can or want to meet. Be forthright, kind, but firm. Happy Labor Day!

Tuesday, September 6 (Moon in Libra) Focus on profession, career, and partnerships. There's a sense of adventure and discovery about today that seizes you. Somehow, you get caught up in the whirlwind and love it.

Wednesday, September 7 (Moon in Libra to Scorpio 2:11 p.m.) With the moon in Scorpio, your emotional experiences leave powerful impressions on you. Your intuitive abilities are exceptional now. Use them.

Thursday, September 8 (Moon in Scorpio) Your willpower is so strong today that it would be to your benefit to meditate. During your meditation, visualize how you want your life to be a year from now. Don't worry about the specifics—just see the vivid mental image. Then carry this image out into the world with you.

Friday, September 9 (Moon in Scorpio to Sagittarius 10:04 p.m.) You're looking for the larger picture, and sometimes that means you have to look within. Mystics say that we already have all the answers we seek; we simply need to look into our own souls, where past, present, and future are one.

Saturday, September 10 (Moon in Sagittarius) If you don't keep a journal, you may want to start, and beginning under the influence of this moon would be excellent. With the moon moving through your twelfth house, your hidden self is much more accessible to you.

Sunday, September 11 (Moon in Sagittarius) While the moon leaves Scorpio today, Venus enters the sign and your love life certainly heats up. This placement favors intense but enjoyable sexual encounters, romance, and love. If you're single or uncommitted, it's possible you meet this person through a group of friends or through a group association.

Monday, September 12 (Moon in Sagittarius to Capricorn 2:57 a.m.) With the moon moving into your sign again, you are resolute and calm, and the pace of life is more to your liking. Your self-confidence is high and pragmatism is your middle name.

Tuesday, September 13 (Moon in Capricorn) Your self-identity seems so strong today that you can convince anyone of virtually anything and get away with it. You may have more than your share of responsibilities today, but even that's okay. You can handle it.

Wednesday, September 14 (Moon in Capricorn to Aquarius 5:03 a.m.) You have a financial opportunity and mull it over for most of the day. By late afternoon, you realize this is an excellent chance to make some additional income and sign up for the deal.

Thursday, September 15 (Moon in Aquarius) You meet with your financial group at your place. This could be a financial astrology group, a theater group, a team of your coworkers, or just some eccentric friends. One way or another, though, the topic turns to money—who has it, who doesn't, and how all of you can make more of it without sacrificing your integrity.

Friday, September 16 (Moon in Aquarius to Pisces 5:25 a.m.) Imagination, color, and deep inspiration are highlighted. Sounds like a prescription for poetry or love.

Saturday, September 17 (Moon in Pisces) You do something today that is completely and utterly pleasurable. The specifications depend entirely on what *you* find pleasurable.

Sunday, September 18 (Moon in Pisces to Aries 5:43 a.m.) Today, one of your children or perhaps your partner or even a parent suggests something thrilling for the family to do. You leap at the opportunity and off you go with your intimate little group.

Monday, September 19 (Moon in Aries) Tempers are short on the domestic front. Passions run high both positively and negatively, and it seems that everyone around you wants something yesterday. Just be patient and quiet, and exercise diligence in doing what you're supposed to do.

Tuesday, September 20 (Moon in Aries to Taurus 7:48 a.m.) Mercury moves into your fifth house, bringing news about your creative endeavors, speculative ventures, and your children. The news is good. And so is your luck.

Wednesday, September 21 (Moon in Taurus) Sensuality is the key note today. It isn't just sexual. It seems to permeate your life, from the foods you eat to the places you visit to the people who grace your life today. Your sensuality awakens a deeper appreciation of the earth and all its bounties.

Thursday, September 22 (Moon in Taurus to Gemini 1:07 p.m.) When the moon moves into your sixth house, you sometimes feel torn between responsibilities and your desire to have fun. Today, go with the fun. You, Capricorn, must be constantly reminded about having fun, of doing something just for the joy of doing it.

Friday, September 23 (Moon in Gemini) You have an opportunity to move in a new direction in your daily routine. It's something you may not have considered, so you're uncertain about it. But this opportunity represents a step in your spiritual evolution. At the very least, explore it.

Saturday, September 24 (Moon in Gemini to Cancer 10:11 p.m.) If you have rental property, your tenant gives you some trouble, possibly about this month's rent. Maybe the property needs repairs. Take care of the problem and get on with the rest of your day.

Sunday, September 25 (Moon in Cancer) Married or single, committed or not, you nurture others today. Your kids need support, your partner or love interest is craving intimacy, and you're perfectly content to sit by a body of water somewhere, dreaming your dreams and pondering a past filled with memories.

Monday, September 26 (Moon in Cancer) The behavior of a coworker or business partner puzzles you. The person seems hostile toward you. Regardless of protocol, you confront the person and the situation is ironed out to your mutual satisfaction. Sometimes, all it takes to resolve an issue is honesty.

Tuesday, September 27 (Moon in Cancer to Leo 10:03 a.m.) Early today, you feel a surge of energy and humanity, a need to connect with the people you love best. So get on the phone. Send e-mails. Don't let other obligations hold you back.

Wednesday, September 28 (Moon in Leo) Are your insurance premiums paid up for the month? Have you been making your quarterly tax payments? Stay on top of your obligations in these areas. And while you're at it, investigate topics like reincarnation. What you find will shock you.

Thursday, September 29 (Moon in Leo to Virgo 10:45 p.m.) Details, details, details. That's what today is about: details related to education, foreigners, foreign countries, and publishing. Get busy. You have problems to solve and your work is cut out for you.

Friday, September 30 (Moon in Virgo) The scent of fall is in the air now. No question that the lazy days of summer are over. And with the change of seasons comes a subtle shift in your worldview, your spiritual beliefs. Are you really so certain that you're right about how the universe works?

OCTOBER 2005

Saturday, October 1 (Moon in Virgo) This month starts with Mars turning retrograde in your fifth house, which favors all creative work. You're in a place now where the creative product is what matters most to you and the financial benefits of your creative work are secondary. Consider this a nine-week window of creative opportunity.

Sunday, October 2 (Moon in Virgo to Libra 10:25 a.m.) The moon joins Jupiter in your tenth house, bolstering experiences and opportunities that concern your profession and career. Your intuition concerning professional relationships is exceptional today. Use it.

Monday, October 3 (Moon in Libra) An invitation from your new romantic interest puts you on top of the world. The arts and music play into your affairs today. Relationships, both personal and professional, are highlighted and your mediation skills may be called upon.

Tuesday, October 4 (Moon in Libra to Scorpio 8:04 p.m.) You investigate a mystery that has baffled you. With the moon in Scorpio, you're able to burrow through miles of information and theories in a thorough but intuitive manner to find the answers you need. Your sexuality is heightened today. People see you as mysterious and charismatic.

Wednesday, October 5 (Moon in Scorpio) You and your partner attend a workshop or seminar on spirituality and discover that your spiritual beliefs and experiences are similar. This common bond deepens your commitment to each other. Your dreams are especially vivid now and can provide you with information and answers about issues that concern you. Keep track of them.

Thursday, October 6 (Moon in Scorpio) You sometimes feel as if you straddle dual worlds: the outer world of ambition and the inner world of spirituality and intuition. You don't have to choose between them—just try to let them blend together.

Friday, October 7 (Moon in Scorpio to Sagittarius 3:28 a.m.) Venus moves into Sagittarius, highlighting creative work done behind the scenes. Your sister, your mother, or another woman plays a role in the scheme of things today. A secret love affair may also be in the offing, but before you get involved, look at the bigger picture.

Saturday, October 8 (Moon in Sagittarius) With Mercury moving into Scorpio, your conscious mind focuses on sex, inner motivations, metaphysics, and investigations. You may be looking for a way to incorporate finances and spirituality. A good place to begin is to become more aware of which companies support or violate the causes you believe in.

Sunday, October 9 (Moon in Sagittarius to Capricorn 8:44 a.m.) With the moon moving into your sign, you feel empowered, your physical energy is strong, and your goals and objectives are crystalline. Use all this positive energy to fulfill your duties and obligations so tomorrow you can begin with a fresh perspective.

Monday, October 10 (Moon in Capricorn) With Uranus in Pisces, still moving retrograde through your third house, you have unconventional ideas that are original and cutting-edge. These ideas attract notice from your bosses and superiors. You may also have some unconventional ideas today regarding sex and anything else that you find pleasurable.

Tuesday, October 11 (Moon in Capricorn to Aquarius 12:05 p.m.) As the moon moves into Aquarius, finances and your earning ability are highlighted. You attend a workshop or seminar on financial planning that proves useful and provides you with information that you need. Don't obsess about finances. Just start stashing ten percent away of everything you earn and watch your savings grow.

Wednesday, October 12 (Moon in Aquarius) You consider a property for investment purposes. Don't make a decision about it today. Wait a day or two. Discuss it with your partner or get a friend's opinion.

Thursday, October 13 (Moon in Aquarius to Pisces 2:06 p.m.) As the moon joins Uranus in your third house, your ideas and your ability to communicate take a newer, more imaginative turn. You're able to work from a deeper place inside yourself to find the answers you need.

Friday, October 14 (Moon in Pisces) Expect news related to your spiritual beliefs, neighbors, or siblings. Your emotions are more out front today than usual and apparent in your communications.

Saturday, October 15 (Moon in Pisces to Aries 3:40 p.m.) By this afternoon, you're ready to get out and about to do something adventurous, perhaps even thrilling. You may be somewhat short-tempered and impatient, especially if family members don't want to go along with your agenda. Slow down. Take other people's opinions and desires into account.

Sunday, October 16 (Moon in Aries) You get into a rush today, perhaps because you're being pressured by someone at home. Ignore the pressure from others and move at your own measured pace. Be sure to turn off the stove, iron, and the coffeepot before leaving the house.

Monday, October 17 (Moon in Aries to Taurus 6:05 p.m.) The moon joins Mars in your fifth house, energizing you toward creative action. You're looking to secure and stabilize ideas and to make the abstract concrete. You're also in a sensual and amorous mood, so you and your partner steal off for a few hours together.

Tuesday, October 18 (Moon in Taurus) Stabilize and secure investments and properties. Your kids look to you to set parameters on their activities. With Mars and the moon touring the fifth house together, you pursue pleasure for the sake of pleasure.

Wednesday, October 19 (Moon in Taurus to Gemini 10:45 p.m.) You're in a high cycle day. Your lucky numbers are 1 and 10. Even if you don't feel like a leader, it's how other people see you today, and this allows you to move forward with your plans. Enlist the help of coworkers.

Thursday, October 20 (Moon in Gemini) Team efforts are called for. Make sure that your team consists of people who know how to speak their minds clearly and that they hold the same values about a project that you do. Listen to other people's opinions and gather all the information you need. Line up your defenses. Tomorrow, make your decision.

Friday, October 21 (Moon in Gemini) Social activities are today's focus. You get together with friends this evening and head out of town for a change of scenery. Your network of friends and acquaintances expands through the Internet and an e-mail loop in which you participate. A close friend provides a lead to information you need.

Saturday, October 22 (Moon in Gemini to Cancer 6:42 a.m.) Your intimate partnerships are highlighted. You and your new romantic interest attend a party and spend the entire evening wrapped up in each other. Is the relationship moving to a deeper level? Are you ready to commit?

Sunday, October 23 (Moon in Cancer) A day at home is heightened by visits from other family members. You feel more emotionally vulnerable than usual and should be careful that you don't take casual remarks as personal affronts.

Monday, October 24 (Moon in Cancer to Leo 5:49 p.m.) You feel extremely generous today; your warmth and magnetism attract new allies, friends, and perhaps even a new lover. A child needs your support and advice, or you consult a child for an opinion on something.

Tuesday, October 25 (Moon in Leo) Jupiter moves into Scorpio today. This brings the focus on your aspirations, your wishes and dreams, and your group associations. To get a sense of what this may mean for you, look back at what was happening in your life twelve years ago. Jupiter always brings expansion and luck to whatever part of your chart it touches.

Wednesday, October 26 (Moon in Leo)   Today you feel a strange sense of relief, as if an inner tectonic plate has shifted. The cause? Pluto, the great transformer, is moving direct again in your twelfth house. It will now be easier for you to use what you've learned these past months about yourself in a focused, powerful way.

Thursday, October 27 (Moon in Leo to Virgo 6:29 a.m.)   As the moon moves into your ninth house, your business expands into the foreign market. It's also possible that foreign-born individuals play important roles in your life today.

Friday, October 28 (Moon in Virgo)   Tend to details today. You're asked to solve a problem, and you're able to do it by using your insight into problem-solving as a process. You ground the problem and find a pragmatic resolution.

Saturday, October 29 (Moon in Virgo to Libra 6:15 p.m.)   Women are helpful in terms of your profession and career. Your mother may even play a role in today's events and experiences, perhaps by doing nothing more than giving you sound advice! Travel related to business is also a distinct possibility.

Sunday, October 30—Daylight Saving Time Ends (Moon in Libra)   Mercury moves into Sagittarius today, joining Pluto in your twelfth house. Your conscious mind turns toward ferreting out issues and concerns, belief or habits, deeply ingrained in your conscious mind. You're looking for the bigger picture of your hidden self right now.

Monday, October 31 (Moon in Libra) Neptune went direct last week in your second house. You're better able to understand the connection now between your spiritual values and your financial values. Happy Halloween!

NOVEMBER 2005

Tuesday, November 1 (Moon in Libra to Scorpio 2:29 a.m.) Early this morning, you get a taste of the kind of cooperation that will be required of you today. It will involve groups, friends, and professional associates. Intense emotional experiences are likely.

Wednesday, November 2 (Moon in Scorpio) You investigate something that has puzzled you about yourself. What are your true motives about an issue or situation? Why do you have this motive? Does this motive benefit you or anyone else? If the belief behind this motive no longer serves you, strive to change it.

Thursday, November 3 (Moon in Scorpio to Sagittarius 8:55 a.m.) You uncover something related to your worldview, politics, or spiritual beliefs that surprises you. This discovery helps you to realign your beliefs and frees up energy that can be used in a positive manner.

Friday, November 4 (Moon in Sagittarius) Jury duty may come calling. Or a legal issue is brewing behind the scenes. If you fall in love today—and there's an excellent possibility that you will—the relationship may be a secret love affair. If you don't mind conducting a relationship hidden from the rest of the world, go for it. Otherwise, you had better question whether this is the right move to make in your personal life.

Saturday, November 5 (Moon in Sagittarius to Capricorn 1:17 p.m.) With the moon in your sign, it's unlikely that you make a wrong move today. Your emotions are right in line with your self-expression, and you may, in fact, be more emotional than you are at other times during the month. That's okay. Just go with the flow.

Sunday, November 6 (Moon in Capricorn) You can win big today as long as you demonstrate self-confidence and self-reliance. It's vital that your personal appearance and elegance stand out in any crowd. You catch the eye of someone you meet under unusual circumstances.

Monday, November 7 (Moon in Capricorn to Aquarius 4:31 p.m.) You find some new Web sites that are gold mines for the work you're doing. The ideas on the sites are fresh and exciting. When you apply these ideas to your own life, especially at home, you are surprised that the ideas actually work!

Tuesday, November 8 (Moon in Aquarius) Your visionary abilities now are strong, and you're able to translate these visions and ideas into concrete realities. You, like the other earth signs, are immensely capable of making the abstract practical and useful.

Wednesday, November 9 (Moon in Aquarius to Pisces 7:23 p.m.) The moon and Uranus are now traveling together through your third house, so expect the unexpected. Sudden events and situations arise that affect you emotionally, but they allow you to shake off outdated habits and beliefs.

Thursday, November 10 (Moon in Pisces) You heal a rift with a sibling or other relatives. Forgive and forget is always the best policy. Too bad our politicians haven't learned that yet!

Friday, November 11 (Moon in Pisces to Aries 10:23 p.m.) Lovely Venus joins Jupiter in your eleventh house today. You may meet a new love interest through a family member or through your friends; the relationship is sexually explosive right from the start. You feel as if a rug has been jerked out from under you, and while the sensation of falling is scary, it's also exhilarating!

Saturday, November 12 (Moon in Aries) Passion runs through your domestic life. This can be the love sort of passion or the temper kind of passion. If it's the latter, resist saying something you'll regret. Keep your bluntness in check and strive to be patient.

Sunday, November 13 (Moon in Aries) You launch new ideas today; some of them have to do with the domestic scene. Maybe it's time for your kids to start doing their part in the household chores. Or perhaps you and your partner need to shuffle around household responsibilities. Just proceed gently, listening to everyone else's opinions.

Monday, November 14 (Moon in Aries to Taurus 2:04 a.m.) Oops, here it comes. Another Mercury retrograde. Communication tends to get fouled up, travel plans can go awry, and it's best not to sign contracts. This one goes retrograde in your twelfth house, indicating that you dive into your own unconscious.

Tuesday, November 15 (Moon in Taurus) You feel a subtle shift in energies today, a definite shift for the better. It's Uranus, going direct finally in your third house. This highlights your communication abilities, relationships with your siblings, other relatives, and neighbors. It's now easier to use your imagination to achieve concrete results.

Wednesday, November 16 (Moon in Taurus to Gemini 7:11 a.m.) A busy workday. Phones ring, e-mails pile up, and it seems you can't work quickly enough to do everything you're supposed to do. Instead of driving yourself nuts, head to the gym on your lunch hour. Do something to keep yourself physically fit.

Thursday, November 17 (Moon in Gemini) News concerning a project and a physical checkup. Both are positive. Your focus now is on routine tasks, books, and communication.

Friday, November 18 (Moon in Gemini to Cancer 2:43 p.m.) With the moon in your seventh house, it's a great weekend to get away with your partner or current love interest. The weekend favors intimate exchanges and being near water.

Saturday, November 19 (Moon in Cancer) If you opted to stay home this weekend, it's time to arrange your office so it's functional and comfortable. Use feng shui principles for the arrangement of furniture and the colors your use for decorating. Pay close attention to the various directions for the placement of objects and colors.

Sunday, November 20 (Moon in Cancer) Your nurturing instincts extend to your animal companions. Take your kids to one of the local pet stores to find holistic products and foods for your pets. This can be an instructional time for the kids. Make the day count.

Monday, November 21 (Moon in Cancer to Leo 1:10 a.m.) Your emotional experiences are powerful. You're attracted to people who cause you to feel things you haven't felt in quite this way before. There may be some conflict over jointly held property.

Tuesday, November 22 (Moon in Leo) Saturn turns retrograde today in Leo, in the eighth house. During this period, which lasts through the end of the year, you may come into conflict with your father, an authority figure, or your spouse about inheritances, jointly held properties, alimony, child support, or taxes. It's not as if all this stuff happens in a single day, but it's to your advantage to be aware that these events are possibilities.

Wednesday, November 23 (Moon in Leo to Virgo 1:42 p.m.) You crave a break from your routine and may call in sick to work or take a vacation day. This is probably a good thing to do in the long run, because you feel restless and unsettled.

Thursday, November 24 (Moon in Virgo) You sign up for a workshop or a seminar. Long-distance travel is also a possibility. News concerning publishing, publicity, or advertising.

Friday, November 25 (Moon in Virgo) On this high cycle day, your thoughts turn to details related to finances, money, and power. Don't be overbearing with others. Embrace the new.

Saturday, November 26 (Moon in Virgo to Libra 1:58 a.m.) You may be tested in a professional sense today. This isn't a negative thing unless you have something to hide or you haven't been forthright with your professional peers and coworkers.

Sunday, November 27 (Moon in Libra) You have your finger on the public pulse right. If you listen carefully to that pulse and deliver what the public wants, you're the winner.

Monday, November 28 (Moon in Libra to Scorpio 11:33 a.m.) Friends are important today. Your emotional connection to a particular group of friends holds together a vital part of your life and spirit. Honor that connection.

Tuesday, November 29 (Moon in Scorpio) Take a good hard look at your goals. Do they fit with where you are in your life today? Do they feel right to you? Are they *your* goals as opposed to goals your family has thrust on you?

Wednesday, November 30 (Moon in Scorpio to Sagittarius 5:33 p.m.) You may withdraw emotionally from others this afternoon. There's nothing wrong with this, as long as you don't withdraw because you want to hide. Besides, right now you've got a lot going on in your life and need to be as up front as possible.

DECEMBER 2005

Thursday, December 1 (Moon in Sagittarius) Be aware that patterns and behaviors laid down in childhood may be surfacing now. If you don't deal with these issues, they can interfere with your present relationships.

Friday, December 2 (Moon in Sagittarius to Capricorn 8:43 p.m.) As the moon moves into your sign tonight, you get into the flow. You feel and think better and become more centered. It's a high cycle day, and your leadership is never questioned.

Saturday, December 3 (Moon in Capricorn) Your goal is harmony. It may be difficult to achieve without cooperation on your part. But if you're willing to listen and at least consider options, you may discover there are other ways of getting a job done or accomplishing a goal. Your way, Capricorn, isn't always the best way! Mercury goes direct today—good news for everyone.

Sunday, December 4 (Moon in Capricorn to Aquarius 10:37 p.m.) Your personal values come under scrutiny or attack today. Either way, you need to defend what you value and to be able to explain why you value what you do. You come out ahead; by the end of the day, you have a deeper understanding of your own values.

Monday, December 5 (Moon in Aquarius) Some unusual events related to money and your finances occur today. Stay abreast of your stock portfolio and your investments. Balance your checkbook. If you don't like the deal you're getting from your bank, find another institution that provides better service or terms.

Tuesday, December 6 (Moon in Aquarius) You can increase your earning potential when the moon moves through your second house. But to do this, you must not be timid about using your imagination to buck the trends.

Wednesday, December 7 (Moon in Aquarius to Pisces 12:45 a.m.) It's a good day to concentrate on immediate and pressing tasks. Don't let opportunities slip away; seize them the moment you recognize them. Siblings and neighbors feature in the picture.

Thursday, December 8 (Moon in Pisces) Narrow your sights today and concentrate on the many small tasks that have to be done before the end of the year. You move around your local area with self-confidence. You may even taken in a couple of stray animals.

Friday, December 9 (Moon in Pisces to Aries 4:03 a.m.) Mars goes direct today in your fifth house. The accent is on your creativity, your children, and everything you do for pleasure. You're likely to enjoy physical exercise today, so a visit to the gym or a yoga class is in order.

Saturday, December 10 (Moon in Aries) As the moon moves into your fourth house, you feel impatient. Today is a great day to work off that restlessness. Take a long drive or go skiing.

Sunday, December 11 (Moon in Aries to Taurus 8:47 a.m.) The day moves along at a steady pace. You have the time and luxury to chat with friends, surf the Net, and then work on your novel or screenplay or fatten up your art portfolio. In other words, today is for pleasure.

Monday, December 12 (Moon in Taurus) This is a sensual placement for the moon, and if you haven't had a chance to indulge yourself in any sensuality lately, you'll do a lot of it today. It won't be just sex, but sensuality in terms of all your senses.

Tuesday, December 13 (Moon in Taurus to Gemini 3:00 p.m.) This afternoon, you move from a rather self-absorbed place to a very social place in your life. Suddenly, you're a people person, flitting around the office to touch base with coworkers, chatting with friends on the phone, and sending e-mails. You're solidifying your network of contacts.

Wednesday, December 14 (Moon in Gemini) A busy day. Your communication skills are nothing short of exceptional, but you may talk and move too quickly. Slow down, take a deep breath, and make a list of what you want to accomplish today. Then move in an organized, systematic fashion.

Thursday, December 15 (Moon in Gemini to Cancer 11:01 p.m.) Venus moves into Aquarius today, blessing you with financial good fortune through the end of the year. With Jupiter moving through your house of wishes and dreams as well, this could mean a windfall in terms of money.

Friday, December 16 (Moon in Cancer) Your partnerships may need attention today. This applies to both personal and professional partnerships, so take stock of which it might be and act accordingly. Your home is also highlighted in some way.

Saturday, December 17 (Moon in Cancer) Steal off with your significant other and get down to the heart of where things stand between you. While you're at it, take the lead in this exchange. Don't be timid about expressing your feeling and beliefs. The more honest you are, the better things work.

Sunday, December 18 (Moon in Cancer to Leo 9:18 a.m.) A domestic issue requires that you listen, cooperate, and compromise. And after you've done that, hit the mall to finish up last-minute shopping.

Monday, December 19 (Moon in Leo) Contact your accountant and find out what tax write-offs you need before the end of the year. Make sure you've paid insurance premiums and taxes.

Tuesday, December 20 (Moon in Leo to Virgo 9:39 p.m.) Your foreign clients need attention today concerning details about your mutual arrangement. You're good at problem-solving, so get to it!

Wednesday, December 21 (Moon in Virgo) The moon in Virgo feels almost as comfortable to you as the moon in Taurus or your own sign. You're able to take abstract thoughts and feelings and make them concrete, practical, and ultimately useful. Face it, Capricorn, you love what is practical!

Thursday, December 22 (Moon in Virgo) As Christmas draws closer, it's time to scrutinize the details of your life and give thanks for all that you have. Spiritual issues and feelings are prevalent today. Give peace a chance.

Friday, December 23 (Moon in Virgo to Libra 10:27 a.m.) Whether you're still at work or on vacation, the moon in your tenth house highlights your profession and professional relationships. You may be put to a test of some kind. Are you up to the challenge? Of course you are. Capricorn always loves a challenge.

Saturday, December 24 (Moon in Libra) With Venus turning retrograde in your second house, you may encounter a glitch in your finances. It can certainly be resolved, but it may take a bit of effort. Be careful that you and your partner don't argue about money.

Sunday, December 25 (Moon in Libra to Scorpio 9:04 p.m.) Merry Christmas! The moon joins Jupiter in your eleventh house. This makes for an enjoyable day, although occasionally emotions will be intense. Your friends are important to you at this time. Honor them.

Monday, December 26 (Moon in Scorpio) An emotionally powerful experience occurs. Ride the waves, Capricorn. This shall pass, but not until you have integrated the emotions into who you are.

Tuesday, December 27 (Moon in Scorpio) You beat out the competition. A boss or a top executive makes a surprise visit and you're prepared. You win kudos for your preparation and knowledge.

Wednesday, December 28 (Moon in Scorpio to Sagittarius 3:45 a.m.) You may be ready for the therapist's couch! After the holidays are over and the visitors have gone home, you feel a bit worn-out and frayed at the edges. If you don't have a therapist, head out of town for some fun!

Thursday, December 29 (Moon in Sagittarius) Organize your thoughts and tasks today. It's a good time to list your goals and resolutions for the new year. Make them reachable!

Friday, December 30 (Moon in Sagittarius to Capricorn 6:36 a.m.) What a great way to end the year, with the moon in your sign. You're on in every sense of the word: speaking and thinking clearly and getting your ideas and your feelings across.

Saturday, December 31 (Moon in Capricorn) Celebrate with the people you love. It doesn't get much simpler than that, does it?

HAPPY NEW YEAR!

JANUARY 2006

Sunday, January 1 (Moon in Capricorn to Aquarius 7:15 a.m.) You greet the day with eagerness and enthusiasm. It's a new year, after all, and you're determined to make this the best year ever. A financial break may come to you in the next few weeks.

Monday, January 2 (Moon in Aquarius) The transiting moon joins Neptune in Aquarius, giving the day a kind of fuzzy, ethereal texture. You have good ideas, though, and the challenge is to get them down on paper. Eccentric neighbors may be dropping by without notice.

Tuesday, January 3 (Moon in Aquarius to Pisces 7:44 a.m.) Mercury moves into your sign today, so your mind is much clearer than yesterday. You're planning and strategizing for the future, but your emotions may get in the way.

Wednesday, January 4 (Moon in Pisces) You delve into your imagination to find the answers you need. You're able to follow your intuition on matters of the heart, and this saves you time and aggravation in the long run. A sibling or another relative plays a large role in your life today.

Thursday, January 5 (Moon in Pisces to Aries 9:45 a.m.) Your mother has something to tell you, and you would do well to listen. Her advice is sound. Even if you've got your own ideas about how to proceed, she has been on the planet a lot longer than you. Resist your own impatience.

Friday, January 6 (Moon in Aries) You're feeling reckless and courageous today. Maybe it's time to get out of town for a breather. If you can leave early from work, by all means do so.

Saturday, January 7 (Moon in Aries to Taurus 2:09 p.m.) With the transiting moon forming a harmonious angle to your sun, you feel more grounded and capable today. Your physical energy is good too, and you tackle projects with a vengeance.

Sunday, January 8 (Moon in Taurus) Creative and romantic passions mark the day. Dust off that manuscript you stuck in a drawer, get out that screenplay, and let your creative passions have their say. And while you're at it, you and your romantic partner should set aside time for yourselves.

Monday, January 9 (Moon in Taurus to Gemini 8:59 p.m.) This evening, you may be feeling out of sorts for a while. Your mind is active, but too focused on work you should have done last week. Forget last week. Focus on now.

Tuesday, January 10 (Moon in Gemini) It's time to get out to do some publicity and promotion for your company or product. Do it before Mercury turns retrograde in early March. You may want to treat yourself to a book you've been eyeing.

Wednesday, January 11 (Moon in Gemini) Yesterday's book is today's joy. You're finding ideas and answers to questions you didn't even know you had. You and a coworker team up for a project, and you keep working after hours. Is romance a possibility?

Thursday, January 12 (Moon in Gemini to Cancer 5:50 a.m.) You wake this morning with partnership issues at the forefront of your mind. You must decide—whether the relationship is business or personal—if it can work. Follow your intuitive guidance on this one.

Friday, January 13 (Moon in Cancer) You and your partner cocoon at home this evening. Neither of you is in a party mood, and you're able to talk honestly with each other about stuff that's been bothering you.

Saturday, January 14 (Moon in Cancer to Leo 4:31 p.m.) You attend a workshop or seminar on something as mundane as taxes and estate planning—or on some esoteric subject that intrigues you. If your partner is experiencing financial difficulties or delays now, don't despair. You'll be able to pick up the slack!

Sunday, January 15 (Moon in Leo) You could be feeling a bit down in the dumps today, maybe because of a demand someone makes on you or due to a responsibility that gets dumped in your lap. Just do the work and move on.

Monday, January 16 (Moon in Leo) With Venus moving retrograde through your sign, your love life may feel confusing. This feeling won't last, however, and you can look forward to a much better time in February. In fact, mark February 4 on your calendar now.

Tuesday, January 17 (Moon in Leo to Virgo 4:49 a.m.) Publishing or higher education is today's issue. Or perhaps you've been called for jury duty. Energy manifests itself early on in the day, though, allowing you to plan accordingly. Take advantage of it.

Wednesday, January 18 (Moon in Virgo) Your attention to detail is extraordinary. You're able to piece together seemingly disparate bits of information and connect the dots. This information may concern your spiritual beliefs or worldview.

Thursday, January 19 (Moon in Virgo to Libra 5:50 p.m.) By late this afternoon, some professional issue surfaces. You aren't sure how to deal with it and put off your decision until tomorrow. That's the smart thing to do.

Friday, January 20 (Moon in Libra) Yesterday's issue now appears in a clear light. You're able to find the right balance and proceed with fairness for all concerned. This evening, you take in a museum or a new art film and let the workweek fall away from you.

Saturday, January 21 (Moon in Libra) You're on the hunt today for a gift for someone special, perhaps a boss or professional peer. You hit bookstores, jewelry shops, garage sales, antique stores. Follow your eye for beauty, Capricorn, and you won't go wrong with the purchase.

Sunday, January 22 (Moon in Libra to Scorpio 5:30 a.m.) Mercury moves into Aquarius today. In the next couple of weeks, news arrives concerning your finances. Your in box is filled to overflowing with e-mails, and it's not just spam! Somewhere in there is an e-mail from someone special!

Monday, January 23 (Moon in Scorpio) Any work you do before the public is well-received. If you're a teacher, it's a terrific day. If you're in sales, your sales increase. The day is about emotional expansion as well.

Tuesday, January 24 (Moon in Scorpio to Sagittarius 1:39 p.m.) This afternoon, you're looking for the bigger picture related to some personal issue. Perhaps you have buried an emotion in the past, and now it's surfacing to haunt you. Deal with it the best way you can.

Wednesday, January 25 (Moon in Sagittarius) You may find the answers you need in a book or through talking to a trusted friend. If you've got the itch to travel now, wait until February, when Venus is moving direct in your sign.

Thursday, January 26 (Moon in Sagittarius to Capricorn 5:32 p.m.) The moon is finally in your sign again, and that makes today a power day! Your inner and outer selves are very much in sync, and gone is the angst that often plagues you. Enjoy!

Friday, January 27 (Moon in Capricorn) Whatever you're planning now demands all your organizational skills. You're the one people call on to get things done. So be flattered rather than annoyed by your additional responsibilities. Remember this is a power day for you. Use it wisely.

Saturday, January 28 (Moon in Capricorn to Aquarius 6:10 p.m.) You may be feeling vulnerable about money, and finances in general. Just keep those dollars stashed away, Capricorn, and watch your savings grow. But remember to have fun too!

Sunday, January 29 (Moon in Aquarius) Some cutting-edge idea seizes you and won't let go. Rather than resist, investigate it. Gather your facts. Explore the idea with friends and family. It may turn out to be something you can use in your business or personal life.

Monday, January 30 (Moon in Aquarius to Pisces 5:32 p.m.) Your emotions today are rather erratic and unpredictable; they feel somewhat uncomfortable to you. Perhaps you need to take a second look at something that's going on in your neighborhood or with your siblings.

Tuesday, January 31 (Moon in Pisces) Indulge your artistic talents today. Get out your easel, your camera, or your dancing shoes! Your imagination is as vast as the Pacific; you can use it to find answers and information that you need. While you're at it, you may want to beautify your home office with new paint and new curtains.

FEBRUARY 2006

Wednesday, February 1 (Moon in Pisces to Aries 5:46 p.m.) If your love life is in disarray, hang on just a little longer. On February 4, Venus turns direct again. On the home front, it's a good day to take your time and nurture patience. You'll need it.

Thursday, February 2 (Moon in Aries) You're feeling daring today; make your affections known. The person to whom you're attracted is also attracted to you. Passions heat up. Is this the beginning of a romance or an affair—does the distinction even matter?

Friday, February 3 (Moon in Aries to Taurus 8:31 p.m.) Venus turns direct today. Welcome news for your finances—and for your love life. For the rest of the month, both your money and your love life improve. Your sensuality is now quite prevalent.

Saturday, February 4 (Moon in Taurus) Be stubborn today about issues that really matter. Don't change your mind just to suit your relatives or neighbors. Once they know you stick to what you believe, they'll back off.

Sunday, February 5 (Moon in Taurus) If other people think you're a pushover, they won't today. Their perspective on you changes. It's actually a great day to chill at home, have a gourmet dinner, and read a good book. You may want to get to the gym too.

Monday, February 6 (Moon in Taurus to Gemini 2:33 a.m.) You're of two minds about work today. Part of you longs for more activity, and another part of you just wants to be get out and socialize. Save the socializing for after hours and don't fall prey to gossip.

Tuesday, February 7 (Moon in Gemini) You're feeling restless and undecided about your work. Is it time to look for daily work that's more satisfying? If so, then get out your résumés, make some calls, and draw on the resources you have.

Wednesday, February 8 (Moon in Gemini to Cancer 11:34 a.m.) Mercury moves into Pisces today, forming a harmonious angle to your sun. Your dreamy mood is noticed by the people around you; they actually enjoy this softer side of you. Avoid overindulgence in food and alcohol. Your intuitive abilities are especially strong today.

Thursday, February 9 (Moon in Cancer) Home, hearth, Mom, and your partner all feature in the day's events. You may be exploring security issues, specifically what makes you feel most safe. Figure out what it is; then try to manifest those conditions in your own life.

Friday, February 10 (Moon in Cancer to Leo 10:45 p.m.) Late today, the moon moves into Leo; dramas begin to unfold in your mind. These dramas creep up on you in the middle of the night, when you lie awake and worry about this and that. Turn over, shut your eyes, and count backward from a hundred. Worrying never solves anything.

Saturday, February 11 (Moon in Leo) Today's venue features both the elderly and the young. How do you fit into this picture? You're called upon to give advice about taxes, insurance, or wills.

Sunday, February 12 (Moon in Leo) You're in a more playful mood today; this doesn't escape the notice of the people with whom you live. Keep the dramas to a minimum, Capricorn. It's Sunday, after all, the day of rest!

Monday, February 13 (Moon in Leo to Virgo 11:14 a.m.) The Virgo moon usually feels comfortable to you. You're more grounded, precise, and detailed in everything you do. The one drawback is that you may be more self-critical or more critical of others. Watch yourself on that last item. The qualities we criticize in others are often the qualities we ourselves have.

Tuesday, February 14 (Moon in Virgo) You may be poring over college brochures or researching colleges online. Higher-education opportunities interest you today. It's also Valentine's Day, so be sure to remember the people you love!

Wednesday, February 15 (Moon in Virgo) If the winter blues have you down, do something special for yourself this afternoon or this evening. Sometimes, special can be as simple as treating yourself to an ice-cream cone or some books.

Thursday, February 16 (Moon in Virgo to Libra 12:10 a.m.) It's a good day to balance things in your career—or, at any rate, to attempt to balance them. You want to be fair and just to everyone involved, but aren't quite sure how to go about it. It's a process, Capricorn. Just go from A to Z.

Friday, February 17 (Moon in Libra) Mars moves into Gemini today, infusing your work routine with new energy. It's kind of like a mental booster rocket that propels you in exciting new directions. Until mid-April, you may be short on patience with coworkers.

Saturday, February 18 (Moon in Libra to Scorpio 12:12 p.m.) Your intensity could get you into trouble today. Back off a little, give the other person space to breathe and think, and revisit the issue on February 24. Tend to your own aspirations. It's safer that way.

Sunday, February 19 (Moon in Scorpio) You're seeking the bottom line concerning a friendship. It could be that one or both of you has outgrown the relationship. That's okay, Capricorn. Change is constant.

Monday, February 20 (Moon in Scorpio to Sagittarius 9:38 p.m.) You spend time today planning a trip for the summer. You're hungry to visit some exotic locale, and right now, you're thinking the more exotic it is, the better! So indulge your fantasy. Do some research online.

Tuesday, February 21 (Moon in Sagittarius) With Mars in Gemini opposed to the moon, you may be feeling temperamental and out of sorts. Get to the root of what makes you feel that way and by February 23, your disposition will be 100 percent improved!

Wednesday, February 22 (Moon in Sagittarius) Your spirituality is something you deal with today. Perhaps a childhood issue that puzzles you comes to light. Now is the time to resolve it, understand it—and release it. Each month, you have a chance to dig deep and clear away cobwebs. Today is one of those days.

Thursday, February 23 (Moon in Sagittarius to Capricorn 3:16 a.m.) With the moon finally moving into your sign early this morning, you awaken refreshed, full of optimism and ambition. Today you can make anything happen—and you probably do!

Friday, February 24 (Moon in Capricorn) Another power day! You're in the driver's seat; as long as you don't let all this power to go to your head, you'll achieve everything you set out to do. You may be so efficient, in fact, that you can knock off early from work.

Saturday, February 25 (Moon in Capricorn to Aquarius 5:15 a.m.) Friends and groups of people are important in the day's scheme. You may be joining a new group of like-minded individuals. You all may not change the world in a single day, but you may change the way one person thinks, and that's a good beginning.

Sunday, February 26 (Moon in Aquarius) How far can you take an idea? It's the day's gauntlet for you,

Capricorn, and you're busy in the back room, brainstorming with coworkers or friends about how to implement something new. It won't all get done today, but you're off to a positive start.

Monday, February 27 (Moon in Aquarius to Pisces 4:56 a.m.) Whenever the moon joins Uranus in Pisces, things feel weird, but not necessarily in a bad way. As with most inner conditions, your perspective determines whether a situation or event is positive or negative.

Tuesday, February 28 (Moon in Pisces) Today you definitely hear the beat of a different drummer. And who's to say you shouldn't follow that tune if you're so inclined? End the month on a positive note and move into March with the notion that you write the script of your own life.

MARCH 2006

Wednesday, March 1 (Moon in Pisces to Aries 4:19 a.m.) Unexpected visitors are a possibility. Even though you don't like disruptions in your schedule, you should enjoy this visit. Try to go with the flow; you'll be happier. Passions heat up at home.

Thursday, March 2 (Moon in Aries) Mercury turns retrograde in Pisces today, the first Mercury retrograde of the year. Until March 26, be absolutely clear in your communications—written or spoken. If you have to sign contracts, do so with the understanding that you may have to revisit the details later. Try to postpone travel plans until after March 28.

Friday, March 3 (Moon in Aries to Taurus 5:23 a.m.) It's a good day for romance, creative endeavors, and pleasure—not necessarily in that order. The transiting moon is forming a harmonious angle with your sun, which is the universe's way of telling you to get out there an enjoy yourself!

Saturday, March 4 (Moon in Taurus) Jupiter turns retrograde in Scorpio today, driving this planet's expansive energy inward. Over the course of the next four months, you'll be rethinking your spiritual beliefs and shifting things around in your worldview.

Sunday, March 5 (Moon in Taurus to Gemini 9:38 a.m.) Venus moves into Aquarius, a nice plus for you in the romance and financial departments. Despite the Mercury retrograde, you're able to move ahead with your personal plans and goals in other areas of your life.

Monday, March 6 (Moon in Gemini) Your mind and intellectual interests rule the day. You're in a talkative mood too, which pleases your coworkers because you come up with ideas that others can use.

Tuesday, March 7 (Moon in Gemini to Cancer 5:39 p.m.) Your intuition soars today, particularly as it relates to your home and children. Your mother may come into the picture today, perhaps with some words of advice or small nuggets of wisdom.

Wednesday, March 8 (Moon in Cancer) Today you explore security issues. You may be feeling vulnerable and want to know exactly why. Are you in a relationship that no longer works smoothly? Is there an issue at home that baffles you? Whatever it is, get to the bottom of it.

Thursday, March 9 (Moon in Cancer) The process that began when Jupiter turned retrograde continues today, part of an internal process that compels you to clarify your personal beliefs. You may just want to keep your thoughts to yourself for a while.

Friday, March 10 (Moon in Cancer to Leo 4:43 a.m.) An elderly relative or friend may need your help and support today. Give freely of your time and energy and remember that what you give returns to you threefold.

Saturday, March 11 (Moon in Leo) Today's events may call for some acting on your part. You can play a role when you need to, and today's role calls for diplomacy. Make it happen!

Sunday, March 12 (Moon in Leo to Virgo 5:24 p.m.) You're more grounded today. You have an agenda, and you are determined to accomplish everything on your life. By the end of the day, you'll have earned some R and R.

Monday, March 13 (Moon in Virgo) It's time for a health checkup and to do some of the things you've been procrastinating about. If you get called for jury duty today or tomorrow, try not to resist. It may prove to be creative fodder at some point in the near future.

Tuesday, March 14 (Moon in Virgo) Another earth sign plays a part in your life today: a Virgo or a Taurus. If just a friend, the person may become something more rather quickly. You don't have any shortage of things to talk about with this new romantic interest, and that's always good.

Wednesday, March 15 (Moon in Virgo to Libra 6:13 a.m.) Early this morning, the moon moves into Libra and your solar tenth house. This transit brings about a need for balance and fairness and heightens your aesthetic tastes. An issue may surface that requires your immediate attention, but you handle it with your usual aplomb.

Thursday, March 16 (Moon in Libra) There's something about this moon that brings out the romantic in you. Who will be the object of your romantic affections? A coworker? A peer? You have plenty of choices!

Friday, March 17 (Moon in Libra to Scorpio 5:59 p.m.) When the moon joins Jupiter in Scorpio, your emotions expand. Some things are blown out of proportion, but your feelings and intuition deepen considerably. Listen closely to what your hunches tell you—then make your move.

Saturday, March 18 (Moon in Scorpio) Friends and groups are highlighted. An emotional issue concerning a friendship could surface today. Simply take it in stride, and promise yourself that tomorrow will be a better day!

Sunday, March 19 (Moon in Scorpio) Your sexuality is heightened today, and someone who has been a friend could become a lover. Don't push things, Capricorn. Let events unfold on their own. In the end, you'll be glad that you did.

Monday, March 20 (Moon in Scorpio to Sagittarius 3:43 a.m.) Put your travel planning on hold until after Mercury turns direct on March 25. Otherwise, you may find that your plans have unraveled and you have to start at the beginning again. In the meantime, do your research. Use the Internet to virtual travel.

Tuesday, March 21 (Moon in Sagittarius) Create a list of stocks you might like to buy. Follow them in the Internet for a month. Study their rises and falls in price. When the moon is in Capricorn, decide which ones to buy. Right after that, when the moon moves into Aquarius, make your purchases—as long as the stocks are performing well, of course!

Wednesday, March 22 (Moon in Sagittarius to Capricorn 10:36 a.m.) Here it is again, a power day! The moon is in your sign, and you're primed for adventure. You feel sexy, other people are attracted to your buoyant personality, and you're pretty much on top of the world.

Thursday, March 23 (Moon in Capricorn) If you don't already have an exercise routine, start one today. Select an activity that you know you can sustain; then go for it. Set a specific length of time—a month, for instance—and then see where you would like to go with the routine after that.

Friday, March 24 (Moon in Capricorn to Aquarius 2:22 p.m.) By this evening, you need recharging. It may be the perfect time to stay at home and chill out on movies, a favorite book, or even with your kids.

Saturday, March 25 (Moon in Aquarius) Mercury turns direct again in Pisces. Life improves now—maybe not in major ways, but certainly in smaller, significant ways that concern daily life. Oh, it's safe to travel and to sit at the barter table once again.

Sunday, March 26 (Moon in Aquarius to Pisces 3:33 p.m.) When the moon joins Mercury in Pisces, your mind and your heart are pretty much in agreement. You may want to plan something special for today.

Monday, March 27 (Moon in Pisces) You could be feeling somewhat erratic today. That's okay. This mood shakes you out of a rut and urges you to think in new, innovative ways.

Tuesday, March 28 (Moon in Pisces to Aries 3:32 p.m.) Your home and personal life are highlighted as the moon moves into Aries. You could be feeling restless and unsettled, so get out and burn up energy.

Wednesday, March 29 (Moon in Aries) Pluto turns retrograde in Sagittarius today. The effects of this movement are subtle, with the planet's powerful energy driven inward. You may be dealing with power issues during the next few months.

Thursday, March 30 (Moon in Aries to Taurus 4:02 p.m.) The moon's transit into sensuous Taurus is a welcome change from the fiery Aries moon. You feel solid, grounded, invincible. You uncover a pleasure that you didn't know you could enjoy!

Friday, March 31 (Moon in Taurus) If you're a freelancer of some kind, today's energies could bring you an agent or manager who is interested in promoting you and your work. Seize the day, Capricorn. You're on your way into the full heart of spring!

APRIL 2006

Saturday, April 1 (Moon in Taurus to Gemini 6:50 p.m.) You feel great under the transiting Taurus moon, more grounded and connected to yourself and your life. So, this evening, when the moon moves into Gemini, you may feel somewhat uneasy initially. However, the Gemini moon is joining Mars in your sixth house; by tomorrow, this casts a whole new light on your daily work routine.

Sunday, April 2—Daylight Saving Time Begins (Moon in Gemini) Mars is the booster rocket for your work today. Even though it's Sunday, you may spend a lot of time on the phone or writing e-mails to clarify points that need to be tackled tomorrow.

Monday, April 3 (Moon in Gemini) You're a speed demon today, moving quickly through all the items on your agenda. You manage to get everything done by the end of the day, though, and should treat yourself to something special this evening.

Tuesday, April 4 (Moon in Gemini to Cancer 2:15 a.m.) You and your partner are ready to ink a deal that has been in negotiations for a long time. Just be sure that you have the full picture and know precisely what the fine print in the contract says.

Wednesday, April 5 (Moon in Cancer) Venus moves into Pisces and remains there through the end of the month. This transit certainly favors a flirtation or a romance with a neighbor or someone you meet through a brother or sister. You feel an intuitive connection with this person. Take it slowly, Capricorn.

Thursday, April 6 (Moon in Cancer to Leo 12:26 p.m.) The transiting moon now joints retrograde Saturn in Leo. This combination may feel a bit uncomfortable. Your emotions run up against the restrictions associated with Saturn and you may feel oppressed—or depressed. An elderly person—perhaps your mother or another female relative—plays a role in the day's events.

Friday, April 7 (Moon in Leo) Be sure that your tax and insurance payments are current. While you're at it, get your tax return in the mail early this year. You may be looking into last-minute ways to save money on your return.

Saturday, April 8 (Moon in Leo) The Virgo moon is more in line with your comfort zone. Get ready for it tomorrow by lining up whatever you want to accomplish over the next two days. Perhaps your heart is telling you to head overseas or somewhere else on a trip. If so, indulge the desire.

Sunday, April 9 (Moon in Leo to Virgo 12:59 a.m.) If you opted to stay home, it's a good day to clean your closets and your office, and to practice some feng shui in the prosperity section of your house (southeast). Head over to your local bookstore for a feng shui book!

Monday, April 10 (Moon in Virgo) Publishing, higher education, and the courts play a role in the day's events. If you're a writer, this transiting moon is excellent for a final scrutiny of your manuscript.

Tuesday, April 11 (Moon in Virgo to Libra 1:47 p.m.) As the transiting moon heads into Libra and your tenth house, your focus is on career matters. You may have to act as a mediator for an issue that surfaces among your peers. This evening, you and your partner or a friend may head to a new restaurant to enjoy a gourmet meal.

Wednesday, April 12 (Moon in Libra) You're in the mood for romance today; it could be with a professional peer or even a boss. Be careful, Capricorn. It may not be wise to mix business with pleasure. A Virgo offers wise counsel.

Thursday, April 13 (Moon in Libra) Mars moves into Cancer today and remains there through the end of the month. This transit stimulates your partnerships. Passions soar. Tempers could be short.

Friday, April 14 (Moon in Libra to Scorpio 1:09 a.m.) The moon joins Jupiter in Scorpio very early today. This combination heightens your intuition, your sexuality, and your emotional life. You may be walking around filled with so many feelings and ideas that you don't know exactly what to do.

Saturday, April 15 (Moon in Scorpio) The astrological energies are a bit smoother today—or perhaps you're just more accustomed to them. You may be doing research that forces you to keep digging until you find the absolute bottom line. It's also tax day!

Sunday, April 16 (Moon in Scorpio to Sagittarius 10:20 a.m.) Mercury moves into Aries and forms a harmonious angle with the moon in Sagittarius. All this fire influence is sure to stimulate interesting conversation at home. Perhaps politics is the topic of discussion. If so, be prepared to hold tight to your position.

Monday, April 17 (Moon in Sagittarius) You're ruminating over stuff today—your stuff, your family's stuff, your partner's stuff. Everyone has issues, Capricorn, and once you accept that people resolve their issues in their own ways—rather than in *your* way—you'll be happier.

Tuesday, April 18 (Moon in Sagittarius to Capricorn 5:14 p.m.) Late this afternoon, you get a boost in energy as the moon moves into your sign. It's another power day. Plan your activities accordingly!

Wednesday, April 19 (Moon in Capricorn) Your sex appeal and charisma are on the rise today; people take notice. You attract the attention of a water sign—Cancer, Scorpio, or Pisces—and the chemistry is tangible for both of you.

Thursday, April 20 (Moon in Capricorn to Aquarius 9:57 p.m.) By this evening, you may be fretting about finances. Or perhaps your finances are fine, but you're worrying about whether you should buy a large-ticket item. What's the best brand? Where can you get the best price? Use the Internet for research; then decide.

Friday, April 21 (Moon in Aquarius) Your personal values are at the center of an issue or situation that comes up today. You defend your position with admirable grace and dignity!

Saturday, April 22 (Moon in Aquarius) Tomorrow, the moon joins Venus in Pisces, a nice combination for romance. Since it's Saturday night, you may still be awake when the moon changes signs. You may get lucky.

Sunday, April 23 (Moon in Aquarius to Pisces 12:44 a.m.) You're in the mood to beautify your neighborhood; start in your own backyard. It's spring, after all, and your yard is screaming for flowers. Maybe you should include a fountain out back this year.

Monday, April 24 (Moon in Pisces) That romance is beginning to heat up now. You and your friend have a genuine connection through your shared interest in the arts, music, or both. Have your respective natal charts drawn up to see just how compatible you are!

Tuesday, April 25 (Moon in Pisces to Aries 2:13 a.m.) Your home is a flurry of activity now. People are coming and going: your kids, partner, neighbors, your parents. All the activity begins to wear you down; by evening, you're ready to hit the gym for some time alone.

Wednesday, April 26 (Moon in Aries) The Aries moon squares your sun, a challenging angle. However, if you can use the fiery energy to your advantage, you should be able to accomplish things that have been on your to-do list for a while.

Thursday, April 27 (Moon in Aries to Taurus 3:28 a.m.) The Taurus moon fits you almost as well as the Capricorn moon. It adds sensuality, stubbornness, and a fixed determination to your personality. Use these qualities in your creative endeavors.

Friday, April 28 (Moon in Taurus) Today's creative endeavor involves children—yours or someone else's—and you may just pack up the cars with the kids and head out of town. You need the time away, and the kids instill in you a fresh sense of purpose and playfulness.

Saturday, April 29 (Moon in Taurus to Gemini 5:58 a.m.) There are lots of discussions around the dinner table tonight. You're in a communicative mood, and you're able to fire up the conversation with little effort. A Libra or a Taurus may play a role in the day's events.

Sunday, April 30 (Moon in Gemini) You wind up the month feeling pretty good about the course of life in general. But you may want to sit down to make a list of goals—personal and professional—and lay out some sort of strategy for attaining them.

MAY 2006

Monday, May 1 (Moon in Gemini to Cancer 11:18 a.m.) The month begins with the focus on your partnerships. You may be attracting some idiosyncratic people into your life who add spice and excitement and compel you to think in a different way. If you resist, you lose! Embrace the experience.

Tuesday, May 2 (Moon in Cancer) What makes you feel most secure emotionally, Capricorn? Today you may find pieces of the answer to that question. Your mother or another nurturing female in your life is helpful in this regard.

Wednesday, May 3 (Moon in Cancer to Leo 8:18 p.m.) Venus moves into Aries today, adding a nice dose of romance to your home life! If you've been trying to sell your home, at some point between now and the end of the month, you may do it. If you're house hunting, you may find the ideal home.

Thursday, May 4 (Moon in Leo) The Leo moon isn't especially comfortable for you, unless you have a fire-sign moon, but it does provide you with an opportunity to feel more expansive and dramatic. It's a good time to start the application process for a mortgage or loan.

Friday, May 5 (Moon in Leo) Mercury moves into Taurus and remains there for the next two weeks. This transit should be positive for you, with a lot of creative impetus. Your mind is unusually clear and creative now; your muse is in full attendance!

Saturday, May 6 (Moon in Leo to Virgo 8:20 a.m) Your creative high continues, and this lunar transit certainly spurs you on. Publishing and higher education are highlighted today and tomorrow. Make use of the energies!

Sunday, May 7 (Moon in Virgo) It's possible that a visitor arrives from abroad—or that you now make plans to go overseas. Today is actually a good day to play a trip because your attention to details is excellent.

Monday, May 8 (Moon in Virgo to Libra 9:10 p.m.) Career issues and concerns come up today. But so do relationship issues. You may be caught between the proverbial rock and the hard place. Mull things over and make your decision on May 16, when the moon is in your sign.

Tuesday, May 9 (Moon in Libra) This should be a good day for romance and the arts. The moon and Venus are close, and their energies are symbiotic. The person you're eyeing may be someone in the same profession or perhaps an allied profession. You'll be surprised to discover the attraction is mutual.

Wednesday, May 10 (Moon in Libra) You may go car hunting today. But instead of spending time on the road, start on the Internet, where you can price, compare, and select the kind of car you're looking for.

Thursday, May 11 (Moon in Libra to Scorpio 8:25 a.m.) You get an opportunity for promotion or publicity that you can't refuse. It could involve some travel, but that's fine with you. You're in the mood for travel, as long as it isn't frivolous.

Friday, May 12 (Moon in Scorpio) A Cancer, a Pisces, or a Scorpio plays into your affairs today. You may find a book or overhear a conversation that sheds light on a question that you have. Remain alert for synchronicities. They're like guideposts that help you make choices in your life.

Saturday, May 13 (Moon in Scorpio to Sagittarius 4:57 p.m.) You're in the mood for some solitude, and it doesn't matter where that solitude happens, as long as it does. Home might be a good spot, but better yet would be a cabin in some remote spot.

Sunday, May 14 (Moon in Sagittarius) Your creative adrenaline is flowing, and you're up to the task at hand. You get plenty of help from Venus, whose sign right now is compatible with that of the transiting moon. Settle in. Enjoy the journey!

Monday, May 15 (Moon in Sagittarius to Capricorn 11:00 p.m.)   As the moon moves into your sign later this evening, you suddenly feel that tomorrow will be a perfect day. Get plenty of rest so that you can begin tomorrow in top form.

Tuesday, May 16 (Moon in Capricorn)   Your sex appeal is on the rise. A flirtation or new romance make take, unexpected turns. Are you ready for commitment? If not, be honest about it.

Wednesday, May 17 (Moon in Capricorn)   Your self-expression is extraordinary. You take the audience by storm; it doesn't matter if the audience is an auditorium of three thousand or your e-mail group.

Thursday, May 18 (Moon in Capricorn to Aquarius 3:20 a.m.)   As the moon moves into Aquarius, you may get an unexpected check. Instead of racing out to spend the money, stash it somewhere, Capricorn, so that at the end of the year, you have cash to burn for the holidays.

Friday, May 19 (Moon in Aquarius)   Mercury moves into Gemini today, a sign that it rules. For the next few weeks, you should have more contact than usual with coworkers. Some of this contact may spill over into time after work.

Saturday, May 20 (Moon in Aquarius to Pisces 6:40 a.m.)   Your mind is exceptionally intuitive today—and also impressionable. Don't fall for a sob story! Your aesthetic sense may prompt you to run out to buy fresh paint to redo one of your rooms. Just make sure you can live with the colors you choose.

Sunday, May 21 (Moon in Pisces)   You should chill today with a good novel or a couple of DVDs you've been eager to see. Let your imagination take you places you've never been. If your muse is helpful, you may feel the need to jot down your ideas at the end of the day.

Monday, May 22 (Moon in Pisces to Aries 9:24 a.m.) Neptune turns retrograde in Aquarius and remains that way for several months. This motion drives the energy of Neptune inward. It's likely that you will be scrutinizing your personal values and your finances from a perspective very different from that which you usually do.

Tuesday, May 23 (Moon in Aries) Home is your focus today. You may have surprise visitors, or tempers may flare for some reason. Just take a deep breath and deal with the situation the way you usually do—in a quick, efficient manner.

Wednesday, May 24 (Moon in Aries to Taurus 12:01 p.m.) You find your footing regarding a creative project or an issue involving one of your kids. You're able to see not only the forest, but the trees. You may spend the evening doing something you love.

Thursday, May 25 (Moon in Taurus) It's time to indulge in whatever makes you happy. You're allowed to have fun, Capricorn; sometimes fun is really the only recourse.

Friday, May 26 (Moon in Taurus to Gemini 3:19 p.m.) The moon joins Mercury in Gemini, focusing your energy on your daily work routine, coworkers, and your health. There's more communication with coworkers today and perhaps some socializing outside of work as well.

Saturday, May 27 (Moon in Gemini) You're feeling social and outgoing; in fact, you may decide to toss a party or invite a few friends over for dinner. The discussions turn lively, and by the evening's end, everyone is raving about your party skills!

Sunday, May 28 (Moon in Gemini to Cancer 8:34 p.m.) The moon joins Mars in Cancer. This interesting combination could indicate the beginning of an affair. Your emotions may be more intense than usual, but this is balanced out by your increased intuitive awareness.

Monday, May 29 (Moon in Cancer) Venus moves into Taurus today. This transit is a wonderful sign of romance, pleasure, and a barrel of laughs and fun. It lasts into June. So enjoy yourself, Capricorn!

Tuesday, May 30 (Moon in Cancer) With the moon in Cancer and Venus in Taurus, you should be feeling exceptionally good today. Both transits are harmonious for you and ease whatever angst and annoyance you may have been feeling lately.

Wednesday, May 31 (Moon in Cancer to Leo 4:52 a.m.) As the moon moves into Leo early this morning, your kids may need additional help and support. Enjoy a day with them.

JUNE 2006

Thursday, June 1 (Moon in Leo) The lazy days of summer will soon be here. Get outside and enjoy the weather—even if it's raining! Do something entertaining with your kids today to celebrate the approach of the end of the school year.

Friday, June 2 (Moon in Leo to Virgo 4:18 p.m.) As the moon enters Virgo, you may be scheduling appointments with doctors and dentists. You better check on monthly payments to make sure you're up-to-date on everything.

Saturday, June 3 (Moon in Virgo) Mercury moves into Cancer, so for the next few weeks, your focus will be on your partnerships. You and your partners should communicate well, agree on major issues, and be able to resolve disputes easily. It's a good time to negotiate and sign contracts too.

Sunday, June 4 (Moon in Virgo) Since Mars moved into Leo yesterday, you could be feeling somewhat feisty today when it comes to *your* belongings. You may be somewhat inclined to criticize or pick on others too. Chill out, Capricorn. Tomorrow really is another day.

Monday, June 5 (Moon in Virgo to Libra 5:10 a.m.) As the moon begins its monthly transit through your tenth house, it may feel a bit lonely for you. It isn't that you're depressed—just that you can't seem to find the right balance between your career obligations and your domestic obligations.

Tuesday, June 6 (Moon in Libra) Same dilemma, different day, except that today you're more accustomed to the lunar energies. You can use this Libra energy to increase your tolerance for people who annoy you, to enhance your visual and artistic perceptions, and to mitigate disputes.

Wednesday, June 7 (Moon in Libra to Scorpio 4:42 p.m.) The moon joins Jupiter in Scorpio. This combination tends to expand what you feel, for both good and bad. Some events or situations may seem more dramatic than they really are.

Thursday, June 8 (Moon in Scorpio) You do well in front of the public. Any promotions or advertising that you do are well-received. You are able to use your intuition to zero in on the bottom line of whatever you're doing.

Friday, June 9 (Moon in Scorpio) Here's a book title for the day: *The Time Traveler's Wife.* It's a perfect Scorpio moon novel! In nonfiction, try *Entanglement,* a layman's guide to string theory. Let these ideas percolate for a while and you won't be looking at the world in the same way.

Saturday, June 10 (Moon in Scorpio to Sagittarius 1:06 a.m.) Solitude is your cup of tea for the day. You may want to settle into solitude with someone special, but if that isn't possible, you're content spending time on your own. You're looking for the larger picture of your own life.

Sunday, June 11 (Moon in Sagittarius) Take a long drive. Go to a town or city where you've never been. Explore on your own. How does this short journey change your perceptions?

Monday, June 12 (Moon in Sagittarius to Capricorn 6:20 a.m.) As the moon moves into your sign, your mood lifts, your sex appeal soars, and your inner and outer selves are in sync. Not too bad for a Monday, right?

Tuesday, June 13 (Moon in Capricorn) Your life sometimes feels like it's on a fast track, but to where? You need a destination, a goal, a plan, and now is the time to come up with one. Where would you like to be six months or five years from now?

Wednesday, June 14 (Moon in Capricorn to Aquarius 9:33 a.m.) Yesterday's questions becomes the day's concerns. And today you're better equipped to do the research, the brainstorming. In fact, you may turn to a group that shares your views and beliefs.

Thursday, June 15 (Moon in Aquarius) Your investments should be in line with your beliefs. Or at any rate, that's what you're feeling today. You may want to join an investment group.

Friday, June 16 (Moon in Aquarius to Pisces 12:06 p.m.) Wonderful things can happen for you when the moon is in Pisces. Shortly after noon, you begin to feel rather dreamy and unfocused. Your imagination takes flight and you're able to carry this feeling through the rest of the day.

Saturday, June 17 (Moon in Pisces) Your compassion reaches a high today. Just be careful that you don't fall for a sob story or a scam. You're more vulnerable now.

Sunday, June 18 (Moon in Pisces to Aries 2:54 p.m.) Uranus turns retrograde in Pisces today. The effect of this motion is subtle, driving its erratic energy inward, so that you may be reviewing your relationships with siblings and other relatives. You may also be mulling over independence issues.

Monday, June 19 (Moon in Aries) This particular moon isn't too comfortable for you, but combined with transiting Mars in Leo, you may have a fire lit beneath you and really speed through whatever you need to accomplish. The combination of these two fire transits could ignite your sexuality too.

Tuesday, June 20 (Moon in Aries to Taurus 6:23 p.m.)   By late this afternoon, you're entering that time of the month when you feel pretty good about yourself in relation to the rest of the world. Put on your best clothes, tuck some money in your pocket, and head out for an evening of fun. You've earned it.

Wednesday, June 21 (Moon in Taurus)   One drawback to the transiting moon in Taurus, at least for you, is that you may overindulge in rich foods. It's hard to resist a gourmet meal and fine wine, but you may want to keep it all in moderation so that you make it to work tomorrow.

Thursday, June 22 (Moon in Taurus to Gemini 10:49 p.m.)   You may spend a lot of today writing memos and e-mails, and talking on the phone. This intercourse could be social, but more than likely it's related to your daily work. You're just trying to get things done.

Friday, June 23 (Moon in Gemini)   Transiting Venus joins the moon in Gemini. This combination is quite nice for a flirtation or romance at work. Whoever the lucky person is, you insist on there being a mental connection between you before anything else transpires. You may feel differently in a couple of days, but that's how you feel right now.

Saturday, June 24 (Moon in Gemini)   Your mind races with ideas that may be related to some project at work. The ideas are so good, you need to jot them down—or use a recorder, if it's easier. This evening, you share the ideas with a Libra or an Aquarius.

Sunday, June 25 (Moon in Gemini to Cancer 4:48 a.m.)   You may find something you misplaced a few weeks ago. In fact, you partner may lead you to it. Follow synchronicities today. Puzzle through them until you get the message.

Monday, June 26 (Moon in Cancer)　　Your mother or another nurturing female in your life may have insights that you need. Listen with an open mind, gather your information from other sources, and then make your decision

Tuesday, June 27 (Moon in Cancer to Leo 1:10 p.m.)　　An elderly person has something to tell you. It could be your tax accountant or insurance broker. *You* aren't the point today; your shared resources are what's important.

Wednesday, June 28 (Moon in Leo)　　Mercury moves into Leo, joining the transiting moon in your solar eighth house. Your mind may turn toward esoteric topics: life after death, reincarnation, communication with the dead. If you haven't read the books by medium John Edwards, head over to your local bookstore. Another good book: *Children's Past Lives* by Carol Bowman.

Thursday, June 29 (Moon in Leo)　　Ah, finally, another moon that's comfortable for you. Take care of details today. If you've been planning an overseas trip, check your schedule and connections. Make sure everything is in order. And don't travel from July 4 to 29.

Friday, June 30 (Moon in Leo to Virgo 12:16 a.m.)　　It's nice to end a month on a day when the astrological energies support you wholeheartedly. And it's a Friday! The world is a moveable feast today.

JULY 2006

Saturday, July 1 (Moon in Virgo)　　Publishing and higher education are the day's highlights. If you've considered returning to college, now is the time to add substance to those considerations. You're good at details, so get to work figuring the angles.

Sunday, July 2 (Moon in Virgo to Libra 1:07 p.m.) Here comes that Libra moon again. It's forming a challenging angle to your sun, but because its energy is as singular as your own, it galvanizes you to action. The area of your life? Career. Get busy, Capricorn!

Monday, July 3 (Moon in Libra) A good Libra beach book? Try anything by Nora Roberts. Her J. D. Robb futuristic series is superb and certain to keep you chilled at the beach!

Tuesday, July 4 (Moon in Libra) Mercury retrogrades force us to reconsider everything that Mercury rules: communication, travel, the conscious mind, and relationships with siblings, relatives, and neighbors. It borders on bad taste that the universe sees fit to begin a Mercury retrograde on a holiday, when family is probably in attendance. Your barbecue could get rained out. Your guests may not arrive—or arrive too soon or too late. The solution? Grin and bear it—not just for today, but for the next two weeks.

Wednesday, July 5 (Moon in Libra to Scorpio 1:14 a.m.) Think positive today. You'll need to be as positive as possible. A friend or someone in your support group balks at what you have to say. But then you and this person go off together and clear the air.

Thursday, July 6 (Moon in Scorpio) Jupiter finally turns direct in Scorpio! It's good news, particularly with the moon also in this sign. Everything with your friends, dreams, and aspirations can now move forward, expanding in ways that will surprise you.

Friday, July 7 (Moon in Scorpio to Sagittarius 10:14 a.m.) The Sagittarius moon loves to party and be with people, but you may not be in the mood. You may not want to be completely alone, either, so make sure you've got support now. Go on the Internet. Communicate through e-mail.

Saturday, July 8 (Moon in Sagittarius) You sleep late and maybe overindulge in the things that you enjoy doing. Take a hike in a wooded area, go parasailing, swim, or walk. Better yet, take a swim with dolphins. You're seeking spiritual connection now, and oddly enough, dolphins may be your ticket to deeper understanding.

Sunday, July 9 (Moon in Sagittarius to Capricorn 3:25 p.m.) Here it is, your power day again! You aren't just *in* the groove—you *are* the groove. For fun and laughs, watch one of the Austin Powers movies.

Monday, July 10 (Moon in Capricorn) Mercury moves into Leo and puts your conscious mind smack in the middle of things you would rather not think about: insurance, taxes, wills, mortgages, loans—take your pick. However, it's possible that you connect mentally with a new romantic interest.

Tuesday, July 11 (Moon in Capricorn to Aquarius 5:46 p.m.) From a friend, you learn about a new investment opportunity. Now you need to gather your facts, check out the investment in other sources, and then make your decision in a few days.

Wednesday, July 12 (Moon in Aquarius) Some days, you may feel that your life is like a commercial. Stuff happens, you puzzle through it, and then a solution appears. Even if it isn't the right solution, that's okay. It moves your mind in new directions.

Thursday, July 13 (Moon in Aquarius to Pisces 7:00 p.m.) Now your imagination can wrap itself around yesterday's wrong solutions and find the right solution. This is progress, Capricorn. You can't always be climbing mountains in the hopes that what lies at the top is the ultimate answer to everything.

Friday, July 14 (Moon in Pisces) How deep can you swim through your own mind? You feel conflicted about something, and you aren't sure what it is. The answer is closer than you think. Rely on your intuition today.

Saturday, July 15 (Moon in Pisces to Aries 8:39 p.m.) This evening, you're feeling antsy, out of sorts. You may pick a fight with someone close to you. Get over it. What's bothering you about others is what's bothering you about yourself.

Sunday, July 16 (Moon in Aries) Passions at home rise up and shock you. You're in the mood for romance and excitement; and if you act recklessly, you may regret it in the morning.

Monday, July 17 (Moon in Aries to Taurus 11:45 p.m.) Here's a comfortable moon day. Pleasure and romance figure prominently in the overall picture. Your creative muse is coaxing you to indulge yourself. Your discipline kicks in. Is it really okay to enjoy myself? Yes, of course. Go for it!

Tuesday, July 18 (Moon in Taurus) Venus moves into Cancer, highlighting romance with your partner for the next several weeks. If you don't have a partner, a new flirtation or romance is likely before this transit ends next month.

Wednesday, July 19 (Moon in Taurus) Today's moon forms a delightful angle with Jupiter. Count on a feel-good day. Friends will figure into anything you do for fun and pleasure. Today's energies are also favorable for all creative endeavors.

Thursday, July 20 (Moon in Taurus to Gemini 4:39 a.m.) Your day is busy with e-mails, phone calls, and meetings. A coworker needs a ride to the office, your kids need rides to the mall, the movies, or the homes of friends, and you're considering taking a week off just to get things done.

Friday, July 21 (Moon in Gemini) It's a good weekend to get away. Pack up the car and the family and head for the hills, Capricorn! Even a day trip will do wonders for your disposition. Let the e-mails pile up in your in box. Everything can wait until Monday.

Saturday, July 22 (Moon in Gemini to Cancer 11:29 a.m.) Mars moves into Virgo, a transit that lasts until September. You suddenly have new opportunities in publishing, higher education, and overseas travel. Try not to speed during the next few months, or you may find yourself paying some hefty speeding tickets.

Sunday, July 23 (Moon in Cancer) The transiting moon and Mars form a harmonious angle to each other today. You and your partner may not stray far from the bedroom. By evening, a romantic dinner for two is called for.

Monday, July 24 (Moon in Cancer to Leo 8:25 p.m.) When the moon joins Saturn in Leo, you may run into rules and restrictions that make you feel oppressed—or depressed. Just go with the flow today, Capricorn. It's easier than resisting the day's energies.

Tuesday, July 25 (Moon in Leo) Look your best today. There's someone you want to impress, and that individual makes snap judgments based on initial impressions. Reds and vivid blues are a good place to start.

Wednesday, July 26 (Moon in Leo) You're onstage today. You don't need to be flashy, just fully present and aware. Be alert for synchronicities that light your path.

Thursday, July 27 (Moon in Leo to Virgo 7:37 a.m.) As the moon joins Mars in Virgo, your focus is on health. If you don't already have a regular exercise routine, start one. If you do have a routine, you might consider expanding it in some way.

Friday, July 28 (Moon in Virgo) Mercury finally turns direct again. It's time to firm up plans, sign contracts, and communicate to your heart's content without fear of being misunderstood. You're better understood by the people around you now.

Saturday, July 29 (Moon in Virgo to Libra 8:28 p.m.) Early this evening, your thoughts turn to career and professional matters. Make your lists tonight for what you want to achieve on Monday. Be prepared. It pays to be organized.

Sunday, July 30 (Moon in Libra) You may decide to rearrange furniture at home or spiff up your home office. Line up your paint, wallpaper, and color schemes so that you can finish the job you start today when the moon moves into your sign in early August.

Monday, July 31 (Moon in Libra) Saturday evening's to-do list serves you well. Even though there are plenty of distractions on the professional front, you're able to get to nearly everything on your list. It's a satisfying way to end the month. And August actually looks very good for you, Capricorn.

AUGUST 2006

Tuesday, August 1 (Moon in Libra to Scorpio 9:08 a.m.) The moon joins Jupiter in Scorpio, expanding your emotions and your inner life. This transit is great for publicity and promotion too. Take advantage of it.

Wednesday, August 2 (Moon in Scorpio) You're determined to get to the bottom line concerning a friendship or publicity issue. Your intuition is strong, so listen to it. Some friendships simply continue; others die away. It's part of the cycle of life.

Thursday, August 3 (Moon in Scorpio to Sagittarius 7:14 p.m.) You're in a somewhat reclusive mood today. You may feel like cleaning your house, your garage, or even your closets. You would benefit from a bit of feng shui addressed to some area of your life where you desire change.

Friday, August 4 (Moon in Sagittarius) The big picture you've been looking for is contained within the smallest details. Connect the dots, and you'll find what you're looking for. Then back up this discovery with belief, and you'll do just fine when the moon enters your sign again.

Saturday, August 5 (Moon in Sagittarius) You head out of town with a friend or partner; even if the journey is just a day trip, the impact on you is considerable. You return refreshed and ready for whatever comes your way tomorrow.

Sunday, August 6 (Moon in Sagittarius to Capricorn 1:20 a.m.) Since the moon moved into your sign, you awaken on top of the world. Before you leap out of bed, spend a few minutes visualizing how you would like your life to unfold, and then plan how you can make your vision come true.

Monday, August 7 (Moon in Capricorn) Another power day and you're ready for it. You're in top form physically, emotionally, and spiritually, and your mind is crisp. The sky is the limit today, Capricorn. Don't waste the opportunity!

Tuesday, August 8 (Moon in Capricorn to Aquarius 3:48 a.m.) Finances and investments are at the forefront of your concerns today. Whether you invest in the stock market or in something else, stay on top of the details. You're a good researcher, so you may want to check out the histories of your stocks on the Internet.

Wednesday, August 9 (Moon in Aquarius) You get together tonight with your investment group to discuss some hot new stock. You're excited about it, but the feeling isn't unanimous. Invest in this one on your own. But before your put your money into the stock, be sure you've got the money to spend!

Thursday, August 10 (Moon in Aquarius to Pisces 4:11 a.m.) Mercury moves into Leo. Your thoughts focus on taxes, insurance, and wills. You also could sign up for a workshop concerning an esoteric topic that interests you. A novel to feed your interests: *Lost in a Good Book* by Jasper Fforde.

Friday, August 11 (Moon in Pisces) When the moon joins Uranus in Pisces, your emotions are less predictable. You also attract idiosyncratic people; one of them may be interested in you! Are you read for a relationship completely different from anything you've experienced before?

Saturday, August 12 (Moon in Pisces to Aries 4:23 a.m.)
Venus joins Mercury in Leo. This combination puts your conscious thoughts squarely on romance. You're looking, but maybe in the wrong places.

Sunday, August 13 (Moon in Aries) Home really is where the heart is, Capricorn. And your home may be in flux. Perhaps you're having renovations done to your house. Or you may be feeling an itch to move. Explore your options, but don't make a decision yet.

Monday, August 14 (Moon in Aries to Taurus 6:01 a.m.) If your passion is good stories, pick up any book by Joseph Campbell. He explains myths as if they were great novels. You may discover something about your personal myths too.

Tuesday, August 15 (Moon in Taurus) The romance in your life is about to take a new, better turn. A flirtation becomes something more as you and another person discover you have many things in commons, including your dedication to a particular hobby.

Wednesday, August 16 (Moon in Taurus to Gemini 10:08 a.m.) You aren't quite with it at work. That's okay. Everyone has an off day once in a while. It's just that your work ethic won't allow anything less than adherence to a rigid work schedule.

Thursday, August 17 (Moon in Gemini) Your head fills up with ideas today, and you aren't sure which one to implement first. Don't worry about getting things in motion. Just jot down the ideas and bring out your list when the moon moves into another earth sign.

Friday, August 18 (Moon in Gemini to Cancer 5:04 p.m.) With the moon in Cancer, it's an ideal weekend to either hang out at home with your partner and family or to head out to a home away from home, wherever that may be. The mountains or the beach? The middle of a city or the middle of nowhere?

Saturday, August 19 (Moon in Cancer) Your intuition hums along today, connecting you with people you haven't thought of or seen in a long time. E-mail connections to these individuals are possible. Be alert for synchronicities.

Sunday, August 20 (Moon in Cancer) Your mother extends an invitation to you and your partner for dinner. This invitation mends a rift or disagreement that has been brewing among you. Enjoy her and be grateful that she's still in your life.

Monday, August 21 (Moon in Cancer to Leo 2:34 a.m.) Here comes that pesky Leo moon. You just have to go with the energy, the fire and passion you feel. Just try not to vent them on someone else.

Tuesday, August 22 (Moon in Leo) You have business with an elderly person. Offer your advice and wisdom, and be glad that you can do so. You may find financial help for this individual.

Wednesday, August 23 (Moon in Leo to Virgo 2:08 p.m.) Okay, here's the earth moon. Bring out your list and get busy. And in the meantime, schedule dentist and doctor appointments. Here's a book suggestion for a Virgo moon day: Louise L. Hay's *You Can Heal Your Life*.

Thursday, August 24 (Moon in Virgo) Details, details—they consume you today. It could be details about work or your love life, but more than likely they concern a long-distance trip you're planning. Be sure about your destinations; play everything out. Even if the trip doesn't go exactly according to your plan, you've got a road map.

Friday, August 25 (Moon in Virgo) A health report returns and everything is in your favor. Your blood pressure and cholesterol are good. Your heart is strong. Keep up your exercise routine, and continue to pay attention to your nutrition. If you have any nagging health complaints, check out their probable emotional cause in Louise L. Hay's *You Can Heal Your Life*.

Saturday, August 26 (Moon in Virgo to Libra 3:01 a.m.) You're mediating a dispute among peers. They look to you because you're the one who always gets things done. Yes, it's flattering, but you're wondering why they can't settle this disagreement themselves.

Sunday, August 27 (Moon in Libra) Mercury moves into Virgo today. This transit certainly favors writing and all sorts of communication. Publishing plays a role in your affairs for the next two weeks. You may travel for spiritual purposes—perhaps to visit a shrine or some other symbol that's important to your beliefs.

Monday, August 28 (Moon in Libra to Scorpio 3:56 p.m.) The Scorpio moon forms a harmonious angle to your sun. When it joins up with Jupiter, your intuition is profound and clear. Listen to this inner guidance. A book suggestion for a Scorpio moon day is Katherine Neville's novel *The Eight*.

Tuesday, August 29 (Moon in Scorpio) Your advertising campaign is a smash! Now you have more clients than you know what to do with it. This compels you to expand your company—and perhaps your physical office as well.

Wednesday, August 30 (Moon in Scorpio) Your nighttime dreams are especially vivid. Before you fall asleep, give yourself suggestions that you'll have a dream that illuminates some concern that you have. Get up at four or five in the morning and jot down your dream.

Thursday, August 31 (Moon in Scorpio to Sagittarius 3:00 a.m.) Your dream recall continues; tonight you get exactly what you need. You may travel abroad for personal reasons, perhaps to expose yourself to other belief systems and cultures that expand your worldview.

SEPTEMBER 2006

Friday, September 1 (Moon in Sagittarius) It's a long weekend, and you would benefit from a trip. Spur-of-the-moment traveling isn't usually comfortable for you, but over the next few days, try to do things you wouldn't do ordinarily. This practice helps you to see events and relationships in a different light.

Saturday, September 2 (Moon in Sagittarius to Capricorn 10:35 a.m.) A power day and what a wonderful time for it to happen! Do whatever you feel like doing. If you want to work, work. If you want to stay in bed all day watching old movies, do so.

Sunday, September 3 (Moon in Capricorn) For the next day and a half, your life hums along at precisely the right speed and pitch. Everything seems to work more smoothly. Your angst is gone.

Monday, September 4 (Moon in Capricorn to Aquarius 2:15 p.m.) Pluto turns direct in Sagittarius. Although this motion is subtle, you'll feel the release of pent-up energy in terms of your own power. You won't be so cautious about speaking your mind now.

Tuesday, September 5 (Moon in Aquarius) The moon joins Neptune in Aquarius. This combination can lead to some fuzzy, unsettled feelings that are tough to pin down. But it can also bring in intuitive and inspired thoughts, particularly where your finances and personal values are concerned.

Wednesday, September 6 (Moon in Aquarius to Pisces 2:57 p.m.) Venus moves into Virgo. This transit, which lasts through the end of the month, favors romance with a foreigner or someone in law, publishing, or higher education. If you take a trip abroad, it will prove to be a memorable and enjoyable trip.

Thursday, September 7 (Moon in Pisces) Mars moves into Libra and adds zest and energy to your career. You may be working longer hours through the end of the month, but your hard work doesn't go unnoticed. A raise or promotion could be possible. Besides, hard work never scares you, Capricorn!

Friday, September 8 (Moon in Pisces to Aries 2:24 p.m.) This afternoon, activity picks up at home. Tempers could be short. Be careful that you—or someone else—doesn't burn the dinner! Your kids may need some structured playtime.

Saturday, September 9 (Moon in Aries) Your impulsiveness is refreshing. You're following your whims, and doing so may lead you into some unexpected adventures and states of mind. Embrace the change in pace.

Sunday, September 10 (Moon in Aries to Taurus 2:31 p.m.) Back to the Taurus moon, your comfort and fun zone! You may get a massage or try a new hairstyle today. You may also spend more time at the gym or extend your yoga practice. The focus is on your body: how you look and feel, and how others see you.

Monday, September 11 (Moon in Taurus)   Your appearance is noticed by others. It's the new you, and it certainly attracts the attention of someone you've had your eye on for quite a while. You're not looking for commitment—just romance and pleasure.

Tuesday, September 12 (Moon in Taurus to Gemini 5:00 p.m.)   Mercury joins Mars in Libra. This transit and this particular combination favor travel for business, a sexual affair as the result of the communion of minds, and lots of talk about you.

Wednesday, September 13 (Moon in Gemini)   The talk continues and some of it could be gossip. That's fine. Let people talk. It's called buzz, Capricorn, and the more buzz there is about you, the greater your chances for a promotion or even a job change. If you do change jobs, it will be to something with higher pay and more in line with your interests and passions.

Thursday, September 14 (Moon in Gemini to Cancer 10:54 p.m.)   The Cancer moon is usually quite comfortable for you, a water sign to your earth. But as the transition happens this evening, you may feel a sudden surge of insecurity about a personal relationship. Roll over and go back to sleep. Tomorrow you won't feel this way.

Friday, September 15 (Moon in Cancer)   You're in the lunar groove, and you have several choices. You can cocoon this weekend with your partner, babysit your grandchildren, or take your own mother out for dinner or shopping. Or you can meditate and take up yoga!

Saturday, September 16 (Moon in Cancer) In October, Mercury turns retrograde, so it's best to negotiate and sign contracts if at all possible. You may be planning a February trip to somewhere warm—like the Caribbean. Will it be a cruise or an adventure tour? You don't have to decide now. But consider all your options.

Sunday, September 17 (Moon in Cancer to Leo 8:15 a.m.) The Leo moon usually puts you on notice that drama is about to unfold in your life. If you have a moon in Leo or another fire sign—Sagittarius or Aries—this transit should be to your liking. But because fire and earth don't get along, this lunar transit usually brings up issues you would rather live without.

Monday, September 18 (Moon in Leo) Now that all of the above has been said, today's Leo moon could bring children into your life in droves: neighborhood kids, children that you teach, or your own kids. Be prepared. Have snacks on hand.

Tuesday, September 19 (Moon in Leo to Virgo 8:07 p.m.) The comfort of the Virgo moon doesn't come about until this evening. However, you're in the mood for its grounding energy. You suddenly feel more in control of your own destiny.

Wednesday, September 20 (Moon in Virgo) You're perfecting yourself today: your habits, your appearance, your nutrition and health practices. Write down everything that you do for yourself in these areas and carry on with these practices throughout the rest of the month.

Thursday, September 21 (Moon in Virgo) Picky, picky. That's how you are today—toward yourself, your living environment, your kids, your partner. Back off, Capricorn. Take it easy. Nowhere is it written that your bed must be made as soon as you get out of it in the morning.

Friday, September 22 (Moon in Virgo to Libra 9:07 a.m.) You take in an art film today and then visit your favorite museum or a music store. Or perhaps a concert is in order. Whatever your pleasure, it involves either the arts, music, or finances.

Saturday, September 23 (Moon in Libra) You may want to take a leisurely drive through the countryside. Not only can you enjoy the beauty, but the drive itself will ease your nerves and put you in a less serious frame of mind.

Sunday, September 24 (Moon in Libra to Scorpio 9:55 p.m.) The Scorpio moon is comfortable for you. With Jupiter in the same sign, though, it tends to deepen and expand your feelings. Remember that when you get upset about something. By Wednesday, whatever upsets you today won't seem as important.

Monday, September 25 (Moon in Scorpio) It's another fine day for you, Capricorn. Your intuition runs through you like a swift-moving river, sweeping out the nonessentials. Your dreams and ambitions may be going through renovation and expansion right now.

Tuesday, September 26 (Moon in Scorpio) Goals that were important to you a year ago may not be on your list anymore. One of the things that Jupiter in Scorpio does for you is expand your vision about your own goals and dreams. This is a good thing. Otherwise, you might get stuck in a single track that doesn't allow you to achieve your potential.

Wednesday, September 27 (Moon in Scorpio to Sagittarius 9:17 a.m.) Sagittarius is a fire sign. Unless you have a moon or ascendant in a fire sign, today won't be particularly comfortable for you. That said, though, it serves a purpose. It provides opportunities for solitude and repose or for travel that possesses a spiritual purpose.

Thursday, September 28 (Moon in Sagittarius) A book suggestion for a Sagittarius moon day is Richard A. Clarke's *Against All Enemies,* which came out in early 2004 and revealed some of the secrets in the Bush administration. Other than that, you may want to delve into travel guides and select a place you would just love to visit.

Friday, September 29 (Moon in Sagittarius to Capricorn 6:02 p.m.) Another power day for you. On your power days, you might enjoy books on how to make a million bucks or how to use feng shui in your home. The day's emphasis is on your appearance and how you feel physically.

Saturday, September 30 (Moon in Capricorn) With Venus moving into Libra, romance comes knocking at your door. When you open it, there stands one of your peers, a person you may not have considered for a romance. Now you take a second look. The next few weeks should be telling.

OCTOBER 2006

Sunday, October 1 (Moon in Capricorn to Aquarius 11:25 p.m.) The month begins with Mercury joining Jupiter in Scorpio. This transit can be especially successful for you, as Jupiter expands your conscious mind, your interests, and your ability to communicate what you feel and think.

Monday, October 2 (Moon in Aquarius) Whenever the moon joins Neptune in Aquarius, you feel somewhat confused about finances and material possessions. Your values and beliefs about money seem to be at odds with each other. It's not a permanent condition, so don't give it too much thought. But be aware of the energies.

Tuesday, October 3 (Moon in Aquarius) Your financial picture may be in flux. It's part of a cycle, but you can control it by adhering to a budget and saving a percentage of everything you earn. It's the only way to accrue savings.

Wednesday, October 4 (Moon in Aquarius to Pisces 1:34 a.m.) The Pisces moon is comfortable for you because Pisces is a water sign that is compatible with your earth sign. However, it's probably the least comfortable of the water moons because it's so ephemeral, dreamy, even mystical. Your imagination and intuition are strong today and allow you to connect with a sibling in a meaningful way.

Thursday, October 5 (Moon in Pisces) Your compassion is profound today, and you're a good listener for people in trouble. A sibling or neighbor comes to you for advice, and even if that person doesn't take your advice, you have listened and the person appreciates it.

Friday, October 6 (Moon in Pisces to Aries 1:33 a.m.) Usually, the Aries moon makes you restless and irritable. Or it ignites passion and tempers at home. Or it may make you courageous, urging you to try something new. You may paint your bedroom a vibrant red. You may tear up your yard. Change—that's the key.

Saturday, October 7 (Moon in Aries) It's early fall and a Saturday, and that lunar energy is urging you to get out, to do something. Go rock climbing somewhere.

Take a photographic expedition into the mountains. Whatever you do, wherever you go, leave your work ethic at home.

Sunday, October 8 (Moon in Aries to Taurus 10:05 a.m.) Today spells fun. If your idea of fun is to make love all day, do that. If it means going to bookstores, movies, antique stores, or garage sales, do that. Recapture your younger, more innocent self. It's okay to enjoy yourself.

Monday, October 9 (Moon in Taurus) You'll have a laid-back day at work, with plenty of stimulus, certainly, but you feel good about yourself and where you are in your life. You feel this despite the fact that your ruler, Saturn, is always whispering for you to work harder and work longer to pay those bills.

Tuesday, October 10 (Moon in Taurus to Gemini 2:06 a.m.) You're talking up a storm with someone at work. You've got a lot to say; so does the other person. It isn't necessarily a disagreement that spurs the conversation, but a meeting of the minds.

Wednesday, October 11 (Moon in Gemini) Your in box is crowded with new e-mails, all demanding an answer yesterday. In your usual efficient manner, you tackle each topic and concern one at a time and manage to work your way through the entire batch by the time you go home for the day.

Thursday, October 12 (Moon in Gemini to Cancer 6:21 a.m.) With the moon moving into Cancer early this morning, you and your partner may decide to start your weekend today. You may want to get into the mountains to see the beginning of autumn. Or if you live in the mountains or in the rural countryside, you may want to do the city. Whichever it is, you're together.

Friday, October 13 (Moon in Cancer)   Sign contracts in the next two weeks, before Mercury turns retrograde on October 28. Your business ventures now seem to be clicking right along, almost as if they are self-sustaining entities. This frees up time for you to do other things.

Saturday, October 14 (Moon in Cancer to Leo 2:38 p.m.)   Early this afternoon, the moon slides into Leo. It's time to check over insurance papers, wills, and tax returns. If you don't have a living will, you should consider getting one.

Sunday, October 15 (Moon in Leo)   Relationships that begin under the transiting Leo moon may have a dramatic flair to them. There could be an intuitive or psychic awareness of past-life connections. Kids may also play a role in the relationship.

Monday, October 16 (Moon in Leo)   With both Venus and Mars still in Libra and the moon in Leo, your romantic life should be pretty intense. It may be difficult to find the right balance between your personal and professional obligations. Part of the challenge is to do everything you need and want to do without feeling divided.

Tuesday, October 17 (Moon in Leo to Virgo 2:16 a.m.)   Your worldview becomes more detailed and precise under the Virgo moon. You may have a chance to communicate your philosophy or beliefs through writing or education. Be concise in what you communicate.

Wednesday, October 18 (Moon in Virgo)   Foreign cultures and people play a role today. Your business interests may begin expanding to overseas markets or into college markets. Stay on top of negotiations, and if there are details that bother you, say so. Speak your mind.

Thursday, October 19 (Moon in Virgo to Libra 3:20 p.m.) The moon joins Venus and Mars in Libra, placing the spotlight squarely on your professional life and on your relationships. A raise or promotion is possible, or if you've been dissatisfied with your profession, a job change may be in the offing.

Friday, October 20 (Moon in Libra) Music, dance, the arts—take your pick. It's Friday and the beginning of the weekend; your soul is in need of some artistic boosts. Perhaps it's time to sign up for a course in painting, writing, or piano lessons. Don't limit yourself.

Saturday, October 21 (Moon in Libra) Women play a major role in your life today. Your mother or a sister extends an invitation for dinner or some other event. Balance is key. Don't feel obligated to do something you don't want to do, but don't hurt anyone's feelings, either.

Sunday, October 22 (Moon in Libra to Scorpio 3:55 a.m.) An emotional issue concerning friends or a group to which you belong may surface. Whatever it is, it may be a precursor to the events that occur tomorrow and Tuesday, when both Mars and Venus join Jupiter in Scorpio. Be alert for signs.

Monday, October 23 (Moon in Scorpio) Mars moves into Scorpio, a sign that it corules. Things with a friend may be very intense between now and December 5. You may also be revising and reworking your goals and aspirations during this time. Romance is a possibility with someone you meet through friends.

Tuesday, October 24 (Moon in Scorpio to Sagittarius 2:54 p.m.) Now Venus joins Mars, Mercury, and Jupiter in Scorpio. This certainly brings a softness to the Scorpio influence, but it can also spell an intense sexual affair. You're ready for something like this, Capricorn. Embrace the adventure.

Wednesday, October 25 (Moon in Sagittarius) Your affair or new romance may be in the solitary stage, where you're getting to know each other before expanding outward to family and friends. If one of you has children, the introductions should wait a little while, until you both feel more comfortable about bringing them into the picture.

Thursday, October 26 (Moon in Sagittarius to Capricorn 11:48 p.m.) As the moon moves into your sign again, you're full of astonishment and wonder at the course of events over the past few months. You're also feeling exceptionally confident and certain of yourself, and that feeling bolsters you if and when you need emotional support or backup.

Friday, October 27 (Moon in Capricorn) Clear off your desk, tie up loose ends, and put unsigned contracts aside. Mercury will be moving retrograde in Scorpio tomorrow, and that may bring about some miscommunications. For today, though, enjoy your feelings of confidence and control.

Saturday, October 28 (Moon in Capricorn) Mercury turns retrograde today in Scorpio, making the final retrograde period of the year. There can be miscommunications with friends, you may be revisiting some of your goals and aspirations. It's time to revise, rewrite, and rework ideas. Friends from the past may surface between now and November 17, when Mercury turns direct again.

Sunday, October 29—Daylight Saving Time Ends (Moon in Capricorn to Aquarius 5:17 a.m.) Your concern over finances is unfounded. You're doing fine financially. In fact, you may want to take some money out of savings or sell off a particular stock to buy a new computer or some other item that you need. Perhaps you've been eyeing a personal digital assistant. Do your research concerning brands and prices online; then buy after November 17.

Monday, October 30 (Moon in Aquarius) A book suggestion for the Aquarius moon: *The Electric Kool-Aid Acid Test,* Tom Wolfe's classic book about Ken Kesey and the 1960s. If nonfiction suits you better today, try Michael Talbot's *The Holographic Universe,* an eye-opener for anyone interested in how the universe really works.

Tuesday, October 31 (Moon in Aquarius to Pisces 9:11 a.m.) Don your costume and get out there to trick or treat with your kids. Be imaginative. Your kids will love this as much as you do. Happy Halloween!

NOVEMBER 2006

Wednesday, November 1 (Moon in Pisces) This lunar transit is wonderful for any kind of writing and communication, but especially for fiction and storytelling. You can draw on the vast wealth of your imagination to create characters and story lines that enthrall readers and listeners. You may want to read any of Joseph Campbell's works about the power and breadth of mythology.

Thursday, November 2 (Moon in Pisces to Aries 10:47 a.m.) Here comes that fire-sign moon again. You're in a feisty mood today, determined to have your way about some personal or domestic issue. You need to sit back, chill out, take a few deep breaths, and rethink your position.

Friday, November 3 (Moon in Aries) Don't try to do it all yourself today. Get help. Enlist the aid of family members. Or if you have to, call in outside experts who know how to do whatever is required. Sometimes, Capricorn, it's wise to delegate!

Saturday, November 4 (Moon in Aries to Taurus 11:05 a.m.) A lazy Saturday at home is called for. Don't push yourself. Everything will get done one way or another. You deserve to pamper yourself today. That means, if you feel like lounging around and reading Internet news all day, you're entitled.

Sunday, November 5 (Moon in Taurus) You have friends in for dinner. It may be as informal as buffet at your kitchen table or as involved and formal as a catered party. It's up to you. The point is to use today's lunar energy to enjoy yourself.

Monday, November 6 (Moon in Taurus to Gemini 11:47 a.m.) Memos have piled up on your desk, your in box is jammed, and you have phone calls to return. It seems you spend much of the day correcting other people's mistakes or trying to explain your own motives and plans.

Tuesday, November 7 (Moon in Gemini) Hang on, Capricorn. In another ten days, Mercury will be moving direct again and many of the communication snafus you've been experiencing will smooth out on their own. In the meantime, control the things you can, and let someone else handle the rest.

Wednesday, November 8 (Moon in Moon in Gemini to Cancer 2:46 p.m.) By early this afternoon, the pressure feels like it's off, and your internal pace slows down. Chaos may still be raging around you, but you can step outside of it. You've learned to keep things to yourself.

Your intuitive awareness is strong, which helps. You instinctively know which situations to avoid.

Thursday, November 9 (Moon in Cancer) Your partnerships are highlighted. You and a business or romantic partner may not see eye to eye on an issue or concern. Engage in calm discussion, lists the pros and cons, and then make your decision after Mercury turns direct on November 17.

Friday, November 10 (Moon in Cancer to Leo 9:35 p.m.) Mercury, Mars, and Jupiter are still in Scorpio, pressuring you to get out more in front of the public. If you have advertising or promotion commitments, your schedule may change without much warning. Go with the flow, Capricorn. Resistance only gives you ulcers!

Saturday, November 11 (Moon in Leo) If your moon is in Leo or another fire sign, or even if you have a natal moon in an air sign, today should be a strong day. Your in charge of your own feelings. If, however, your moon is, like your sun, in an earth sign, today could be troublesome.

Sunday, November 12 (Moon in Leo) You feel conflicted about resources that you share with someone else. Your partner's income may be in a state of flux, requiring you to work longer hours. Try not to feel resentful. Support and cooperation will get you much farther.

Monday, November 13 (Moon in Leo to Virgo 8:20 a.m.) Breathe, Capricorn. Your life evens out for a couple of days. The Virgo moon prompts you to clean up your office and toss out old files that you no longer need. If you have income tax returns that are older than five years, shred them and send them out with the trash.

Tuesday, November 14 (Moon in Virgo) You continue to make room for the new by purging your life of things you no longer need or which have outlived their usefulness. You may be planning a holiday trip. Tend to the details concerning the journey, but don't make your reservations until after November 17.

Wednesday, November 15 (Moon in Virgo to Libra 9:15 p.m.) By this evening, you're ready for meetings and social obligations tomorrow. You've learned to have your agenda prepared, your schedule set. A relationship with a peer or boss may be a bit bumpy.

Thursday, November 16 (Moon in Libra) You can feel it. Communications are starting to clear up. Mercury will turn direct tomorrow. For today, make a list of what you would like to accomplish tomorrow. For tonight, though, kick back and watch a movie that will make you laugh out loud.

Friday, November 17 (Moon in Libra) It's a big day. Mercury turns direct, and Venus moves into Sagittarius. The Venus transit lasts until mid-December; during this time, it's possible that you will have a secret romance. The reasons for secrecy are known only to you. But by the time Venus moves into your sign in December, the affair will either come out into the open—or be over.

Saturday, November 18 (Moon in Libra to Scorpio 9:48 a.m.) The transiting moon joins Mars and Jupiter in Scorpio. This transit enhances your sexuality and makes you attractive to someone you meet through friends or through a group to which you belong. Your physical energy in front of groups is impressive; you're forceful enough to be convincing as well as inspirational.

Sunday, November 19 (Moon in Scorpio) Uranus moves direct in Pisces today, a welcome change. Even though the effect is subtle, it releases energy that you can now integrate into your writing or speaking engagements. Your spirituality and your creativity should be stronger.

Monday, November 20 (Moon in Scorpio to Sagittarius 8:16 p.m.) The moon joins Venus in Sagittarius. This interesting combination focuses on romantic feelings and usually indicates that women play more prominent roles in your activities. Even if you're feeling a bit reclusive, your aesthetic senses are more attuned today.

Tuesday, November 21 (Moon in Sagittarius) Your spirituality and your urge to travel may result in a quick trip to another town to see a shrine or some other landmark that is personally meaningful. Or you may be doing virtual traveling tonight, clicking through sites on the Internet for specific information.

Wednesday, November 22 (Moon in Sagittarius) As the holidays draw nearer, your spirits lift. You may hit the mall after work to get an early jump on holiday shopping. You're after special gifts this year, and you don't intend to buy just anything for the people you love.

Thursday, November 23 (Moon in Sagittarius to Capricorn 4:26 a.m.) It's a big day in the stars! Not only is the moon in your sign, but Jupiter moves into Sagittarius. This transit lasts about a year and should bring enormous internal changes and expansion for you. You're going to be clearing your life of excess baggage: relationships, old issues, situations, and feelings.

Friday, November 24 (Moon in Capricorn) With Jupiter and Venus both in Sagittarius and the moon in your sign, your romance swells and enters a whole new stage. One of you is asking for commitment. Are you ready, Capricorn?

Saturday, November 25 (Moon in Capricorn to Aquarius 10:41 a.m.) You invest in a company whose products and policies are in line with your personal beliefs. In other words, if you're into women's issues and rights, you probably won't invest or shop at a company where women are underpaid. If outsourcing enrages you, you won't invest in companies that practice it.

Sunday, November 26 (Moon in Aquarius) You and your investment group meet. You can't make up your mind about a particular stock or mutual fund. But after spirited discussion, you reach a consensus.

Monday, November 27 (Moon in Aquarius to Pisces 3:21 p.m.) With Uranus moving direct in Pisces, you begin to attract unique artistic types. Perhaps you meet these individuals in your own backyard!

Tuesday, November 28 (Moon in Pisces) Get busy on that novel or screenplay you stuck in a drawer months ago. With the moon in mystical Pisces, you can move full steam ahead. Try working to music that you like. This often gets the creative adrenaline flowing.

Wednesday, November 29 (Moon in Pisces to Aries 6:30 p.m.) If your ascendant or moon is in Aries or another fire sign, you'll like whatever happens this evening. Otherwise, the Aries moon may make you uncomfortable. Passion are inflamed.

Thursday, November 30 (Moon in Aries) You and your family head out of town early for the weekend. Maybe a cabin in the woods, with a roaring fireplace and the smell of pine in the air, is the perfect way to end the month.

DECEMBER 2006

Friday, December 1 (Moon in Aries to Taurus 8:27 p.m.) You're feeling sensuous this evening. It's time to get dressed up, take in a concert, and have a long, leisurely meal afterward with someone you love. Be careful, though, that you don't overindulge in rich foods.

Saturday, December 2 (Moon in Taurus) You're relentless today in your search for answers. It may be an intellectual answer that you're looking for or something as simple as the special gift for the right person. Whatever it is, you don't give up until you find it.

Sunday, December 3 (Moon in Taurus to Gemini 10:06 p.m.) It's a chatty day. You're on the phone or writing e-mail or playing around with oracles in an attempt to get information. Try the *I Ching* and then the tarot for a different perspective on the same question.

Monday, December 4 (Moon in Gemini) Yesterday's search yields results. You know exactly how to handle whatever comes up at work. Now that Mercury is moving direct, your holiday getaway plans are coming together nicely. You're confident about an intellectual issue.

Tuesday, December 5 (Moon in Gemini) Mars moves into Sagittarius, joining Venus and Jupiter there. This interesting trio of planets can bring to light some long-buried issue you've had since childhood or even something from a past life. It's time to deal with whatever it is so that you can move on.

Wednesday, December 6 (Moon in Gemini to Cancer 1:02 a.m.) With three planets in Sagittarius and a moon in Cancer, you're looking to the past for answers. Your mother may have something that you need in this regard. Talk to her about. What she says could surprise.

Thursday, December 7 (Moon in Cancer) Your partner is supportive of your search and may offer good advice. Take it. Right now, you need whatever you can get in terms of information. A female coworker may have something to say about it all too. Seems pretty mysterious, doesn't it?

Friday, December 8 (Moon in Cancer to Leo 6:53 a.m.) Mercury now joins Jupiter, Mars, and Venus in Sagittarius. You're certainly looking for the big picture regarding a romance, your sexuality, and childhood stuff you've buried. It's all wound together somehow. Find one piece and the rest fall into place. Therapy, meditation, and dream recall are all excellent venues for uncovering whatever this is.

Saturday, December 9 (Moon in Leo) You're feeling a whole lot better today. The Leo moon forms a harmonious angle with all those planets in Sagittarius, and it's now easier to see your way through the forest. You know you're on the right track in this search. Children or an older person may prove helpful.

Sunday, December 10 (Moon in Leo to Virgo 4:32 p.m.) By this afternoon, you're far more grounded than you have been. You're able to gain some distance from a relationship or issue by scrutinizing the details. It sounds like a dichotomy, but it really isn't. Sometimes, answers come to us through a study of the most minute details.

Monday, December 11 (Moon in Virgo) Life takes a sudden and pleasant upswing. With Venus moving into your sign, where it remains throughout the rest of the year, you're in heaven. Your love life takes off in a major way, you may get a promotion or raise at work, and new opportunities come to you. Part of your good fortune is that you feel so good about yourself, you attract other people.

Tuesday, December 12 (Moon in Virgo) It's a great time for a trip abroad. Mercury is moving direct, the moon is in a sign where it feels comfortable for you, and you've got some money to burn. Why not be daring? Head up, up, and away!

Wednesday, December 13 (Moon in Virgo to Libra 5:01 a.m.) The holiday spirit benefits you professionally. Any social events you go to today and tomorrow allow you to make new contacts. These contacts will be helpful in the new year.

Thursday, December 14 (Moon in Libra) You and your friends shop for the holidays. Everyone is in a spending mood and some of the gifts are extravagant. You may feel a bit guilty afterward, but you really shouldn't. You deserve to spend some money.

Friday, December 15 (Moon in Libra to Scorpio 5:43 p.m.) The intense Scorpio moon brings issues to the surface today that you have to confront and deal with. It's not really as intense as some of the things you've been through this year, so just relax and allow your intuition to guide you.

Saturday, December 16 (Moon in Scorpio) Good books for a Scorpio moon day include the biographies of several notable Scorpio women: Sylvia Plath and Anne Sexton. What motivated these women? How did both of them end up as suicides? Big questions.

Sunday, December 17 (Moon in Scorpio) Your mind and your emotions run along parallel courses today. There are no major bumps, no major glitches. It's as if you intuit your way through the day.

Monday, December 18 (Moon in Scorpio to Sagittarius 4:10 a.m.) As the moon links up with Jupiter, Mars, and Mercury in Sagittarius, you're feeling energized and optimistic. You've settled and resolved issues this year, and you are delving now into your spiritual beliefs. Are the beliefs you hold your own or are they leftovers from childhood?

Tuesday, December 19 (Moon in Sagittarius) Foreign visitors arrive. You may not be in the mood, but resolve to make the best of the situation. By the end of the day, you realize you actually enjoy having people around right now. They are considerate of your schedule and space.

Wednesday, December 20 (Moon in Sagittarius to Capricorn 11:39 a.m.) Another power day, and this time, the moon links up with Venus in Capricorn. This wonderful combination really puts you on top of the world. You can do anything today, achieve anything, and still have energy left over for the people you love.

Thursday, December 21 (Moon in Capricorn) Your partner is talking marriage. Or if you're already married, the relationship is about to reach an even deeper and more connected level. One of your kids is in need of advice and nurturing.

Friday, December 22 (Moon in Capricorn to Aquarius 4:49 p.m.) In a flurry of last-minute shopping, you find all the gifts you want for the special people in your life—and in the lives of your kids and partner. In other words, today you're shopping for friends, teachers, coworkers, and bosses.

Saturday, December 23 (Moon in Aquarius) Some of the best things in life come in small packages. Today you receive one of those packages and aren't sure how you feel about it. Ecstatic? Astonished? Well, forget the analysis. Go with the flow.

Sunday, December 24 (Moon in Aquarius to Pisces 8:44 p.m.)   This Christmas Eve, your imagination is soaring, your compassion is deep, and your heart is swelling with goodwill and love for everyone around you. Quite a combination of emotions. Enjoy it.

Monday, December 25 (Moon in Pisces)   Your storytelling abilities take off today, as you sit around making up stories for the younger kids in your family group. Maybe this is a talent you should explore in greater depth.

Tuesday, December 26 (Moon in Pisces)   Hopefully, you've taken time off from work and can indulge yourself in all the things that you and your family and neighbors enjoy. If there's snow on the ground where you live, get outside, go skiing, or enjoy other winter sports.

Wednesday, December 27 (Moon in Pisces to Aries 12:05 a.m.)   Mercury now joins Venus in Capricorn and you're delighted. Your mind and your heart are no longer at odds. You know exactly where you're headed in the new year, and you're eager to implement your plans, goals, and dreams.

Thursday, December 28 (Moon in Aries)   If you're still on vacation, you're going to be out and about today, perhaps preparing for New Year's Eve or returning gifts. There's a lot of activity at home, and you may want to get off by yourself for a little while to enjoy your solitude.

Friday, December 29 (Moon in Aries to Taurus 3:09 a.m.)   As the moon moves into sensuous Taurus, you're in the mood for more fun and romance. It's going to be a little challenging to come off the high you've been on. But you'll do it when the time comes.

Saturday, December 30 (Moon in Taurus) You and your family and friends make preparations for New Year's Eve. The party is going to be at your place. When you have time, send e-mail cards to friends in other places, wishing them the best for 2007.

Sunday, December 31 (Moon in Taurus to Gemini 6:17 a.m.) Early this morning, the moon moves into Gemini, and you're in a party mood, eager to greet the new year with open arms. Be sure to have your resolutions handy. At the strike of midnight, give thanks for all that you have.

HAPPY NEW YEAR!

SYDNEY OMARR

Born on August 5, 1926, in Philadelphia, Pennsylvania, Sydney Omarr was the only person ever given full-time duty in the U.S. Army as an astrologer. He is regarded as the most erudite astrologer of our time and the best known, through his syndicated column and his radio and television programs (he was Merv Griffin's "resident astrologer"). Omarr has been called the most "knowledgeable astrologer since Evangeline Adams." His forecasts of Nixon's downfall, the end of World War II in mid-August of 1945, the assassination of John F. Kennedy, Roosevelt's election for a fourth term and his death in office . . . these and many others are on the record and quoted enough to be considered "legendary."

ABOUT THE SERIES

This is one of a series of twelve Sydney Omarr® Day-by-Day Astrological Guides for the signs of 2006. For questions and comments about the book, e-mail tjmacgregor@booktalk.com.

⊘ SIGNET

WHAT'S IN THE STARS FOR YOU THIS YEAR?

SYDNEY OMARR'S® DAY-BY-DAY ASTROLOGICAL GUIDES FOR 2006

TRISH MACGREGOR WITH CAROL TONSING

Let Sydney Omarr's astrology guide you into the new year with amazingly accurate predictions—available for every sign.

Aquarius	0-451-21533-8
Pisces	0-451-21534-6
Aries	0-451-21536-2
Taurus	0-451-21535-4
Gemini	0-451-21537-0
Cancer	0-451-21538-9
Leo	0-451-21539-7
Virgo	0-451-21540-0
Scorpio	0-451-21542-7
Sagittarius	0-451-21544-3
Capricorn	0-451-21543-5
Libra	0-451-21541-9

Available wherever books are sold or at
www.penguin.com

S454/Omarr